RULES
FOR
DEFEATING
RADICALS

COUNTERING THE ALINSKY STRATEGY IN POLITICS AND CULTURE

CHRISTOPHER G. ADAMO

Printed in the United States of America
First Printing 2019
First Edition 2019

ISBN: 978-1-7332182-0-7

DEDICATION

Whether Saul Alinsky's original dedication of *"Rules for Radicals"* to "Lucifer" was merely intended to be an outrageous and provocative affront to the traditional culture he hated, or as a sincere acknowledgment of the kindred forces warring alongside him against the American ideal, it set the tone both for his writing, and for the havoc it wreaked. So, with that in mind, I dedicate this book to all those willing to brave the sinister tides engulfing our nation; the people across America in the coffee shops, break rooms, and pulpits, who refuse to bend to the lies of the counterculture, but instead stand firmly on the truth. It is by their courage and steadfastness that this nation can be resuscitated from the death spiral into which the leftist counterculture would take us.

And also to my wife, Thea Adamo, whose unwavering determination to stand for truth inspired me to write this.

TABLE OF CONTENTS

INTRODUCTION...*i*

CHAPTER ONE.. 1
  ARROGANCE: THE PRIMARY MOTIVATION OF LIBERALS

CHAPTER TWO...19
  HYPOCRISY: NOT A LIABILITY TO LEFTISTS

CHAPTER THREE.. 37
  HYPOCRISY AS A STRATEGY

CHAPTER FOUR.. 55
  BRANDING HEROES AND VILLAINS: THE POWER OF LABELS

CHAPTER FIVE.. 101
  LEFTIST MANTRAS: ESTABLISHING "TRUTH" BY PRESUMPTION

CHAPTER SIX...125
  THE STRATEGIC IMPORTANCE OF DESTROYING OUR MORAL CERTITUDE

CHAPTER SEVEN... 161
  RINOS: THE ESSENTIAL ALINSKY FIFTH COLUMN

CHAPTER EIGHT...185
  THE RULES, PART I

CHAPTER NINE.. 211
  THE RULES, PART II

CHAPTER TEN..239
  CONCLUSION

INTRODUCTION

Another day dawns, and with it comes another malignant leftist assault on America's founding principles, which were established as a firewall against efforts to subvert and destroy our nation and our way of life from within. For several decades, the good people of America have been appalled to watch their once-great country being dismantled before their eyes, as one institution after another is systematically targeted, attacked, and destroyed under a relentless onslaught from the leftist counterculture. In each ensuing episode, a formerly untenable leftist precept is suddenly elevated to center-stage and any opposition to it deemed first "controversial," and soon thereafter, verboten. Eventually, all remaining vestiges of resistance to it crumble, leaving every liberal notion, from the absurd to the abhorrent, proclaimed as the new "mainstream" of society.

But far from being a crazed and random onslaught, this detestable pattern is fully premeditated and purposefully implemented with liberal politicians, academia, "news" media outlets, and entertainment industry icons playing their specified and scripted roles like the foot-soldiers of an advancing army. With even a superficial understanding of their tactics, their moves become entirely predictable. Yet among far too many on the right, the attack appears to be unstoppable. America has, at times, seemed destined to be dragged down into an abyss of moral, social, and economic collapse.

While the forces of societal decay have been a plague on the human condition throughout all of history, certain modern proponents of disorder and dystopia stand out as key figures in the movement, possessing a degree of evil "genius" that sets them apart from typical revolutionaries and anarchists. Certainly, in the modern era, Karl Marx occupies the dubious preeminent position among such subversives. But close in his shadow, and much more recently, the leftist ideology of Saul Alinsky and his pivotal work *"Rules For Radicals"* has done more to destructively transform America than any rampaging foreign army could ever have hoped to accomplish. Beginning in 1971 when it was first published, Alinsky's *"Rules"* has been adopted as the principal battle plan of the leftist counterculture. And any honest assessment of its impact must concede its devastating effectiveness. Without a doubt, the Alinsky strategy has succeeded far beyond the wildest dreams of its original acolytes. The scars borne across present day America, from its nightmarish inner cities, to its disastrously failing government schools, to its struggling and broken families, grimly attest to no less.

Unfortunately, little concerted effort was ever actually made to adequately counter the Alinsky strategy, once it became the core of Democrat Party politicking. And as a result, the concept of sincerely and legitimately debating any issue, regardless of its merits or liabilities, and despite the likelihood of negative repercussions to the nation, has been thoroughly supplanted by a preemptive barrage of fierce attacks against anyone daring to oppose the liberal position. Though conservatives should be accustomed to this sordid game plan by now, they are instead repeatedly blindsided by it. Rather than being able to weigh the pros and cons of a particular agenda item in the public arena (which would shift the debate unquestionably in their direction), conservatives find themselves the targets of vile and baseless slander, to which they invariably react defensively and are thus rendered politically impotent.

So effective has this approach proven to be for liberals that during the past quarter century, despite which party officially holds majority status in the Congress, and even with a two-term Republican president in the White House at the opening of the twenty first century, the detestable Democrat "vision" for America's future advanced virtually unhindered. Any new policy initiative from leftists is essentially guaranteed implementation, as Democrats increasingly assume the role

of "agenda party," while Republicans are relegated to being merely the party of "tweaking and window dressing." This is a role that many modern Republicans are all too willing to accept, in order to have something... *anything* to offer their constituents back home as proof of their worthiness to be reelected. And under such circumstances, the eventual demise of our Constitution, and the great nation it birthed, becomes all but inevitable.

Nevertheless, all hope for America is not lost. The profound truth of the Alinsky strategy is that it is far from invincible. It has no guarantee of ultimate triumph. Rather, a proper recognition of the specific tactics at play, and their inherent weaknesses, can render even a protracted Alinsky onslaught completely ineffective, or better yet, cause it to politically implode upon its perpetrators. However, prevailing over the political left in such circumstances is absolutely contingent on a deliberate course of action by those being targeted. It is to their shame that so many prominent individuals, ostensibly on the "right," completely fail to rise to the occasion and thus needlessly cede ground to the liberal agenda.

This book is an effort to identify the reality of the Alinsky strategy, both in its "strengths" as portrayed in *"Rules for Radicals,"* but more importantly the limits on what can be accomplished through it, in the face of a principled and properly structured opposition. With that in mind, it is important to understand that the scope of this work is not strictly limited to Alinsky's *"Rules,"* but is intended as a counter to the entire collection of underhanded tactics being rampantly employed in rapid fire fashion by liberals in current day political and cultural contests. The goal is not merely to create a treatise on Saul Alinsky or his sordid tactics, which would limit conservatives to a strictly defensive posture. At best, such an approach would only amount to "Damage Control," and America is in dire need of much more at this time. Furthermore, as it becomes apparent that the Alinsky strategy has metastasized over the past several decades, a successful counter strategy

cannot be shackled to his dictates and tactics as presented forty-eight years ago.

Rather, the ultimate goal is to properly equip those Americans who recognize the disastrous threat Alinsky's end game poses, and seek to prevent it from becoming a tragic reality for the nation. In that same vein, no great purpose would be accomplished by merely compiling a vast compendium of historical evidence against Alinsky or his minions. Such an informational reference is not essential to making the case against the leftist onslaught and its strategic elements. Rather, the focus is on sufficiently establishing the pattern of Alinsky attacks, so that readers can gain an understanding of their nature, and be able to recognize their presence in current and future political confrontations. By doing so, counter strategies can be much more quickly and effectively established.

A certain segment of conservative activists have proffered that Alinsky's "Rules" should be embraced by the political right to be used against the left, which is a largely untenable idea. At its core, the Alinsky strategy necessitates lying, intimidation, and exploiting the lowest and basest failings of human character. While such precepts are at the heart of liberalism, they fundamentally conflict with real conservatism. Thus, for one example, a liberal lie cannot be countered with a "conservative lie," but only with the *truth*. Liberal bullying must be countered with courage, based on principle, and not by unethical tactics which could not be credibly conducted or defended in the name of virtue and the Constitution.

When researching and presenting evidence of the Alinsky strategy at work, it would have been easy to pick out ongoing daily examples, since they are abundant in America's current political arena, within the inarguably leftist climate of public education, and on the nightly news. But it is important to understand that this phenomenon is not limited to current events, no matter how detestable and glaring the underhanded

machinations of leftist state and federal power brokers have become in recent years. It is instead more crucial to recognize how leftists have operated and achieved so much unwarranted success over the last half-century, despite the disasters that invariably ensue whenever and wherever they gain uncontested power.

Although fraud, duplicity, intimidation, and abuses of the public trust have been endemic to every corrupt political organization throughout all of human history, the institutionalized practice of Alinsky's *"Rules"* as unofficial but wholly deliberate Democrat party "policy" can be traced back to the first term of Bill Clinton, commencing in January of 1993, with less coordinated but equally fervent efforts preceding that date by several decades. And not coincidentally, America's sudden lurch into its current, seemingly inexorable decline can be also tracked to those same milestones.

Of course any such undertaking required a thorough reexamination of Alinsky's original work, which not surprisingly proved to be an extremely distasteful task. Aside from being a dismal reminder of just how detestable Alinsky's guiding philosophy has been, it also brought a renewed focus on the sheer ugliness in the souls of those who ascribe to it, whose dishonesty and venom are now regularly on display from the highest levels of government to every other locale where leftists have acquired political power. Yet in the process, the consistent emergence of potentially fatal flaws in the strategy, if principled opponents can muster sufficient courage and resolve to seize upon them, gives reason to hope for something better. The entire Alinsky worldview is predicated on exploiting the darkest impulses and weaknesses of the human character. However, America was built on higher and nobler ideals. Thus, a determined break from the currently entrenched standards of behavior and propriety, as defined by the leftist counterculture, is absolutely necessary if America is to change course. Such a prospect, while daunting, is entirely possible. The leftist monster can be slain, if it is recognized for what it truly is, and confronted as such.

A thorough awareness of the underlying forces that drive leftists was profoundly enlightening when considering their track record of despicable and sordid behavior. Of particular significance was Alinsky's highly elevated opinion of himself and his presumed "virtue" in employing the most detestable and underhanded tactics to advance his "cause." Only when one fully grasps the consuming nature of such arrogance can the actions of leftists, completely devoid of any normal tenet of "conscience," begin to make sense. Throughout the text of *"Rules,"* Alinsky's own arrogance thoroughly permeates his worldview. In every verbal confrontation, he's unquestionably convinced he has the best retorts, and that he *never* loses the moral and intellectual "upper hand." In every situation, his motives are the most pure. And the glaring moral inconsistencies that invariably emerge from his fulminations are an inconvenience with which he refuses to distract himself. Even his occasional mention of the disreputable actions of other contemporaries, such as terrorist bombings and violence from fellow leftists of the era, elicit tepid criticism that is completely conditional. In the end, his only real contention with such abhorrent behavior was that he considered it bad publicity, and thus not beneficial to the cause. And on that basis alone he opposed them.

It is inevitable that, to the degree such a work as this might gain any widespread notoriety, it will be lampooned and denigrated in the most severe terms. That, in itself, is a manifestation of the Alinsky strategy, and thus can be rightly construed as validation. While a secondary goal of any honest author is to help pay the grocery and electric bills, the temptation to moderate the tone, thus avoiding particularly controversial topics, would be an undue concession to those on the left whose disreputable actions need to be bluntly identified and neutralized. In a very real sense, such a retreat from truth would be its own acquiescence to the leftist counterculture, and thus another Alinsky success.

So although no effort has been made to be deliberately and unnecessarily provocative, neither was any important topic intentionally sidestepped in order to soften the tone, or appease those on the left who will castigate and condemn any and every attempt to appraise their battle plan and develop an antidote, regardless of how delicately one seeks to buffer the facts. Therefore, the focus of this work has remained instead on reaching those principled and sincere individuals who desire an honest and effective resource to be utilized in service to the nation's restoration. In contrast, the larger body of ostensibly "conservative" advocacy can remain on its "politically safe" turf, as it continues to feign concern for the future of the country while studiously avoiding the hard battles that need to be fought if, in fact, America is to be salvaged. And thus its key players can be content accepting the ongoing defeat of the policies which they profess to uphold.

Those patriots who took up arms on Lexington Common did not do so with a primary focus of self-aggrandizement or even self-preservation, but with a firm resolve to defend and advance the dream of a free and enduring America. We in the current age can do no less.

CHAPTER ONE
ARROGANCE: THE PRIMARY MOTIVATION OF LIBERALS

When one considers the glaring evidence of liberalism's universal failures, and how so many institutions of America's greatness have been devastated by the political left, it might seem strange that the self-evident disaster of the leftist agenda isn't obvious to those who perpetrated it. However, while such thinking may be typical for rational and introspective individuals, it is a wholly foreign concept to leftists. From the time they first networked with fellow leftists, their presumption of inherent superiority over the common rabble and the realities of life that surround them has completely dominated the alternate universe in which they live. No room even exists in their thought processes to consider the cause and effect relationship of their policies to the disastrous results that inevitably ensue. Rather, their self-professed virtue is of such profound worthiness that no time or conscience even exists within which to ponder the dismal consequences of their policies.

Such thinking defines them and ultimately inoculates them against the contravening evidence that would totally demoralize them, were they to give it even a little attention. Whether in conclaves of fellow leftists, or sitting under the tutelage of the hard-left dominated public "education" system, the message is incessantly pounded into them that their worldview is elevated far above the reasoning of those narrow-minded and backwards people who raise them, feed them, and foot the bill for their intellectual enrichment.

Among the most infamous aspects of Saul Alinsky's *"Rules For Radicals"* was its dedication to "the first radical known to man who rebelled against the establishment and did it so effectively that he at least won his own kingdom-- *Lucifer*." By the nature of the rest of his text,

Alinsky makes it clear that his intent was not in any way spiritual, but only to be outrageous, as an emboldening bit of humor for his acolytes to thoroughly enjoy as an "In your face" affront to their opponents on the right who would most certainly recoil at such an abhorrent testimonial. Yet throughout the rest of *"Rules,"* a disturbing pattern emerges in which it becomes apparent that Alinsky believed himself to be the ultimate philanthropist, whose impact on society was so noble that his methodology was unhindered from any boundaries whatsoever, including common decency. This is presented against a backdrop of moral purity (from his perspective) which seeks to recast the sheer nastiness of his strategy in such terms as "beauty" and "meaning."

Along with its stated purpose of remaking the world, *"Rules"* represents the ultimate testament to Alinsky's belief in his undisputed superiority over modern society. The arrogance with which he extols his goals and achievements wafts obnoxiously from its pages like cheap perfume.

This mindset has been diligently instilled in both devoted liberal activists and any who fall, even temporarily, under their dominion (the largest such group being students in government schools). Once they've bought into the notions of their "higher" levels of reason and intellect, the blinding allegiance to their cause is increasingly detached from any assessment of its repercussions; a pattern that is absolutely essential to maintaining their level of commitment. Among such people the "end" (liberal utopia) clearly and inarguably justifies the means. And so they operate totally unshackled from such quaint notions as honesty or mutual respect. It is fundamentally important to understand this aspect of how they function, since it gives leftists an inherent and often decisive advantage whenever they are able to succeed at having political contests conducted on their turf.

It has now become evident exactly why America's government schools worked so tirelessly during recent decades to instill a mindless concept of "self-esteem" in young people, even while their social skills and actual academic performance deteriorated significantly during that same period. In truth, time and effort that should have been devoted to scholastic advancement (were it actually the goal) was diverted to convincing students of the ultimate worthiness of themselves and their imprinted notions of reality, which inevitably prevented many of them from actually achieving academically as they otherwise might have. By being kept ignorant of the facts and lacking in even the most basic critical thinking skills, young people are more easily convinced that they have all the answers when obediently regurgitating leftist mantras and platitudes. And while not everyone within the education system is intentionally supportive of such practices, a look at any platform of the National Education Association (NEA) in recent decades makes it impossible to dispute the fact that, on an institutional basis, instilling leftist ideology in students and conditioning them to reflexively adopt it takes total precedence over any other goal.

From their first years in school to the post graduate levels of "higher education," students are no longer taught how to critically think, or even what to think, but rather what to "believe." This, when combined with a toxic level of "self-esteem" renders them the ideal minions of a leftist plan to remake America, along with the rest of Western Civilization, despite the glaring evidence of liberalism's thoroughly consistent track record of failure. Rendered clueless, for the most part, as to how America became a bastion of freedom and liberty, they are instead marinated with a leftist litany of its imperfections and failings, which they tout with an unbridled confidence and a sanctimony that is so consuming, the increasingly dismal results of leftist policies surrounding them, rarely have even the slightest sobering influence on their world-view. They have been assured of the inherent superiority of leftist ideology ever since its tenets were originally trumpeted as a wondrous fix to all the ills and failures of traditional America, and that's all that matters.

In so-called "higher education," this situation is far more dire. Any efforts to quantitatively evaluate liberal theorizing, and the actual validity of its rosy but ultimately empty promises, by anyone, from university administrations and professors to the trustees and state governments who provide the enormous funding demanded by modern colleges, has been largely nullified under an incessant mantra of "academic freedom." In place of accountability, wholly autonomous leftist fiefdoms have taken over. Their version of "academic freedom" is a perverse caricature of what free thinking has ever been. Now, the leftist ideology permeates and dominates every conceivable course and subject. So dogmatic have college teaching staffs become that such quaint past notions as "differing schools of thought" have been totally marginalized and eradicated. Instead, ideas are presented in terms of orthodoxy and heresy.

> Students are no longer taught how to
> critically think, or even what to think,
> but rather what to "*believe.*"

In regards to "climate change" for example, the differing camps are characterized as "settled science," versus "deniers." Students who unquestioningly accept the notion that the earth is inexorably warming, and that disaster will ensue unless liberals quash the excesses of freedom, are deemed knowledgeable. While any attempt to substantively assess the validity of such claims (or, in reality, the lack of any objective, quantifiable evidence) represents ignorance and sacrilege. The same pattern applies to capitalism versus socialism, the traditional (Judeo-Christian) morality on which the nation was founded as opposed to the bankruptcy of the modern counterculture, and any other matter in which a liberal versus conservative undercurrent can be established. In this, the once unrivaled U.S. education system now more closely resembles Maoist "retraining camps" than the former openness, inquisitiveness, innovation, and ingenuity of American academe. Nevertheless, the product of those schools moves forth into society, largely clueless as to causes and effects that constitute reality, while mindlessly asserting its unquestioned superiority over the primitive notions of former generations.

Elsewhere in our world, this pattern is no less pernicious. Consider the degree of indoctrination being perpetrated by the so-called entertainment media. America's greatest generation can well remember a time, not long ago, when the overwhelming purpose of the "Silver Screen" was to provide an escape from the drudgery of the Great Depression and dreadful events of the Second World War. In ugly contrast, an enormous bulk of modern media is strictly devoted to social causes, addressed from an inflexibly leftist perspective, of course.

From the time of Shakespeare, playwrights resorted to having actors "speak aside" to audiences, particularly in comedies, as a means of giving information to those audiences that put them at an advantage over the rest of the players who, for effect, were often to remain buffoonish and ignorant of their circumstances. This technique has, of course, become much more sophisticated over the past four centuries. These days, TV and movie plot lines are interwoven with suggestions, at every turn, of who is "right" and who is "wrong" on the given topic being addressed. Some producers attempt to be subtle and insidious, while others engage in glaring rewrites of history that can be easily refuted with even a little effort. Their gamble is that most audience members will focus on the story as presented and absorb it as intended, while comparatively few will devote the necessary energy to determine the reality behind the propaganda.

It is inevitable that, from such a toxic and deceptive environment, total falsehoods can gain widespread traction and a fiercely devoted following, especially among the youth, who are far more prone to connecting emotionally with a story rather than logically assessing it.

Given this timeless aspect of the human condition, it is hardly a coincidence that from the start of his book, Alinsky openly focused on the youth of America, ostensibly because of their energy and idealism, while even a cursory analysis reveals that their actual value to him and his movement was on account of their gullibility and fervor.

We have all glimpsed an isolated, but telling effect of this current overall climate on young people when watching those popular televised national talent competitions. In what is intended as comedy (if one ignores the sinister undertones), contestants who clearly lack talent are purposely put on display, as they audition with inarguably dismal performances. Yet when they fail to impress judges and are rejected from advancing to the next round, the frequent response is total shock and outrage. Once again, they are absolutely oblivious to the reality of their limited or nonexistent abilities; a fact which certainly must have been glaringly apparent to friends and teachers. Instead, they are stunned and angry (sometimes, violently so) that their baseless self-image isn't blindly accepted by the judges.

While such is the nature of modern "reality TV," and talent shows are not the events on which a nation's future hinges, these situations do reveal a widespread mindset that, at one time, would have been deemed socially dysfunctional, but is now becoming the "norm." Such thinking, in combination with starkly slanted leftist caricatures of current events, history, and science, has resulted in a generation of young people who have no concept of the world they live in. Nevertheless, they believe themselves to be experts, and are instantly ready and willing to confidently go on the attack against anyone who dares to challenge the worldview that has been pounded into them.

So it is that, despite the devastation that has been wreaked upon their world, resulting in a clear loss of freedom and economic opportunity, they continue to trumpet the leftist party line and are often virulently opposed to any effort to point out its absolute failure to deliver on its promises to them. Instead, even the most transparent obfuscations, when delivered by leftist icons, are instantly embraced as validation that as the leftist agenda has advanced, the nation has been on a worthwhile course from which it simply cannot deviate in the slightest. And any such suggestion of doing so is instantly rejected and condemned under the monotonously predictable banners of "hate" and "insensitivity" (which terms will be specifically dealt with in later chapters).

Nor is this pattern confined to America's youth. At this point, several generations have been subjected to some degree of leftist indoctrination. Furthermore, the hard-left infiltration of American "academe" is so complete that no institution can be presumed immune to it merely on the basis of status or previous reputation. Even older Americans, many of whom were able to benefit from the momentum of that former time when honesty, hard-work, and patriotism made for a "land of opportunity," have remained blissfully ignorant of the encroaching forces that will eventually destroy the comfort and ease they've enjoyed.

> Hard-left infiltration of American "academe" is so complete that no institution can be presumed immune to it merely on the basis of status or previous reputation.

As can be readily gleaned from Saul Alinsky's generous self-appraisal in *"Rules,"* the goals of leftists are, in their minds, so worthy and virtuous that facts need not be included in any assessment of their value. Only malice and hate can possibly be at the root of any opposition. Moreover, since such opposition is instantly rendered abhorrent according to this thought process, blanket condemnation of critics is automatic. It deems as "guilty" those who offer even the slightest suggestion that an accurate assessment of the leftist agenda should be determined solely on the basis of the results it yields. So it is inevitable that any deviation from the liberal orthodoxy is unquestionably "evil." In contrast, all avenues to achieving liberals' end game are, by nature of their stated purpose, inherently worthwhile.

Alarmingly, this coordinated undermining of reason by leftists descends to even lower levels. In order for their "rank and file" to maintain the arrogant perch to which leftists in leadership consign them, they are regularly required to engage in what would otherwise be characterized as thoroughly demeaning professions of loyalty to the orthodoxy. In a breathtaking contradiction to their professed monopoly of "tolerance" and "open mindedness," the regular blunders and other revelations of ineptitude and corruption among liberal leaders, any one of which ought to be deemed thoroughly disqualifying, are instead easily dismissed in the most juvenile of terms which, under even cursory scrutiny, are typically condescending and embarrassingly devoid of substance. But woe unto the underling who dares peer behind the curtain and focus, even briefly, on the truth. For their efforts they can expect to be savaged with shocking brutality, to either be brought back into the fold of the willingly blind, or thereafter be expunged from the ranks of the faithful. Under such circumstances, leftists have proliferated in positions for which they are grossly unqualified. Yet again, their abysmal performances remain beyond serious scrutiny, as their self-assessment is not determined by the content of their work, but instead entirely from their grotesquely bloated opinions of themselves, and the general agreement among their peers of the superiority of their worldview.

Consider the harm suffered by the nation under liberal presidential administrations when an individual is appointed to a high level policy making position, convinced of his economic "expertise" after having completed an Ivy League education, but who is in fact as devoid of talent and ability in his field as that tone-deaf singing contestant, yet just as consumed with the same level of blind arrogance. A seemingly profound economic policy (esteemed as such solely on the basis of pedigree and accolades from similarly credentialed cohorts) may prove to be horribly damaging in practice. Yet the reflexive response to any disapproval is to spew angry epithets and baseless allegations of nefarious motives on the part of critics. Even the plight of those harmed by it, who are typically the "little people" leftists publicly claim to champion, is dismissed as an infuriating distraction.

In the 2004 presidential contest, Democrat challenger John Kerry regularly exhibited glaring ineptitude not only as a potential leader, but even as a political campaigner. Carrying the unflattering baggage of his persona (throughout his public life, Kerry has epitomized the wholly unwarranted arrogance of left-wing elitists described in this chapter), along with such pathetic pandering efforts as his pseudo-Redneck "git me a huntin' license" photo-op, and that infamous "I actually did vote for the $87 billion [Iraq war funding] before I voted against it," Kerry's campaign began to seriously falter. In response, the liberal media became desperate and sought damage control by proclaiming to America that Kerry's public comments were too "nuanced" for common people to properly comprehend. While it is difficult (and not entirely relevant) to determine who originated the notion, it was immediately adopted and widely repeated throughout the remainder of Kerry's campaign.

Any honest appraisal of such an idea would quickly dismiss it as contemptible and demeaning to the American people. But Kerry's staunchest supporters were faced with the options of either renouncing his ineptitude, or accepting their role (along with the rest of America) as pitifully inferior and unable to operate on his stratospheric intellectual level. So, as leftist minions, they easily opted for the latter, since it preserved their mantra of being on the correct side of the issues. Once again, the fact that by embracing such a premise they thoroughly demeaned themselves, is of no consequence. The facade of superiority, which is all that they have, is maintained only as long as no one among their ranks dares to question it; a demand to which, as a result of their studious indoctrination, they dutifully complied.

As a fortunate side note, this flimsy veneer was insufficient to totally fool the American people, and Kerry was defeated at the ballot box in November of 2004. Yet as Secretary of State under Barack Obama, Kerry maintained a highly influential position in government that wholly belied his actual abilities. And, along with his successor Hillary Clinton, it will be a long time before America recovers from the harm that resulted from his starry-eyed leftist notions of international relations and the blind arrogance with which they were put into practice.

Among the most pernicious and condescending statements of recent decades was then House Speaker Nancy Pelosi's unforgettable 2010 assertion "We have to pass the [Obamacare] bill so that you can find out what is in it." Frequently mocked to this day, and cited as an example of the vacuous nature of the Democrat agenda, it is not sufficiently recognized that those most demeaned by Pelosi's statement were not the opponents of Obamacare, but the bill's gullible supporters. Specifically, presumed advocates of Obamacare were targeted as needing to be kept in the fold by any means possible, which motivated Pelosi to spew her indefensible diatribe. Yet again, rather than rebelling against such condescension by demanding a more substantive defense of Obamacare (since none was possible), rank and file liberals largely sidestepped Pelosi's embarrassing statement, and pressed forward with the Obamacare disaster as if all was well. The straight-faced denial of any problem, the repeated professions of ensuing leftist utopia, and when all else failed, the vicious condemnation of those opposing the bliss of "free healthcare for everyone" were all the political ammunition they had. But given their mental conditioning, it proved to be enough for them to stick to the plan.

During the 1990s, as Bill Clinton's pathological dishonesty became inescapable and loomed as a potential liability for the Democrats, their "public relations" machine was forced to concoct a defense for his actions. Remaining firmly in character, they put forth the mantra that "Bill Clinton had to lie to get elected." This blatant and unapologetic denigration of Clinton's voting base sprang from the notion that, once again, the leftist "cause" was universally understood to be so worthwhile for the nation that any means of advancing it would be eventually accepted as valid. Unhindered by quaint and debilitating trifles such as honesty, the leftist agenda and its chief standard-bearer of the day, Bill Clinton, would yield so much goodness for the American people that the deceit could not only eventually be forgiven, America would ultimately be grateful for Clinton's willingness to further their interests in the manner that he did.

Also on Bill Clinton's watch, a single comment delivered during a January 1999 speech in Buffalo New York spotlighted the consuming arrogance of leftists to an unparalleled degree. Asked why he wouldn't consider reducing taxes in the wake of a budget surplus, Clinton explained "We could give it all back to you and hope you spend it right. But if you don't spend it right, here's what's going to happen..." In essence, Clinton was telling the crowd that only the federal government could be counted upon to use the money wisely, and further, that letting common rubes keep the fruits of their labors would cause hardship to future generations, per the usual liberal warnings of impending disaster in a free market society.

> Too few people recoiled at
> Bill Clinton's contempt for them,
> which was so plainly on display.

From his perch, Bill Clinton informed the lowly rabble that his own insights as to how to utilize their property were far superior to such selfish and short-sighted notions as earning and spending it on their own. Equally despicable, his presentation was predictably crafted to stoke the sanctimonious notion of "contributing" to his noble cause as the only respectable option, while denigrating any departure from his collectivist ideology. Given those choices, too few people recoiled at Clinton's contempt for them, which was so plainly on display. Instead, a sizable number of Americans embraced his condescension despite the extent to which it specifically disparaged them. Most significantly, as a result of their thorough indoctrination in leftist sanctimony, they accepted the pronouncement of themselves as being totally vindicated and thus, morally superior, for buying into Clinton's demeaning statist pablum.

Consider how thoroughly incapacitating this pathological arrogance has become in modern Europe. Faced with glaring daily occurrences of rape and murder at the hands of invading Islamists, a situation that should cause any sane society to take immediate and decisive action for the protection of its citizens, Europe is instead paralyzed by the debilitating effects of the "political correctness" in which it is mired. Abhorrently frequent accounts of assaults by "immigrants" from the Middle-East are first denied and even suppressed by the "news media," while outraged Europeans are denigrated and accused of responding out of "fear and bigotry," the standard terms of leftists. Meanwhile, this disaster is disguised in noble sounding platitudes such as providing a safe haven for "refugees."

The insidious cycle and debilitating effects of such arrogance are truly appalling. Rather than letting themselves be shaken into acceptance of reality by the latest ensuing attack, these fully brainwashed and conditioned Euro-lefties actually embrace each new assault as an *opportunity* to once again flaunt their "tolerance" and moral superiority in front of fellow citizens. As is the case elsewhere, among such leftist conclaves, the devotion to "political correctness" is so all consuming that it has essentially become a "contest" among them, to see who can be most sanctimonious in denying the reality that glares at them. Consequently, foreign attackers are essentially shielded, and any "backlash" they might have otherwise received is redirected against those most abominably victimized by the attacks. For far too many, this effect of their preprogrammed arrogance threatens to maintain their culture in a state of willful blindness and total defenselessness until it is too late to recover from the societal debasement that has ensued, or the cultural suicide that increasingly appears to be their fate.

This pattern continues, even as leftists are certainly to be counted among the victims. Yet until an individual actually faces a personal attack, it is seemingly safer and thus "preferable" to go along with the leftist mantra and be applauded as culturally sensitive and caring, rather than warn of a real and burgeoning danger, which will result in immediate ridicule, condemnation, and marginalization from the "powers that be" on the left. This leftist pack mentality has been so thoroughly ingrained that any who seek to break free from it are instantly ostracized in order to prevent even the slightest deviation from the dictates of the orthodoxy, lest they open their eyes and eventually leave the fold.

On this side of the Atlantic, the games are varied somewhat, and the societal decay not quite as advanced. But be assured that things are heading in the same direction. The primary roadblocks faced by the left are those pillars of Americanism put in place by the Founders, who foresaw the possibility of a moral and cultural threat at some point in the future. So of course those very principles and their authors are being systematically targeted for destruction.

A widely held misconception is that leftists who decry America's greatness and seek parity with the rest of the world by eradicating it are consumed with "guilt," over the advantage they've enjoyed, and can only be vindicated by virtue of the exorbitant degree of "humility" they exhibit (when grandstanding in front of the cameras). This guilt is the presumed motivation of their professed desire to implement "fixes" for the past transgressions of Western Culture and American society in particular. As evidence of this, an excellent book by Dr. Shelby Steele entitled *"White Guilt,"* with the subtitle *"How Blacks and Whites Together Destroyed the Promise of the Civil Rights Era,"* is often cited. But although Dr. Steele does an outstanding job dealing with his specific topic, the notion of pervasive "guilt" as a widespread motivator among leftists is vastly misapplied elsewhere. Once again, their actual impetus for promoting the leftist agenda is hardly "guilt," but is in fact the most extreme example of arrogance.

It cannot be stated emphatically enough that the notion of leftists ever feeling "guilt" over the inequities and injustices of life, or their acting on it in such circumstances, is *entirely a myth*. In virtually every circumstance where leftists express "guilt," it is *not* an admission of wrongdoing on their own part, but a *projection* of accused guilt onto some other person or institution, invariably tied to the political right, who from the leftist perspective *should* feel guilty, but isn't sufficiently enlightened (according to their precepts of righteousness) to do so. The examples are endless, but the pattern is invariably the same. A leftist icon will "apologize" for some heinous wrong that has been perpetrated against society, then immediately point a sanctimonious finger of blame at someone, or something else.

To reemphasize, projected "guilt" is *never guilt*. Finger pointing, especially when it is perpetrated with such shamelessness and hypocrisy, is the antithesis of either guilt or humility. Rather, it is the epitome of arrogance and sanctimony. It not only presumes that the particular issue in question should be universally recognized as wrong, simply because a leftist says so, it also carries with it a baseless presumption that leftists are uniquely capable of comprehending and identifying such wrongful actions, and therefore must relentlessly point them out to the rest of society, lest such things otherwise go unnoticed.

Finger pointing, especially when it is perpetrated
with such shamelessness and hypocrisy,
is the antithesis of either guilt or humility.

But just as predictably, this pattern of behavior completely exempts them from taking any action to correct the injustices of life, other than to pontificate about it and demand that somebody else make sacrifices to implement a fix. Here, Saul Alinsky's own deeds represented a sterling example, though they are hardly alone.

A quick read of Alinsky's biography tells of all the noble causes in which he endeavored to "improve life" for others. But while Alinsky's efforts to "organize" disparate groups and motivate them to take action are abundant, any evidence of his own physical contributions to feed the hungry or clothe the naked is virtually impossible to find. This was no "Mother Theresa" who actually shared of his own property to help others, but in contrast he embodied the glaring double standards of Democrat politicians who extol their own virtue for being so "caring and generous" when "sharing" (confiscating and redistributing) the property of others.

In this sense, Alinsky's behavior was a striking precursor to the haughtiness of Clinton Vice-President Al Gore, who gained worldwide notoriety as an environmental philanthropist and savior, despite living in an expansive mansion that was tremendously expensive to heat in the winter and keep cool in the summer. Gore never deprived himself of any opulence as he enriched himself, flying from one "climate summit" to another in the lap of luxury on private and chartered jets. Clearly, the enormity of Gore's "carbon footprint" was of no consequence, since the supposed worthiness of his cause vastly outweighed the pollution that resulted from his extravagant lifestyle. Yet let a common citizen seek to own an SUV in order to safely navigate winter roads, and that individual becomes the target of condemnation in the severest of terms since, we are incessantly told by Gore and his kind, such inexcusable excesses would surely put the planet in peril.

President Bill Clinton, in Uganda in 1998 famously "apologized" for slavery which, coming from other individuals of real character might have carried an element of true contrition. However, in Clinton's case, it epitomized the empty grandstanding of liberals who seek to elevate themselves above the unrefined and selfish interests of the unenlightened right. Conspicuous by their total absence in Clinton's words and consciousness were any references to his own mistreatment of people in his realm, and particularly those women whom he sexually harassed and exploited. Nor did he ever exhibit the least remorse for embracing and lauding known segregationists such as his one-time idol J. William Fulbright. Though Clinton was vigorously lauded by fellow leftists for his feigned compassion towards minorities and even women (which seems comical in retrospect), the overall pattern of his words, as opposed to his totally self-indulgent actions, puts the lie to any notions of real contrition in the "guilt" which he publicly assumed, but more accurately assigned to others.

Of course, when it comes to faux "apologizing," it is unlikely that any character in American history could ever compete with Barack Obama who, throughout his time in the White House, deftly "apologized" at every opportunity for America's unbroken track record of flaws and failures (in his worldview). It is beyond any stretch of reason to deem Obama's consuming narcissism and antipathy towards America as "humility." But while Obama carried this conduct to a ludicrous extreme, by no means did he hold a monopoly on it. The list of leftist competitors in this game of egos could go on forever. It should be increasingly evident that such faux "guilt" is inseparable from the arrogant mindset that readily and enthusiastically inflicts harmful policies on others, loudly claiming to be their champions, while invariably rigging the game in order to remain immune to the inevitable and dire consequences of those policies.

The willingness of Congressional Democrats to jubilantly extol the virtues of Obamacare, while totally exempting themselves from participation in it on the basis that its members could not endure the hardships resulting from it, was among the most glaring of examples, but hardly the only one. Yet leftist arrogance is not without its strategic liabilities. But this is only true if conservatives possess the necessary diligence to identify it, along with the fortitude to confront it, unhindered by self-doubt. And thus far, that is where leftists have held a decisive advantage.

By now it should be readily apparent, though admittedly discouraging, that mere intellectual engagement with modern day leftists is ultimately pointless. And this is especially true of those in positions of leadership. Directly confronting their arrogance, and expecting them to retreat from their chosen course as a result, is a fruitless endeavor. But this does not suggest that their mindset constitutes an impenetrable armor against which any conservative opposition will ultimately prove futile. Rather it highlights the specific manner in which conservatives must engage the left in order to be effective. And the short version of this counter strategy demands that it *not* be conducted on terms dictated by them, despite the skill with which Alinsky acolytes have learned to frame every issue in a manner that inarguably favors their position.

This need not be the end of the story. Arrogance only empowers the left when we leave its presumptions uncontested. If, on the other hand, we recognize it as empty, and capably dismantle it as such, it loses its power. Based as it is on unsubstantiated assertions of intrinsic superiority, and owing such assertions only to the assumed virtue of leftist ideology *as stated by leftists*, it is a complete "house of cards" that is ultimately vulnerable. The Achilles' Heel of the Alinsky strategy, which will be reemphasized throughout this text, is that it *only works on those who allow it*.

As the particular details of the leftist onslaught and how it can be effectively neutralized are presented, the manner in which this counterattack must take place will increasingly reveal itself.

CHAPTER TWO
HYPOCRISY: NOT A LIABILITY TO LEFTISTS

Having so thoroughly convinced themselves of the unassailable greatness of their cause, a mentality which is the direct byproduct of their consuming arrogance, leftists are thereafter totally justified in their minds invoking any words, and engaging in any actions necessary to advance that cause. It is an understatement to say that truth itself is the first casualty of such thinking. Rather, truth is the greatest stumbling block to their agenda, which requires that it be circumvented as quickly and thoroughly as possible in order for them to move forward. This mindset immediately manifests itself in the glaring hypocrisy with which leftists shamelessly but relentlessly attempt to establish one set of rules for themselves (essentially amounting to no limitations whatsoever), while dictating a wholly different and deliberately stringent set of standards by which to hamstring their conservative opposition. Only in this manner can they expect to maintain their presumed dominance of the "moral high ground."

On such a basis, continuing victories are all but assured, since the unsuspecting right is all too often sufficiently foolish as to accept arbitrarily contrived restraints upon itself. Sadly, for too many on the right, the unwillingness to flatly call out liberal hypocrisy for what it is, and thereafter refuse to accept it as legitimate, leaves a severely lopsided "playing field" in which conservatives continually find themselves outmaneuvered by leftists with their flagrant duplicity and lies. Defeat becomes inevitable in any engagement with the left on these absurdly unbalanced terms. It's as if leftists are somehow allowed to advance their ideology as a bunch of marauding vandals with spray paint, while piously demanding that conservatives color strictly "within the lines."

Worse yet, it is the leftists who confer upon themselves the sole authority to determine where those lines exist.

Merely calling out the political left for these glaring inequities is completely pointless. In the end, the goal of leftists is not to win fairly or honorably, but simply *to win*. Their "mandate" is not that their ideology has prevailed with any "consent of the governed" (since it is most often masked), but just that *they prevailed*. And in each such case where leftists succeed, the whimpering complaints of disingenuousness leveled against them from the right, if not backed by decisive action to deal with their fraud, only serve to embolden them in their inevitable next venture.

> In the end, the goal of leftists
> is not to win fairly or honorably,
> but simply to win.

In June of 1954, when defending a young associate with known ties to American communists, Joseph Welch uttered his famous indictment of Senator Joseph McCarthy "Have you no sense of decency sir, at long last? Have you left no sense of decency?" Irrespective of the facts at hand, it was the boldness and ferocity of Welch's attack on Senator McCarthy that ultimately turned the tables on him, and eventually drove him, as well as his entire effort to root out communist infiltrators, into a completely defensive posture from which it never recovered. To this day, Welch's accusation stands as its own testament against any ostensibly overbearing efforts to expose and confront seditious insurgencies operating on behalf of the political left.

However, no such pronouncement against the left, regardless of massive corroborating evidence, will ever induce its players to waiver in their tactics for even a moment. In contrast to the reaction Joseph Welch elicited, if current day liberals were to ever face a similar question of whether or not they have any shame over their glaring hypocrisy and moral bankruptcy (and assuming that any among them even felt compelled to respond), the answer would be a flippant "No," after which they would press forward without the slightest hesitation. For although among civilized and honorable people, hypocrisy reflects a flaw that demands correction, to leftists it is an enabling advantage; a tool by which they can always deal themselves a winning hand. Until this disparity between the two camps is recognized by those on the right, and thereafter properly rebutted in every circumstance where it is manifested, it will remain a political weapon giving the left an undeserved and decisive edge, while simultaneously being a crippling handicap to those on the right.

Leftist hypocrisy is rampant throughout every realm of political discourse and in every contest between left and right, from political debates on Capitol Hill, to the "coverage" of such events on the nightly news, to the revisionist "history" in the government "education" system wherein young minds are rendered susceptible to accepting leftist ideology as legitimate. And, of course, the mindless liberals of Hollywood can always be counted upon to reflect their warped worldview as "fact" on television and in the movies.

While this dire set of circumstances is grim and formidable, it also reveals a potentially decisive weakness in the leftist onslaught, since their agenda can only be advanced under an all-encompassing cloak of lies. The stridency of their efforts to present a monolithic front while prohibiting any opposition is proof of an Achilles' Heel. Confront that facade with truth on a diligent and unapologetic basis, and it will inevitably fracture and eventually crumble. Nobody is more aware of this than the leftists themselves, which is why they are so fervent in their efforts to enshroud every situation in a meticulously structured mantle of deceit. Without a total monopoly on "the facts" as defined by leftists, they cannot hope to credibly make their case. Thus, their obsession with maintaining a monopolistic control over the flow of information, from government school curricula to the suppression of opposing viewpoints on the public airwaves and in print, to the meticulously scripted talking points among leftist political figures. And while deceit is a pernicious element of the human condition and has been so since the first adversarial encounters between individuals, in recent decades it has been elevated to a virtual "science" by the left. The evidence is massive, to the point of justifying an entire book on that subject alone. However, only a few of the more egregious and pernicious examples need to be recalled so as to establish the sordid and ongoing pattern.

In the latter days of the Vietnam war, when the efforts of America's anti-war radicals reached their peak, leftists zealously condemned American military personnel as "baby killers." Yet these same people were silent in regards to the massive genocide that ensued at the hands of the North Vietnamese in the wake of American evacuation of South Vietnam, or of even worse genocides committed by such notably vile communist regimes as Cambodia's Khmer Rouge, who slaughtered as much as a quarter of that nation's population, possibly totaling three million people. Yet, to hear it from American leftists, the 1968 "My Lai Massacre," in which between three and five hundred Vietnamese were killed by an Army detachment under the command of Lieutenant William Calley, was the defining event and nadir of inhumanity of the Vietnam War and the entire region. From the leftist perspective, My Lai not only stood as the ultimate testament to the inherent immorality of America and its efforts to prevent the spread of communism in Southeast Asia, it gave a blanket justification to every barbaric act by the communist monsters of that region.

From this disparity, it is apparent that the civilian lives lost in Southeast Asia were only of importance to the left insofar as they could be invoked to validate the liberal condemnation of the evils of America, while communist tyrannies that slaughtered millions, were given a total pass. The same unbroken pattern holds to this day, as leftist activists and media outlets spotlight individual incidents as they attempt to make the case that innocent urban minorities are wantonly and regularly gunned down by rogue police officers. Yet they completely ignore the rampant mayhem and death that occurs on an appallingly frequent basis, and in enormously greater numbers, at the hands of the gangs and criminals of America's inner cities.

Any expectation that actual concern for human lives, whether in the jungles of the Far East, or among America's urban war zones, might prompt the leftist media to clean up its act are naive or delusional. The lies and fraud from which their alternative reality is contrived have become so ingrained, leftists have been rendered virtually unable to even absorb any refuting evidence. Leftist bias and selective "moralizing" of so-called "news" outlets have become the sole perspective from which they present their views of the world. Double standards have degenerated from deliberate to reflexive, with no room left for any proper consideration of evidence.

> Leftist double standards have degenerated
> from deliberate to reflexive, with no room left
> for any proper consideration of evidence.

During a January 1994 episode of Nightline, host Ted Koppel introduced Lt. Colonel Oliver North, who was running for the United States Senate in Virginia, with the blunt characterization of North as "an accomplished liar." Koppel's epithet was given in response to North's admitted misleading testimony before the Congress during the Iran-Contra affair. While the initial public reaction to Koppel might be one of justification, particularly in light of how the leftist media has incessantly painted Iran-Contra as sordid and indefensible, several other facts need to be included in this situation in order to gain a complete perspective of it.

For starters, consider the timeline of Koppel's comment. This was the beginning of the second year of the presidency of Bill "I did not inhale" Clinton. Between his 1992 campaign and his initial year in the White House, Bill Clinton had thoroughly established himself on the national stage as a pathological liar (Arkansans were well aware of Governor Bill Clinton's predisposition for lying many years prior). Enshrouded in scandal and corruption, Clinton already had an almost comical reputation for prevarication. Yet on no occasion did Koppel ever offer any assessment of Clinton bearing even the slightest hint in that direction. Instead, Koppel has since lamented that Clinton didn't receive the "credit" for his time in office that Koppel felt was his due.

More recently, Koppel appeared as a "Special Correspondent" on *The Rock Center* during its 2011-2013 run. The host of that program was none other than the serially delusional Brian Williams, who is infamous for essentially destroying his career when caught in a series of blatant, self-aggrandizing lies. And this occurred after Koppel had also appeared as a reporter for the NBC Nightly News when Williams was Anchor. So it is inarguable that Koppel has worked on numerous occasions in close contact with Williams, and is completely familiar with Williams' habitual fabrications. Nevertheless, as with Clinton, Koppel had nothing disparaging to say about Williams' behavior that might be even the slightest bit comparable to the unrestrained contempt he exhibited towards Oliver North. Instead, Koppel dismissed Williams' congenital dishonesty, insisting that Williams had merely "slipped," and "has more than paid the price," whatever that was supposed to mean.

Koppel's situation is hardly a random fluke, but is enormously significant for several reasons. First, it reveals the thoroughly selective and agenda-driven nature of "morality" espoused by the leftist media, which epitomizes the pervasive hypocrisy of leftists. Furthermore, given that Koppel's denunciation of Oliver North occurred back in 1994, it reflects circumstances that conservatives have had to face for decades, and which have seriously degenerated ever since. Leftists are totally matter of fact as they capriciously determine who is worthy of condemnation, and who deserves "absolution" and praise. It is under just such premises that brazen perjurers like Hillary Clinton grant themselves a "pass" (with total media concurrence) on the basis that she "may have short circuited" when the reality is that she flatly lies about her conduct and her own official assessments of it. The Koppel "standard" grants Hillary and her kind sufficient latitude to make such claims without fear of repercussions or accountability of any kind.

More significantly, Ted Koppel is by no means regarded as a hardcore leftist. Rather, he is touted, even by the Republican Establishment, as thoroughly "mainstream." With such skewed standards generally accepted by the GOP, it is no wonder that even the glaring leftist radicalism of such entities as CNN and MSNBC are unlikely to be relegated to the extreme leftist fringe where they belong, but instead enjoy seeming credibility that bears no connection to their actual conduct. Consequently, their thoroughly contorted worldview often gains wholly undeserved traction among the general population. As long as standards for "objectivity," are so jaundiced, and overtly biased individuals like Ted Koppel are treated with near deference by those who should be flatly dismissing them, the remainder of hard left propagandists can benefit from "coat tails" such as his. And the situation only deteriorates from there.

Other examples of leftist media bias abound, and have arguably worsened enormously in recent years. Several patterns have emerged during this time which, when the specifics are sufficiently analyzed, reveal a sinister undercurrent of straight-faced presumption and judgment, all from the hard-left perspective. Ignoring *any* of these indicators allows their faux assessments to be cemented as objectivity and even "fact," despite the transparency of their leftward slant.

Contrast some prominent recent episodes of twenty-first century security breaches, and how both liberal media and posturing leftist political players responded to them. First, recall the notorious "outing" of CIA employee Valerie Plame Wilson, during the term of President George W. Bush. Then consider it in contrast to a more recent occurrence, which is the still unsettled scandal of the illegal, unsecured e-mail server used by Hillary Clinton to conduct her sordid "private business" of selling official influence, below the radar, while serving as Secretary of State.

In early 2002, on the heels of the September 11 World Trade Center terrorist attacks, former Ambassador Joe Wilson was commissioned by the CIA to investigate possible Uranium purchases in Niger, Africa by Iraqi dictator Saddam Hussein. Upon returning to America, Wilson wrote an article for the New York Times, in which he claimed to refute such actions by Hussein. One week later, columnist Robert Novak published the name of Wilson's wife, Valerie Plame, as a CIA operative. And from that truly inconsequential event, Democrats in Washington caterwauled with accusations of the most horrific compromise of American security since Benedict Arnold tried to give West Point to the British.

Given Wilson's total lack of technical qualifications for his "mission" (other than the ability to rub diplomatic elbows), it doesn't require the deductive abilities of Werner Von Braun to conclude that Wilson must have had some special connection within the CIA to receive such an "assignment." And under those circumstances, nepotism would hardly be out of the question. Moreover Plame's CIA status, at the time her identity was disclosed, was as an employee working at the organization's Langley Virginia headquarters! What this means is that, apart from the possibility of her disappearing down a "telephone booth" elevator at some obscure parking garage on the way to work, anyone standing anywhere along her daily commute, and possessing the ability to read the license plates on her car, could have easily determined her identity with full knowledge of her employer.

Nevertheless, leftist cries of "foul play" reached such a crescendo that President George W. Bush appointed Patrick Fitzgerald as an Independent Prosecutor to investigate the "breach" and determine the culprits. Two years later, and after expending huge sums of money and wasting enormous amounts of Bush Administration time as it sought to comply with demands for information from Fitzgerald's office, Fitzgerald secured five indictments of Lewis I. "Scooter" Libby, none of which contended that he had divulged Plame's identity or status. In short, Libby was "guilty" of failing to recall, with absolute precision, conversations in which he had participated months earlier. Yet he was fined $250,000 and disbarred. Had it not been for a belated presidential pardon, he would also have had to serve thirty months in prison.

Upon Libby's indictment, leftists on Capitol Hill and in the media responded with unfettered triumph and jubilation. Fitzgerald delivered the announcement of his "findings" with shameless bravado, asserting that by bringing the hammer of justice down on Libby, "I think what we see here today, when a vice president's chief of staff is charged with perjury and obstruction of justice, it does show the world that this is a country that takes its law seriously; that all citizens are bound by the law." Later he heroically added "I can say that for the people who work at the CIA and work at other places, they have to expect that when they do their jobs that classified information will be protected."

Celebratory leftist "news" accounts of Libby's indictment treated the event as if the greatest all time threat to America's security had been successfully thwarted, with salivating speculation that Libby's crimes would inevitably lead to Vice-President Dick Cheney. Emboldened Democrats weren't hiding the political agenda which was at the root of the Plame affair. Eventually, it would become evident that politics alone was their motivation.

Responding in 2007 to President Bush's commutation of Libby's prison sentence, then House Speaker Nancy Pelosi lamented with righteous insincerity that "The President's commutation of Scooter Libby's prison sentence does not serve justice, condones criminal conduct, and is a betrayal of the trust of the American people." She further accused Bush of having "abandoned all sense of fairness when it comes to justice" and failure to "uphold the law."

Predictably, those history revisionists in Hollywood took up the issue, repackaging it and presenting it to the public in 2010 with the movie "Fair Game" (based on Plame's account of the episode). Not surprisingly, Plame was portrayed as a cross between James Bond and Wonder Woman who was ostensibly involved in covert operations at the highest levels to save the world, until her cover was maliciously blown.

The nitpicking problem with this event, and all the leftist sanctimony surrounding it, was that it was based on a total lie. Patrick Fitzgerald's "investigation" commenced in the fall of 2003. Shortly thereafter, Deputy Secretary of State Richard Armitage informed Fitzgerald that is was *he* who had divulged Plame's identity to Novak (a detail entirely missing from the plot of "Fair Game"). Nevertheless, Fitzgerald continued his "investigation," from that point forward under totally false premises, for another two years! Throughout that period, Armitage remained silent at the bidding of Fitzgerald, whose real motivations and intentions are anybody's guess. Ultimately, despite the vilification of Libby, the single individual most guilty of perpetrating a fraud, suppressing evidence, engaging in a baseless witch-hunt, and by the aggregate of such actions, lying to the American people, was Patrick Fitzgerald himself. If such is the real regard which Fitzgerald and his liberal cheering section hold for the enshrined "law" and its weaponized purpose, then nobody is safe, the moment their lives and actions become an irritation to the state. Worst of all, the greatest casualty of such actions is national security itself, which was reduced to little more than a political football as a direct result of Fitzgerald's misbegotten "investigation," and the pandemic of leftist grandstanding over it.

As to that epic cinematic achievement "Fair Game" (which netted less than half of its $22 million production costs), the only passing reference to Armitage came in the *postscript!* For a sobering perspective, try imagining a "historical" movie on the assassination of Abraham Lincoln, in which the only mention of John Wilkes Booth occurs in the closing credits. It would be an understatement to refer to such duplicity as "agenda driven."

> The greatest casualty of such actions is national security itself, which was reduced to little more than a political football as a direct result of Fitzgerald's misbegotten "investigation."

The purpose in revisiting the Plame episode in such excruciating detail is not to give an exhaustive account, but to highlight the hypocritical manner in which leftists will cry "foul" when they believe some political advantage is to be gained by doing so. No rational person can truly believe that liberals are, in any manner, preoccupied with maintaining national security, or in maintaining the cover of operatives in that most reviled of organizations (in their world), the CIA. To be sure, the entire occurrence was and is merely political theater. In May of 2014, in the middle of Barack Obama's second term, the identity of the CIA "Chief of Station" in Kabul, Afghanistan, Gregory Vogel, was revealed in a statement to the press coinciding with Obama's visit to the region. Operating in such a forward area, Vogel risked immediate and possibly mortal danger as a result of the security compromise. Nevertheless, the event was dismissed by the Obama White House as a "mistake," and little further discussion ever followed. Case closed.

Roll forward to 2015, when the public learned of the massive and quantifiable security breach that resulted from Hillary Clinton's deliberate misuse of classified State Department information. Between 2009 and 2013, during her tenure as Secretary of state, she casually shared highly sensitive material with whomever she pleased on a private e-mail server, with total disdain for the grave implications to America's security. And while a comprehensive discussion of "Plamegate," were it pertinent to the current discussion, might require several pages, entire books can (and no doubt will) be written on the vast web of crime and collusion that is the Hillary Clinton e-mail scandal. But only a few relevant points need to be mentioned, in order to establish the shameless duplicity and hypocrisy that characterizes everyone involved up and down the ladder, from Hillary herself to collaborating enablers such as Attorney General Loretta Lynch, FBI Director James Comey, and ultimately their boss, Barack Obama.

Whereas no actual harm to Plame ever occurred as a result of her identity being released, Hillary's malfeasance was most likely directly culpable in the death of Shahram Amiri, an Iranian nuclear scientist who had collaborated with U.S. intelligence agents. A reference to Amiri as "our friend," in Hillary's unsecured e-mails was easily sufficient grounds for the Iranians to hang Amiri as a spy in August of 2016. Of course leftists have fervently denied any link, as if the only acceptable validation would have to come from the Iranians themselves. But Iranian hackers are certainly more adept at "connecting the dots" than criminally partisan leftist politicians who remain stubbornly in denial, along with their willfully blind enablers in the media.

During a three hour session with the FBI in July of 2016 regarding her criminal misuse of the private e-mail server, Hillary Clinton dodged straightforward FBI inquiries *forty times* with her glaring "Don't recall" deflection, a tactic she made famous as she obfuscated when being questioned by investigators back during Bill Clinton's presidency. It is noteworthy that, had Scooter Libby been granted similar latitude for evasion with the same excuse in a mere *four* responses, he could have completely skated free. Nevertheless, throughout the entire Clinton e-mail debacle, leftists have doggedly insisted that *nothing* wrong ever occurred. And, per their standard pattern of going hard on the offensive in order to take the focus off of themselves, they loudly and indignantly rebut the mountains of evidence amassed against Hillary by hurling accusations of nefarious motivations on the part of her accusers. Herein is Hillary's "Vast Right Wing conspiracy" deflection of the 1990s revisited. And it is here that their strategy, based in the principles of Alinsky's "*Rules*," has on yet another occasion enjoyed unwarranted success when it should have blown up in their faces.

When Texas Congressman Trey Gowdy released the report from the Benghazi committee he chaired, he had the prime opportunity to fully characterize Hillary Clinton's behavior, both during the attack on the American Consulate, and in its aftermath, as *criminally* fraudulent. Doing so in completely unambiguous terms could have so thoroughly set the stage for her eventual indictment that it would have been virtually impossible for Obama Administration pawns, such as Attorney General Loretta Lynch, to turn a blind eye to the rest of her vast, intertwined web of malfeasance. Instead, Gowdy showed a greater concern for dodging the inevitable liberal backlash and charges of bias on his part, than of decisively driving home the relevant point that Clinton had indeed engaged in horrendous violations before, during, and after the Benghazi attack. So Gowdy offered no direct determination of Clinton's guilt, but instead delivered this non-statement: "Now I simply ask the American people to read this report for themselves, look to the evidence we have collected, and reach their own conclusions."

Given this ample wiggle room, the leftist press eagerly and predictably heralded Gowdy's restraint as a declaration of Hillary's total exoneration. In like manner, James Comey readily echoed those sentiments and similarly provided cover for Hillary shortly thereafter when the FBI delivered its own token report. Taking an unprecedented stand, Comey delivered the bizarre assertion that despite voluminous evidence of criminal actions, no "proof" of intent could be determined, so he was not recommending indictment. Of course this sordid saga continues. Since Comey's faux "exoneration," everyone who rallied to Hillary's defense has been further tainted with the inevitable constant stream of Clinton corruption, with no end in sight. Nevertheless, having been successful with their total juxtaposition of innocence and guilt in the Plame episode, leftists within the highest levels of government had no problem continuing the charade, and entangling any real efforts at pursuing justice in their endlessly ongoing Mueller "investigation."

So throughout the 2006 mid-term elections, and into the 2008 presidential race, liberals invoked "Plamegate" as though it was both a heinous crime which inflicted irreparable harm on American security, and a defining event that characterized the hopelessly corrupt administration of George W. Bush. Yet despite such shrill appraisals, no such reaction was warranted. However, the magnitude of their glaring hypocrisy can only be grasped when one considers the breathtaking scope of Hillary Clinton's e-mail scandal. Hardly the inadvertent disclosure of a single tidbit of information, Clinton brazenly engaged in a course of soliciting bribes, selling influence (the two are overwhelmingly synonymous), subordinating America's security to her personal gain, destroying *subpoenaed evidence*, committing perjury when questioned on the matter, and engaging collaborators within the FBI and Department of Justice to assist in the cover-up of her felonious actions. Since that time, both Democrat politicians and their media parrots refuse to appropriately address the massive accumulation of further evidence of Hillary Clinton's deliberate compromise of classified State Department information, as well as her flagrant obstruction of any and every attempt at investigation.

Worst of all, in the current climate, Republicans are more fearful of accusations of "partisanship" or being deemed "mean spirited," than of allowing Democrat criminals and traitors to walk. Thus is leftist hypocrisy enabled by those on the right. It is difficult to fully grasp the starkness of the contrast that exists between such eggshell-walking from the right, as opposed to the unrestrained "hard ball" tactics of the left. Yet the pattern is entrenched on both sides, as it has been throughout the latter part of the last century.

Blatant corruption during both of Bill Clinton's terms in the White House eventually resulted in Senate investigations and calls for a special counsel. To the astonishment of Senators on the investigating committee, then Attorney General Janet Reno covered Clinton's tracks at times so openly that key investigating Senators called for an independent counsel to bypass Reno's efforts to run interference for Clinton. In a move that vastly eclipsed any Nixon efforts to thwart investigators during Watergate, Reno turned a blind eye to the otherwise inescapable evidence of Clinton wrongdoing, and instead attempted to deflect attention from Clinton by making accusations against RNC Chairman Haley Barbour. Thus was the pattern set whereby Republicans, despite holding a winning hand, were put on the defensive, and like a cadre of battered wives, tacitly accepted such glaring miscarriages of justice as their rightful and apparently inevitable place.

In the current climate, Republicans are more fearful of accusations of "partisanship" or being deemed "mean spirited," than of allowing Democrat criminals and traitors to walk.

Ultimately, in none of these episodes has the focus remained on identifying corrupt behavior at the highest levels of government and expunging it for the good of the country. Rather every legal engagement has purposely devolved into a detestable "Chess match," with guilt and innocence having no basis in fact, but instead reflecting the willingness of the left to advance its political fortunes as a result of its sheer brazenness, which is further enabled by the timidity of the GOP. The hypocrisy of the left can be characterized in the severest of terms, but since its adherents are without shame on account of it, they are not likely to be distracted from their ultimate aim, which is to politically dominate.

At this point, it may seem appropriate to launch into a comprehensive list of leftist hypocritical infractions ranging from the sanctimony of leftists in government, to the disconnect between supposed champions of the environment and their lavish lifestyles, to those elitists in Hollywood and professional sports who excoriate and denigrate the nation that has made them incomprehensibly wealthy and famous. However, while it is necessary to clearly establish the pattern of empty sanctimony exhibited by leftists, which is most often in complete contradiction to their actions, the most important objective is to comprehend such behavior as a pattern, and recognize it wherever it manifests itself. Only then can the vehement pontificating of leftists be seen in its truly ugly and duplicitous nature, not as a means of improving life for anyone, but as an avenue to power, for the sole benefit of those who thrive on power.

Among present day leftist politicians, the propensity for hypocrisy is reaching depths previously unknown outside of banana republics and nightmarish tyrannies. And this is its natural, wholly predictable course. Thoroughly privy to the facts, leftists in government are without excuse for the blatant lies they officially spew onto an unknowing public which they clearly intend to preserve in its unenlightened and pliable stupor. Far from believing themselves as accountable and heroic guardians of the people (and despite any platitudes of such that they may occasionally offer), they prove by their actions that they hold the common citizen in absolute contempt. Moreover, they recognize their institutionalized ability to defraud the public as an empowering asset, which they value above any other dominating weapon.

Nevertheless, the problem is twofold. A conservative "opposition" that accepts this political and journalistic fraud as its inescapable fate, rather than seeking ways to circumvent it, consigns itself to surrender and failure. However, these grim circumstances and the course for America they portend are not so much an inescapable fate as they are a reflection of the defeatist attitude of too many on the right who currently hold positions of power. Here again, the leftist tactics are only as potent as compliant targets expect them to be.

The Alinsky strategy is only effective against those who allow it. But rising above such things requires courage and a commitment to principle that puts justice and truth ahead of conventional political pragmatism. Otherwise, "business as usual" will prevail, which portends an unending pattern of political retreat. And the American people will continue to pay the price.

CHAPTER THREE
HYPOCRISY AS A STRATEGY

Among conservatives and Republicans, one of the darkest political episodes of recent decades was "Watergate," spanning from June of 1972 when the break-in at Democrat National Committee headquarters first occurred, to the resignation of Richard Nixon in August of 1974. Throughout those twenty-six months, Democrats relentlessly lectured the nation on the rule of law, the sanctity of justice, the integrity of the Constitution, and the need to preserve America from the mortal threats posed to it if such ideals weren't diligently upheld. When evidence of malfeasance in the Nixon Administration exceeded standards of reasonable doubt, Republicans joined Democrat calls for Nixon to leave office. In the end, their only choice was to renounce the corruption and act decisively against it, or be forever tainted as complicit. Given the circumstances, they had no other option.

Unfortunately, too many of them believed the profuse and strident Democrat sanctimony of the Watergate era to be sincere. Barely two decades later, they would learn the ugly truth. During the presidency of Bill Clinton, a literal avalanche of flagrant corruption proceeded to pour forth, ranging from money laundering inside the White House, to shady land deals, to the sale of American nuclear and missile technology to the Chinese, to abuses of official power against individuals who fell into disfavor with the Clinton political machine, to the almost regular appearances of bodies, such as the apparent "suicide" of Deputy White House Counsel Vince Foster, and the dubious circumstances surrounding his death. However, the frequent expectations of Bill Clinton's "Waterloo" moment consistently amounted to nothing, specifically due to a total lack of interest on the part of the liberal media, combined with a stunning ability of Democrat politicians to look directly into cameras and assert, with totally straight faces, "nothing to see here." In stark contrast to their heated assertions that America couldn't possibly survive if the hammer of justice were not severely lowered on anyone and everyone associated with Watergate, Democrats glibly deflected all concern over the scope of Clinton corruption with such trite rejoinders as "It's all about sex," and assertions of the inconsequential nature of Bill Clinton's "private life."

To properly assess the astronomical difference in scope, consider the matter of FBI files, the misuse of a *single* one of which during Watergate sufficed to send Nixon Special Counsel Chuck Colson to prison for seven months. Yet on Clinton's watch, an episode eventually nicknamed "Filegate" involved as many as twelve hundred such FBI files, many containing sensitive personal information on members of previous presidential administrations. These files apparently traveled all over the Clinton White House, at times even coming within the clutches of Hillary Clinton. Yet after incessant stonewalling and deflection from the Clinton cabal, no official determination of wrongdoing was ever established. In the end, the flagrantly illegal presence of those files in the hands of such shady operatives as Hillary Clinton henchman Craig Livingstone was dismissed as a "bureaucratic mistake." More significantly perhaps was, again, the total lack of "interest" by a liberal media machine whose primary goal was to exonerate the Clintons and continue to enable their agenda of dragging America to the left.

No less despicable and hypocritical was the coordinated effort of media and Democrat players to protect Bill Clinton from any consequences of the sordid and disgraceful Monica Lewinsky affair. Remaining on course through pure shamelessness throughout the entire episode, Clinton and his defenders instantly switched from the deflection of "never happened" to "doesn't matter," the moment Lewinsky's infamous blue dress and its incontrovertible DNA evidence made further denials impossible. But while Republicans had wallowed in guilt and self-reproach for ever having supported Richard Nixon, the Clinton cabal and its media propagandists simply reverted to marketing and "public relations" strategies of recasting the situation as a giant meaningless distraction, laying their convoluted version of "guilt" at the feet of the Republicans. Any standards of right and wrong, the misogynistic exploitation of a young intern, perjury under oath, and the abuse of power to suppress evidence became "irrelevant" according to the left, while the real injustice, asserted by that moral paragon Bill Clinton himself, was the so called "politics of personal destruction" being fomented by partisan Republicans, which he and his Democrat parakeets shamelessly decried as the only significant issue needing to be addressed and corrected.

From these episodes, and so many others that could be recounted, it should be obvious that, from their most fundamental building blocks of what ostensibly constitutes "right and wrong," the contrast between the ideologies of the left and right are as starkly divided as night and day. Thus, it stands to reason that the respective approaches of each political camp to achieving social and political goals will likewise be drastically different. Some on the right embrace the misbegotten notion that honesty and forthrightness puts them at a disadvantage, therefore compelling them to adopt underhanded leftist strategies in order to triumph over their liberal opposition. From the start, this idea is doomed to fail, since it represents a total contradiction of professed motivations and tactics. The Scriptures plainly state that a bad tree cannot bear good fruit. And this precept is just as relevant in the physical and political realms as it is in the spiritual. However, this does not suggest that conservatives should naively allow themselves to be paralyzed by restrictions indiscriminately placed on them in the name of "virtue," especially when those restrictions are dictated by their morally bankrupt leftist rivals.

Unfortunately, just such a pattern has been established over the past several decades, and particularly since the advent of the Alinsky strategy. In far too many cases, conservatives are unwittingly and unnecessarily prevented from truly confronting their opposition, simply because they allow themselves to be distracted by phony "moralizing" from the left. Introspection can be a good thing, but only when it results from a sincere personal effort to ensure one is saying and doing what is right. It should *never* be undertaken at the bidding of the liberal political opposition whose sole purpose it to confuse and hamstring effective conservative strategizing. Accepting the premises of leftist hypocrites only serves to neutralize conservative momentum, which insidiously puts those leftists in complete control. And *nothing* good or "moral" can come from that.

> Introspection can be a good thing, but only when it results from a sincere personal effort to ensure one is saying and doing what is right.

What must be thoroughly understood is that leftists, having become completely comfortable with hypocrisy and deceit as political assets, feel no guilt whatsoever over their duplicity. Thus, they are not dissuaded from their agenda when confronted by these things. Instead, they employ such human failings as an arsenal to be invoked when convenient, then denied and even denounced if the tide shifts and they can make a case, even on the flimsiest basis, that their conservative opponents are less than absolutely pure and honorable. By such means, they continually assert their sordid ideology from a contrived perch on the moral high ground, and remain shamelessly on the offensive, despite the abundance of contradictory evidence.

In the 2011 "Tuscon Massacre" Jared Loughner, a mentally ill (and left leaning) individual opened fire in a Safeway parking lot, killing six people and injuring sixteen others including Congresswoman Gabby

Giffords. Immediately, leftists jubilantly and predictably went on another "politically correct" rampage. Claiming they had evidence of right wing rhetoric inciting violence (Giffords is a Democrat), they flooded the airwaves with blanket accusations against conservatism, hurling specific charges at such notable conservatives as Sarah Palin. In particular, Palin was castigated for having previously used a graphic that showed Democrat House members (including Giffords) targeted with cross hairs, by which she signified that a viable effort could be made to remove them from office in the next ensuing election.

Liberal politicians and media types engaged in a feeding frenzy, spurred on by irresponsible assertions from such individuals as Pima County Sheriff Clarence Dupnik, who decried "vitriol that comes out of certain mouths about tearing down the government." Dupnik further condemned as outrageous "the anger, the hatred, the bigotry that goes on in this country." But Dupnik was hardly alone. The blinding and consuming sanctimony of the left was glaringly evident in the shameless moralizing rant of New York Times columnist Paul Krugman, who eagerly seized upon the horrific event for his January 9, 2011 sermon entitled "Climate of Hate."

"When you heard the terrible news from Arizona, were you completely surprised? Or were you, at some level, expecting something like this atrocity to happen? Put me in the latter category. I've had a sick feeling in the pit of my stomach ever since the final stages of the 2008 campaign. I remembered the upsurge in political hatred after Bill Clinton's election in 1992 — an upsurge that culminated in the Oklahoma City bombing. And you could see, just by watching the crowds at McCain-Palin rallies, that it was ready to happen again. The Department of Homeland Security reached the same conclusion: in April 2009 an internal report warned that right-wing extremism was on the rise, with a growing potential for violence."

What must be clearly understood here is that absolutely none of these blanket condemnations from the left were aimed at Jared

Loughner, but were instead leveled against conservatism in its entirety. Despite claiming to be opposed to hateful rhetoric and malicious language that might incite violence, it was those very leftists who spewed such venom in abundance, not on account of any actual wrongs committed by conservatives, but simply because conservatives had dared, as free Americans, to dispute and oppose the leftist agenda. In Krugman's world, merely disagreeing with Bill Clinton and Barack Obama was tantamount to advocating the slaughter of innocent people. While pretending to denounce "hate," it was (and is) Krugman and his leftist kindred who prove themselves thoroughly capable of the most noxious and unbridled hate. Yet they remain deliberately oblivious to the degree that their accusations contradict their professed virtue, owing to the fact that leftist sanctimony has totally overwhelmed any sense of conscience and blinded them to reality.

Of even greater significance was the degree to which leftists virtually abandoned the actual victims of the Tuscon slaughter, and perversely exploited the situation, with palpable exuberance, as an opportunity to address the issue that really troubled them, that being the return of the Congress, only days prior, to a Republican majority. Eventually, the truth leaked out that Loughner was, in fact, a leftist and that he was not motivated to violence in any degree by conservative ideology. Even Sheriff Dupnik was at length compelled to concede that absolutely no evidence existed to connect Loughner with any groundswell of conservatism.

Nevertheless, the Tuscon massacre had made an enormous emotional impact on America, and the left was not about to let such an opportunity slip by without fully exploiting it. Correcting the record would gain nothing for the left. Democrat partisans on Capitol Hill and liberals in the media had their bludgeon, and they intended to maximize its use against the resurgent Republicans. Through brazen political twisting and contorting, they concocted a link between Tuscon and "partisanship," as well as "incivility," back in Washington.

After winning control of the House and Senate in 2006, Democrats had proceeded to rule with a heavy hand, under hyper-partisans Harry Reid and Nancy Pelosi. In January of 2009, as Barack Obama prepared to kick-off his term in office by squandering nearly a trillion dollars on his bogus "Stimulus Package" (a vast expenditure that was ultimately ineffective at its stated "purpose" of boosting the economy), Obama had dismissed Republican efforts to curtail his extravagance with the words "I won." So, once Republicans had regained the Congress in 2010, it was clear to liberals that they needed to undermine any Republican momentum which might be used against them in a partisan manner similar to their own. The Tuscon shootings came at exactly the right time to save faltering Democrat political fortunes. And, as if on cue, Republicans joined in the calls for bipartisanship, and thereby validated Democrat duplicity. Consequently, they essentially abdicated the purpose for which the grassroots had rallied to restore them to majority status.

It is entirely noteworthy that, shortly afterwards, any pretense of collegiality and civility by Democrats and their media minions evaporated into thin air. In the immediate aftermath of the shootings, a few on the left had briefly tried to abide by such admonitions. As calls for conservatives to abandon any speech that might be construed as fomenting violence reached their intended "fevered pitch," MSNBC commentator Keith Olbermann actually attempted to apologize for possibly inappropriate statements, "Violence, or the threat of violence, has no place in our Democracy, and I apologize for and repudiate any act or any thing in my past that may have even inadvertently encouraged violence." Other pundits stumbled in mid sentence as they sought to avoid such words as "target," "hit," and "fire," that might possibly be construed to suggest violent overtones.

However, the moment it became clear to them that any real conformity to their phony piety would prove difficult and encumber them along with conservatives, the effort was quietly but quickly abandoned. In its place, the focus was redirected towards gun confiscation, and other similar measures, with such notables as Democrat Senator Chuck Schumer of New York and Representative Carolyn McCarthy, another Democrat from New York's Fourth House District, pushing legislation to restrict the size of magazines.

In a sane world (and the toxic atmosphere inside the Beltway clearly does not qualify), Republicans would have righteously and fiercely hit back at Democrat efforts to taint them on account of a crazed lone gunman in Arizona, only to change the subject when politically expedient. However, having been marinated in the notion that their majority status on Capitol Hill was fragile, and that maintaining majority status would be completely contingent on doing as little as possible to be noticed, they abandoned any pretense of real leadership, and instead attempted to prove that their motives and efforts were not nearly as malicious as claimed by their Democrat accusers. And from that point forward, the House of Representatives was effectively neutered as a force to rein in the abuses of Obama and Senate Democrats.

Another memorable series of events several years prior completely puts the lie to every leftist assertion of advancing the standing of women in American society. When Anita Hill had accused Supreme Court nominee Clarence Thomas of "sexual harassment" in 1991, her grounds were so tenuous, and the "evidence" so inconsistent, that in the short term, the effort to derail his nomination failed. Thomas was confirmed by the Senate, despite Democrats holding a majority. Nevertheless, liberals made a determination to exploit the episode as clear evidence of Republican indifference to Hill's supposed plight, and thus their hostility to women in general. Hill's case was flimsy and transparent at best, as evidenced by her willingness to follow Thomas into subsequent job situations in which she remained in a role that was subservient (and ostensibly vulnerable) to him, long after his supposedly unseemly and unwanted advances. But instead of focusing on the facts, leftists instigated a huge ruckus over the manner in which Hill's assertions were rebutted. Rather than conceding the weakness of their effort to discredit Thomas (the true purpose of which was to prevent the confirmation of a reliable constitutional champion on the court), leftists pounded home the message that Thomas, and all of his Republican supporters, had proven themselves to be callous oppressors and abusers of women.

So of course conservatives assumed, only a few years later, that those on the left would never be willing to stand by the flagrant and numerous instances of serial sexual assaults by Bill Clinton, once the evidence against him became inescapable. In comparison to the few flimsy accusations of supposedly improper acts of Justice Thomas, Clinton had established a long track record, corroborated by numerous extremely credible underlings including Arkansas State Troopers, of flagrant sexual exploitation and assault. The two most notable cases (early on) involved Paula Jones and Juanita Broaddrick. Jones was summoned to Clinton's presence by officials during his tenure as Arkansas Governor, whereupon he exposed himself and demanded sexual favors. Prior to this, Juanita Broaddrick, a prominent Arkansas businesswoman and nurse, very credibly accused Clinton of having brutally raped her while serving as Arkansas Attorney General.

Unlike Anita Hill's accusations against Justice Thomas, which appeared out of the clear blue and were totally uncharacteristic of Thomas's well-established demeanor of honor and respect towards *everyone* in his work environment, Clinton's reprehensible conduct and maltreatment of women had been well established. So it might seem inevitable that those Democrats and liberal media critics who had most loudly decried Thomas, at the bidding of his sole accuser, would certainly deem Clinton's behavior wholly unacceptable. To the astonishment and amazement of conservatives, the reaction of Clinton's supporters, both male and female, in the media and on Capitol Hill was more deflection, excuses, and denigration of any who criticized Clinton.

Most telling were the juvenile rebuttals of notable "feminist" activists, who had staked their public reputations on the ability to skewer masculinity in general. Over the years, they had established a pattern of condemnation of males, even for merely noticing in any manner, traits in women reflective of their gender. Of course these banshees, upon realizing just how disgracefully Clinton had treated so many women within his grasp, would thoroughly renounce him and demand punitive measures be taken against him. But here again, the defining characteristics of the left took precedence over any supposed allegiance to the fairer sex. Rather than properly excoriating Clinton (And who can doubt they would have *demanded* the immediate resignation, followed by public caning, of any Republican found guilty of similar malfeasance), they invented bizarre and contorted definitions of "sexual harassment" that somehow managed to exclude Bill Clinton's despicable conduct. Above any other consideration, Bill Clinton stridently supported abortion (What exploitative male, so prone to "sowing wild oats," would do otherwise?). In their world, that prospect thoroughly supplanted any other consideration, including his actual treatment of women.

So, in summation, the same leftists who would have us believe Clarence Thomas to be an indefensible misogynist, based on the weak and inconsistent testimony of a single accuser, would deem Bill Clinton to be innocent and virtuous. By so doing, they virtually guaranteed Clinton's continued demeaning treatment of their leftist "sisters." And on just such grounds, leftists confer upon themselves, with totally straight faces, the mantle of being "champions of women."

The stunning level of leftist hypocrisy was by no means confined to the Clinton era. Consider the following examples of glaring leftist hypocrisy, not only from the perspective of how these episodes should have instantly discredited their liberal perpetrators (as such action would certainly have done to conservatives engaging in similar abuses), but more significantly, how they instead served as "ammunition" for the left, by which it actually gained ground.

In light of this, an understanding of future events of this nature means they can be rapidly identified and properly characterized. Responding in this manner will significantly enhance the ability of our side to effectively neutralize them.

The advent of the "Tea Party" movement in early 2009 was deliberately and disgustingly denigrated by network and cable "news reporters," who childishly contrived the title of "Tea Baggers" to describe members of the movement. The term was exuberantly applied, and rapidly spread across virtually the entire cabal of leftist "news" outlets. It actually alludes to perverse sexual behavior, and has absolutely no bearing on the real ideology and motivation of Tea Party members, who had sought to recapture the sentiments of those Revolutionary War era participants in the original Boston Tea Party. The same leftist media that, when expedient, castigates conservatives for an ostensible "lack of civility" and "cheapening of the discourse" behaved in a manner that thoroughly debunked their pretense of objectivity, while proving themselves the most vile examples of incivility and cheapened discourse.

Perhaps the most glaring example of institutionalized leftist hypocrisy was the determination by the Congress and Senate to enact Obama's absurdly misnamed "Affordable Care and Patient Protection Act" (more widely known as "Obamacare"), under every sanctimonious and phony pretense of compassion and concern for the American people, with promises of its unbounded and utopian benefits to all. Yet those same Democrats who thoroughly trashed the Constitution when forcing the Obamacare fiasco on the lowly peasantry (that's us) were diligent to officially exempt themselves and their staff members from it, at times even publicly defending their near-criminal duplicity by explaining that participating in it would inflict "hardships" on them. In the very next breath, without even breaking stride, they were back to assuring America that Obamacare was being established in the nation's best interests and with the purest of motives, and that any who contended otherwise were heartless and uncaring. Here, as in every other situation, it was their stunning degree of shamelessness which *empowered* them to present such glaring contradictions without batting an eye.

This mindset has given them the ability to boldly promote illegality and direct assaults on the American ideal by framing situations on premises that are wholly contrived and ultimately irrelevant. Consider the entire debate over voter ID. The real goal of those who advocate proper identification of voters is clearly to ensure legitimate elections. Case closed. Yet it is inescapably obvious that the *sole* reason leftists oppose even the most benign efforts to ensure legitimate voting is that they have historically achieved so many illicit electoral "victories" through rampant cheating.

Nevertheless, they could count on fellow leftists to shamelessly look directly into the cameras and insist that the matter was strictly an issue of "racism" and "intimidation" of minority voters. This, despite the fact that in every single case, voter ID laws would apply universally to every voter, regardless of race. Yet over the years, leftists have squalled incessantly at the mere suggestion of proper monitoring of voter eligibility. The willingness of a thoroughly politicized (and thus corrupt) Obama Department of Justice to overlook the many instances of vote tampering throughout his two terms in office only proved that such fraud has been institutional in scope. In 2016 Barack Obama even encouraged illegal aliens to vote, assuring them that no action against them would be taken.

Regardless of the evidence, whenever a serious effort is made to clean up voting rolls by validating the identities of potential voters, the universal response from the left is to hysterically hurl accusations of "racism" and "minority voter suppression." Since any genuine investigation of voting irregularities would quickly reveal a criminal pattern of fake balloting, the left is compelled to entirely revert the discussion to one of its most reliable and proven strongholds: race. From this point forward, any effort to uphold the law is subordinated to leftist claims that doing so would unfairly compel minorities to present the sort of identification that is required throughout the rest of society for such trivial actions as opening a bank account, applying for a credit card, or even buying a beer or pack of cigarettes. Yet, we are told, providing basic proof of one's identity unfairly burdens minorities.

Consider the scope of what leftists accomplish here, by virtue of their unfettered hypocrisy. Claiming, with nearly comical sanctimony, to be champions of the common citizen and valiant protectors of democracy, they promote a practice that totally corrupts and ultimately negates the actual will of the people. Yet their shameless sanctimony doesn't discredit them but instead, in the face of a timid and feckless opposition, has given them near total dominance of the issue.

In each of these situations, the actual events were of no concern to the left, and only deemed consequential (or not) in light of their expected usefulness to Democrat politicking. To presume all of the leftist grandstanding as anything more substantive or sincere than that is to accept a leftist political ruse contrived for the sole purpose of gaining leverage. Alleged victims of abuse from conservatives are a useful political tool, and are diligently spotlighted. Meanwhile, real victims of well-established assaults (and worse) by leftist politicians are rarely given credence, with the bulk of leftist energies devoted to either discrediting them, or deflecting attention with claims that such behavior is a universal trait of "all" politicians.

Not surprisingly, the willingness of leftists to engage in flagrant hypocrisy and then leverage their perch on their phony "moral high ground" goes much further. Given how easy it has been for them to establish their comically lopsided double-standards and still be taken seriously, they step their game up even further and project their moral duplicity with the broadest of brushes, eventually asserting guilt and innocence on any topic, based entirely on political affiliation. This insinuated "guilt through political ideology" ruse, which they pursue with clockwork predictability, is at the root of their public demands for mass renunciation in the wake of any major event which leftists find objectionable. Furthermore, for this renunciation to be deemed "acceptable," it must be delivered according to terms which leftists stipulate. Let a conservative say something to which the left can successfully attach negative connotations, whether real or concocted, and the incessant, fevered condemnation from liberal politicians and their media parrots will quickly reach cosmic proportions.

When expedient, even the slightest alleged breach of liberal decorum or violation of "politically correct" dogma quickly morphs into a monumental "atrocity" against all of humanity, promptly followed by media demands that it be universally renounced. The next step involves liberal media types seeking "comments" from any and every notable conservative, which quickly devolve into demands that the conservative condemn the offensive action or words, and disassociate with the perpetrator, or face similar castigation.

When expedient, even the slightest alleged breach of liberal decorum or violation of "politically correct" dogma quickly morphs into a monumental "atrocity" against all of humanity.

These demands carry with them an unspoken suggestion that conservatives in general secretly support the objectionable behavior. But the element of hypocrisy here goes deeper still. This snare, into which conservatives fall all too frequently, yields two distinct political benefits to the left. First, it advances the Alinsky tactic of "freezing and isolating" an individual on the right, who is then often thwarted from advancing the conservative agenda, or worse yet, is undermined in an electoral contest. Secondly, with each misbegotten conservative assent to the leftist premise, that premise is further solidified and validated as "mainstream," no matter how hypocritical and extreme it may actually be.

Such universal renunciations are *never* demanded from liberal public figures. When the amassing evidence of each of Bill Clinton's misogynistic episodes became irrefutable, the last thing leftist media types wanted in the public eye was an assessment of his behavior by fellow Democrats, since they would either have to distance themselves from Clinton's malfeasance, or tacitly condone it and in so doing bear some level of complicity. Thus, with zero concern for those victimized by Clinton, or for any other women who would eventually face similar assaults as a result of such acts being "normalized," the media would simply change the subject.

On those extremely rare occasions when leftists find themselves briefly "cornered" by circumstances that focus a spotlight on them, they shamelessly offer some manner of excuse and justification. When Timothy McVeigh bombed the Murrah Building in Oklahoma City on April 19, 1995, leftists from then President Bill Clinton down to every nightly news anchor across the nation reacted with Pavlovian predictability, targeting their favorite conservative nemesis as a defacto accomplice, without a shred of evidence that McVeigh was influenced by any of them. And this was irrespective of the loud and sincere condemnation of McVeigh by every conservative with access to a public forum. Yet when Ted Kyzinski, the notorious "Unabomber" was finally identified and apprehended, the mountain of evidence of leftist ideology as his motivation was actually excused and dismissed on the basis that Kyzinski had a valid reason for his feelings, if not entirely for his actions.

The significance of this pattern is far greater than being mere proof of more leftist hypocrisy. It embodies an essential element of the Alinsky Strategy. Among Alinsky's most effective tactics are those which "freeze and isolate" intended targets. Despite the obvious and provable insincerity of feigned leftist outrage in any given situation, the moment those on the right react to leftist attacks with defensiveness, or even the slightest degree of concurrence, the leftist stance is thereafter deemed totally heartfelt and legitimate. End of discussion. From that point forward, a "snowballing" effect takes place. Leftist grandstanding increases in shrillness. The offending individual or premise is increasingly marginalized. Eventually, the leftist narrative totally dominates all ensuing discussion, with even the minutest deviation condemned as being sympathetic to the perpetrator and thus instantly silenced. In stark contrast, the tacit refusal of conservatives to stridently denounce leftist moral degeneracy and hypocrisy, mainly for fear of the inevitable backlash and contrived firestorms of protest, too often renders leftists immune to thoroughly deserved criticism when real episodes of their moral depravity and criminal corruption surface. Under such circumstances, the leftist cabal is able to retain a cohesiveness that gives it unwarranted validity.

In this manner, leftists have all-too-often rebounded from what should have been wholly indefensible positions on issues and controversies, and amazingly, have even proceeded to make political hay from their circumstances. Massive volumes could be written, merely cataloging episodes of flagrant liberal hypocrisy in great detail, since the practice is rampant and has been so for years. However, the purpose here is not to provide a comprehensive historical reference, but to highlight the sordid manner in which leftists have resorted to such tactics and thereby achieved successes on virtually every front of the political and social debate. It is more important and necessary to focus on how this behavior actually empowers the left by unfettering it from any pretense of decency or intellectual honesty, while hampering real conservative opposition by placing constraints on conservatives to which leftists would never abide. And this point is particularly prescient since it represents a major building block of Alinsky's Rules. Once it becomes thoroughly apparent how widespread and predictable this ploy has become, those who will inevitably be targeted in this manner can learn to quickly recognize the actual dynamics that are in play, thus enabling a more effective rejection of them. Consequently, all conservatives can avoid such contrived controversy, remaining focused on the real issues at hand and how to properly advance them in spite of leftist distractions.

In many ways, leftists have gotten away with so much because they've essentially been "allowed" by our side to do so. The manner in which the political "establishment," including complicit Republicans, has set this stage will be dealt with in greater detail in Chapter 7. The goal at this point is to thoroughly grasp the degree to which leftists have succeeded in advancing an agenda, against the will of the American people, simply by evading any accountability, dodging truth, and thus remaining politically on "offense." And although these admittedly abhorrent circumstances may initially be discouraging, what should instead be gleaned from them is that while leftists have indeed gained significant ground, the choice of whether or not to allow them any further successes lies primarily with those on our side.

Chapter Four
Branding Heroes and Villains: The Power of Labels

By engaging in unfettered hypocrisy that is devoid of any shame or remorse, leftists have been able to conduct an ongoing political onslaught built on a foundation of absolute lies and glaring contradictions. And since too few on the right are willing to bluntly and consistently call them out on it, or to cease from further discourse with them until a modicum of honesty in debate is established, leftists too often successfully ply their case through wholly fabricated precepts. Such behavior is not perpetrated with any goal of addressing real problems or offering feasible solutions, but only for the purpose of swaying popular opinion through manipulation, with the end goal being to dominate the supposed "moral high ground" by *any* available means. Perhaps more than any other single aspect of the Alinsky strategy, the ability of the left to create this pretense of moral "superiority" has enabled it to infiltrate every area of our society with seeming credibility that never should have been allowed. Thus it remains politically viable while engaging in unspeakable behavior, spewing the vilest of epithets and fraudulent accusations, and when all else fails, overwhelming its political opposition with violence, all while still parading its phony mantle of "virtue."

The strategic value of this position to leftists cannot be stressed strongly enough. It is by such means that their agenda garners enormous momentum, though any reasoned assessment of the principles they actually embrace, and the historically disastrous results their ideologies reap, should quickly shut them down. In the "public relations" battle, where they will most often begin their onslaught, it is highly advantageous to be perceived as the undisputed and objective arbiters of virtue.

Unlike conservatives, leftists waste no time on introspection or assessing intellectual honesty. Rather, the intent is solely to convince a significant segment of the general public of the supposedly "self-evident" and inarguable superiority of the leftist position. If winners and losers in a political contest can be determined without actual merit, but merely by the names and insinuations leftists initially attach to people and policies, they need not worry themselves over their historically indefensible positions or the abysmal record of the policies they actually implement.

Essential to this strategy is the usage of labels and mantras at the outset of a debate, by which leftists seek to construct an impenetrable foundation of "right and wrong" that paints their position as one of unassailable goodness, while thoroughly vilifying even the slightest opposition to it. Obviously, these labels and mantras fall into two basic categories, those which confer a mantle of faux "virtue" on the leftist position and its advocates, as opposed to those which carry an implicit condemnation of the "evil" conservative position. Consequently, by the mere manner in which topics are discussed, leftists have succeeded in positioning themselves as "judge, jury, and executioner" before any real consideration of the factual pros and cons of a particular matter are even considered.

> By the mere manner in which topics are discussed, leftists have succeeded in positioning themselves as "judge, jury, and executioner."

Of critical importance to leftists is that all further "debate" be maintained within this framework. Otherwise, that despised element of *reality* may enter a discussion, at which point their position is severely weakened. To prevent this possibility, leftist terminology is rapidly embraced and repeated in every forum from the political podium to the anchor chair of the nightly news, to the political "round tables," to academia, to the scripted and tedious pontificating of "entertainers" in

Hollywood (but of course this is *not* a coordinated effort, we are told). In this manner, an issue can be defined as unwinnable for those on the right, providing they accept the premise or aren't successful in redirecting debate to actual facts and realities.

This ruse, like too many others, has enjoyed enormous success in recent years, to the point that many on our side almost reflexively abandon fundamental issues of right and wrong, believing them to be both unwinnable and too politically costly, the moment leftists have thus framed them in their own terms. Unless this tactic is properly confronted and neutralized, the prospects of conservatism prevailing in this environment become extremely bleak. A leftist agenda that cannot be honestly and objectively discussed is far more likely to remain intact, despite its glaring deficiencies, if conservative opponents fail to deal with it honestly and forthrightly, but instead seek to retreat to a politically "safe" position which, in actuality, was dictated to them by leftists whose goal is to ensure no real debate ever ensues.

Admittedly, it is infuriating that as a result of incessant repetition of trite platitudes that are wholly lacking in substance, leftists have been able to create an illusion of social and political momentum out of thin air. Nevertheless, their facade of worthiness is anything but invulnerable. Once again, as with the rest of the Alinsky strategy, the frustrating nature of this situation should not be construed as an invincible stronghold. Rather, it reflects an enormous weakness for leftists, if only our side will properly seize upon it and exploit it. While the intention of their labeling is to fabricate an "Achilles' Heel" to mock and castigate even the slightest disagreement, thus stalling conservative momentum, a response of unabashed truth from our side can completely turn the tables, and instead create precisely that same situation for them; a severely weakened position from which they must struggle to recover. And truth, if steadfastly asserted, is far more difficult to counteract than puerile leftist name-calling.

Consider, for only one example, how touchy Democrats become, whenever their political machine is identified as the "Democrat Party" rather than their preferred moniker, the "*Democratic* Party." Their aim here is to have every mention of it carry a message of how it ostensibly operates, specifically being benevolent and respectful of all; the essence of "democratic." But as the "Democrat Party," its name instead merely indicates a party full of leftists who call themselves Democrats. Of course, any objective appraisal of who they really are, and how they operate, must conclude that the latter is the "shoe" which fits. Their hypersensitivity to such a minor infraction reveals an extremely fragile public image that cannot be maintained in the face of even mild scrutiny. What is intended as a badge of honor can easily be recast as something far less, and once the truth is known becomes a major liability which puts them on the defensive.

It may seem, at first glance, that such considerations are inconsequential and that the "adults in the room" should not allow themselves to be dragged down to a juvenile level of quibbling over trivialities. However, what must be understood is that each of these points represents an individual building block, all of which are essential to the success of an expansive strategy. And the ultimate purpose of that strategy is to implement an abhorrent agenda that runs contrary to the will and heritage of the American people. Were it not the case, the proponents of this political movement would conduct themselves with dignity and forthrightness. Their descent into such pettiness on so many fronts allows them to succeed when they should otherwise have been dispatched in shame from the public arena. It is extremely important to note that the labels which leftists always attempt to attach to issues and people they dislike are overwhelmingly, if not universally baseless. Consequently, as with the rest of the Alinsky strategy, they can *only be effective if their intended targets allow it.*

It is therefore crucial that conservatives learn to instantly recognize when these tactics are in play, and diligently deal with them as such. The moment leftists are forced to contend for their agenda in honest and objective terms, they fight from a greatly weakened position, and face likely, if not inevitable defeat. In light of this, a wide-ranging discussion of specific leftist labels and mantras is necessary to an understanding of how they operate, in order to avoid the manufactured snares and pitfalls they represent. However, it is far more important to fully grasp *how such tactics work*, rather than to simply learn all of them on an item-by-item basis.

For starters, no mere list of previously invoked leftist mantras and labels can be comprehensive. Furthermore, since this is such a major component of leftist strategizing, new ones are being added daily. So although a wide-ranging collection of the more common examples may help conservatives to spot specific instances of leftists as they resort to such tactics, it is far more beneficial to recognize the strategy itself, despite the particular words being used on any given occasion. Once conservatives reach a point of identifying this ruse the moment it occurs, and are able to counter the baseless presuppositions it is intended to create, its power to sway and manipulate diminishes significantly. In the end, if leftists are forced back to a place where they must contend for their sordid "cause" in sincere and truthful terms, their game is over and their loss becomes virtually inevitable.

It is far more important to fully grasp *how such tactics work*, rather than to simply learn all of them on an item-by-item basis.

It also bears mentioning that the historical and philosophical roots of these terms are not pertinent to this discussion. Rather, it is their usage in the modern context in which leftists invoke them that is of overriding significance. With that in mind, several of the most common examples, along with an explanation of their intended purposes and inherent flaws, are offered here.

Hate/Hatred: Undoubtedly the most common leftist reaction to any opposing viewpoint is to instantly brand it as some form of "hate." With a predictability that borders on the Pavlovian, leftists will invoke the accusation of "hatred" as the primary conservative motivation for virtually any effort to impede or deviate from the leftist agenda, whether the topic is the right to life of the unborn, the protection of America's traditional (Judeo-Christian) founding principles, or apprehension over the dreadful consequences of socialism.

Of course any discussion of leftists and the concept of "hate" must mention their flagrantly expanded characterization of it, including their time tested accusation of "hate speech." While real hate would involve malicious actions that inflict harm on victims and damage to their property, the accusation of "hate speech" need not be accompanied by any supporting evidence, other than that somebody claims to have been emotionally harmed by it. By expanding this accusation to include mere statements which liberals define as "hateful," even restrained and thoughtful opposition to the leftist agenda can be successfully deflected with no substantive basis. It is no exaggeration that in the minds of leftists, truth itself is the ultimate "hate speech." In the leftist world, no other moral component of any issue or debate should ever be considered, the moment they get the accusation to stick that the "real motivation" of conservatives who disagree with them on any given topic is "hate."

Leftists have all too frequently celebrated the successes of this baseless charge, as conservatives time and again back down from their principles, in futile and misbegotten efforts to prove *to the leftists* that the accusation of "hate" isn't warranted. Not surprisingly, the response from the left is to expand its reach and to level the accusation even more stridently. In regards to several issues on which the left would otherwise find itself in a totally indefensible position, the accusation of "hate," and the diligent labeling of any who attempt to resist leftist intent as "haters," takes on an elementary school playground nature that could be almost comical, were its consequences not so Orwellian.

As they have enjoyed ever growing political clout, based on what should be a flimsy, easily dispelled notion, leftists have continued to encroach on their real target; traditional (Judeo-Christian) morality which, somewhat ironically, they attack with the most vile and unfettered exhibitions of real *hate*. Increasingly, leftists assert that even calling sin "sin" makes one guilty of "hate." At that point they deem themselves fully justified in shutting down free speech, and suppressing religious freedom, in total contradiction to the First Amendment. With characteristic sanctimony, they assert that it is their moral obligation to oppose, by any available means, "haters" on the right.

> As they have enjoyed ever growing political clout,
> leftists have continued to encroach on their real target;
> traditional (Judeo-Christian) morality.

Sadly, their targets on the right are generally more prone to retreating from this epithet than to point out the glaring hypocrisy, and actual *hatred*, that it represents. The real malevolence is invariably expressed by leftists, who are clearly given to attacking on a personal basis, and spewing malicious accusations, the moment they sense an opportunity for political advantage.

A few notable examples incontrovertibly make this case. Anyone residing in the Rocky Mountain region in October of 1998 can well remember the firestorm that ensued in the wake of the murder of Matthew Shepard. But while the perpetrators of the crime were quickly apprehended, tried, convicted, and are serving jail time to this day, none of this was sufficient to appease the insatiable appetite for vengeance of the leftist counterculture against those it truly *hates*.

Matthew Shepard was a homosexual, which instantly made his plight a weapon for the leftist counterculture. Commentaries, passed off as "news" reporting by leftist opinion makers, painted with the broadest possible "brush," those they blamed on completely spurious grounds for Shepard's death. For weeks, these "reports" were rife with accusations leveled at virtually the entire population of the region. The local culture, presumed to be conservative and traditional in its views, was universally and vehemently condemned as the real culprits. It wasn't until years later that the reality of the Matthew Shepard situation came to light, having nothing to do with his sexual practices, it was instead fomented by contentious drug deals.

Heralded as the preeminent "hate crime" of the era, and invoked ever since as "judge, jury, and executioner" to condemn the people of the heartland, it turns out that the actual manifestation of hatred for people of differing lifestyles was that which the leftist counterculture vomited onto anyone and everyone who happened to be living in the same geographical region where Shepard's murder occurred.

In a similar manner, leftists are quick to re-brand any opposition to abortion, under any and all circumstances, as irrefutable evidence of "hatred towards women." The flagrant and widespread victimization of women by the abortion industry constitutes abundant evidence of a truly mercenary and exploitative attitude that denigrates and abuses women who are in a state of extreme vulnerability, and the abortion industry "money trail" glares forth as the inarguable motivation. Yet leftists simply choose to callously ignore such inconvenient facts, and to remain wholly indifferent to the plight of women who are brutally exploited in those situations.

The horrors of an industry that thrives on the destruction of the unborn, as epitomized by the nightmarish conditions in the abortion mills of convicted abortionist "Dr." Kermit Gosnell and the monstrous marketing of human flesh conducted by Planned Parenthood, all at the expense of women who must bear the emotional and physical scars alone, is ignored and even ridiculed by leftists in politics and the media. Yet to assert that a young woman may want to keep and bear her child under less than optimal circumstances is somehow an affront to all things decent, and in the thoroughly twisted leftist worldview, the epitome of "hate" towards that woman.

A popular trend among leftist "news" reporters is to characterize Christian organizations that seek to uphold traditional values as "hate groups," while giving a complete pass to the nefarious and hateful actions of leftists which have been occurring with increasing frequency. Considering the unwillingness of leftist mouthpieces to condemn such things, it is clear that like everything else leftists claim to decry, they are not concerned with stopping real hate, and the behavior that ensues as a result of it. For leftists, the terms "hate" and "hatred" are mere tools, selectively employed to gain leverage in political and cultural debates.

Bigot/Racist: Whenever any racial element can be included in a policy discussion, no matter how oblique or irrelevant race may actually be to the topic at hand, the accusation of "bigot/bigotry" is sure to follow. From the leftist perspective, the requirement for conservatives to back down at this point is absolute. Even the slightest hesitance to concede is treated as inarguable proof that conservatives heartily endorse every prejudicial action going back to the slave traders of the eighteenth century.

Of course reality paints a far different picture. It is the political left that instantly reverts to the vilest racial slurs and stereotypes, the moment any conservative who happens to be black, dares to wander from the liberal plantation. Such notables as 2016 presidential candidate Dr. Ben Carson, Supreme Court Justice Clarence Thomas, former National Security Adviser Condoleezza Rice, and former Secretary of State Colin Powell can attest (though characterizing some of them as "conservative" might be a stretch). Nevertheless, at one time or another, they didn't embrace the leftist "orthodoxy" with absolute fidelity, so in the eyes of leftists they are fair game to be demeaned as "Uncle Tom," "Aunt Jemima," or any other flagrantly bigoted and demeaning racial term in the leftist lexicon.

It is critically important to fully understand what this pattern represents. Despite leftist claims of being champions of minorities, their actual behavior proves *exactly the opposite*. Leftist "support" of minorities is completely conditional, based solely on whether or not an individual in question is aiding the liberal agenda or represents an impediment to it, in which case it's open season on them. Despite leftist sanctimony, it is not the ethnicity or personal dignity of any individual that is of importance to them, but only the political "value" of that person, which of course presumes that they subordinate themselves to the leftist ideology. Assertions that leftist race pandering results from lingering guilt felt by liberals over past wrongs, or sympathy at the current plight of minorities in America, are thus proven to be entirely baseless. Rather, the left operates from a position of pure bigotry, only pandering to particular groups or individuals as long as they continue to "deliver the goods" demanded by the Democrat Party. In bygone days, this was accomplished by working in the fields. Now the requirement is to toe the party line and publicly endorse a straight Democrat ticket. Yet at the slightest "infraction," the public flogging of these individuals ensues. And any pretense of sympathy or multicultural "sensitivity" instantly vanishes.

> Leftist "support" of minorities is completely conditional, based solely on whether or not an individual in question is aiding the liberal agenda or represents an impediment to it.

Nevertheless, among conservatives, the looming possibility of being labeled "racist" is scary enough to drive far too many of them into full retreat. It is widely speculated by many conservatives that this threat alone was ultimately responsible for the fact that neither Congressional Republicans, who gained a majority in 2010, nor their Senate counterparts, were willing to impede any portion of Barack Obama's disastrous agenda.

Fairness: In order for the nihilism of the sixties generation to propagate, it was imperative to completely destroy the time honored societal concepts of "right and wrong." Leftists diligently insisted that such ideals were wholly arbitrary and had been forcibly imposed on humanity, usually be a "patriarchal culture" or some other such sinister entity. Instead, we were told that such quaint notions were based on nothing more significant than humanity's mindless devotion to tradition or religious despotism. Sadly, the strategy was implemented with such ferocity that it eventually took root and is now widely accepted.

Having enjoyed overwhelming success at eradicating such foundational concepts of a healthy society, their next step was to supplant traditional convention with edicts of their own making. To institute such precepts, they needed only to find justifying substitutes for the hated concepts of right and wrong, but which didn't sound quite so domineering. Thus, such terms as "fairness" and "unfairness" quickly supplanted traditional morality, with their actual definitions being dictated by the leftist counterculture. Any issue that the left sought to advance as a defining moral precept was deemed "fair," while the opposing ideology was denigrated and dismissed as "unfair." As this pattern has been allowed to stand, leftists increasingly hand down their rulings of what is or isn't "fair" with an iron-fisted "certainty" that would make medieval inquisitors green with envy.

In this manner, leftists have since established an entire perverse moral framework, entirely on the pretense of their own inherent virtue, while effortlessly reverting to their former contradictory assertions that "right and wrong don't exist" in the very next breath. In short, the right and wrong of American tradition, as well as its Biblical foundation, are dismissed as personal opinion, which paves the way for the leftist agenda to be relentlessly advanced on the basis that it embodies some superior and universal concept of "fairness" as an inarguable moral absolute. Sadly, this particular aspect of the leftist assault on the American ideal has not only faced little opposition, it has all-too-often been embraced to some degree by such institutions as the Church, where it has wreaked enormous havoc and severely tainted the faith of many.

Sensitivity/Insensitivity: Like "fairness," these terms presume some sort of moral "absolute," based entirely on the presumed emotional impact of a topic on individuals, most often with no supporting evidence whatsoever, other than their assertions of such. The moment a leftist minion sees an opportunity to claim "offense" over an issue, the assumption is that any further discourse represents a virtual "attack" on that individual. Truth is no longer of any consequence. Moreover, leftists have no problem deeming truth itself to be "insensitive," which elevates their feelings to supremacy, even over reality.

Of course such concepts are determined entirely along ideological lines, with leftists as their sole and unchallenged arbiters. For example, they are free to denigrate and attack Christian principles under the auspices of exercising "free speech," with no recourse, and certainly with no consideration of their insensitivity; a prospect that poses a grave and direct threat to the First Amendment. Conversely, any anti-Christian premise they dare to promote is deemed "off limits" to criticism, particularly from Christians, since doing so would be "insensitive." Furthermore, any expectation of sensitivity to Christian principle, particularly in the public arena, is decried as a violation of their enshrined "separation of Church and state."

Attempts by conservatives to play this game invariably prove futile, since those leftists who will cry the loudest over any supposed "offense" against them or their ideology are the very same ones who dismiss offended conservatives as "whiners."

Unacceptable/Intolerable: As leftists demand that society conform to their self-proclaimed concept of "fairness," they often need to stifle the beliefs and prohibit the actions of others which conflict with their worldview. So in the same manner that they have established "fairness" and its counterpart "unfairness" as the legitimizing grounds for their point of view, they also must maintain the ability to issue condemnations of disparate viewpoints, again sidestepping their glaring hypocrisy, and without conceding the existence of moral and ethical absolutes. In a very similar manner, the terms "unacceptable" and "intolerable" are invoked to denigrate any idea or behavior with which they disagree, in order to suggest that something other than their own opinions have made this determination.

Conspicuous by its total absence in the bulk of such discussions is the nature and authority of just who casts the judgment of what is, or is not "acceptable." The intended presumption is that "everybody knows" something to be a "truth." Yet the actual identity of "everybody" is left as an open ended question. Thus can an issue be deemed wrong in the most absolutist of terms, while the actual entity making that determination enjoys a status of being both omnipresent and nonexistent. Of course an honest and forthright answer of who hands down such judgments would point directly to the leftist "moralizers" who deem themselves alone to be in a position to do so. But absent any diligent pursuit of this component of the debate, it is simply glossed over, with leftists presuming to hold one more portion of the "moral high ground" on no substantive basis whatsoever.

Tolerance: It may initially seem a bit redundant to discuss the term "tolerance" separately from the above mention of that which leftists deem "intolerable." However, given the intellectual dishonesty of the left, and their resulting verbal gymnastics and contradictions of reason, the manner in which tolerance is most often employed merits further examination. And in the determination of both that which must be accepted on the basis of "tolerance," and whatever is deemed "intolerable," leftists presume the authority to selectively hand down such judgments, with the ultimate goal being that they always remain unquestionably in control.

To hear leftists explain it, tolerance is the ultimate virtue. With each new affront to time honored and historically validated precepts of right and wrong, the thunderous demand of traditional America by the leftist counterculture is of tolerance. By continually focusing the discourse on "tolerance," leftists can promote the most insane perversions of right and wrong without ever facing the pitfalls of marginalization that the Alinsky strategy directs at its ideological foes.

Conversely, any conservative response that focuses on the downside of the leftist countercultural agenda is instantly deemed to be evidence of "intolerance," which is intoned as being every bit as universally evil as "hate." Thus "intolerance" is to be vehemently condemned, and its purveyors relegated to the fringes of society. So diligent and obsessive have leftists been at implanting and codifying this mindset in the American psyche that it has permeated the Church. Yet even a cursory reading of the Scriptures flatly refutes the notion of "tolerance" as the ultimate "virtue." Tolerance of evil is not lauded in any manner as being virtuous, but is instead deemed an evil all its own.

Still, leftists must have sufficient wiggle room within their faux "moral code" to grant themselves exceptions. So, while they demand universal tolerance from conservatives and will condemn any who dare dispute the notion, they must have a means to just as loudly condemn actions or beliefs with which they disagree. So it is that they have established the concept of "zero tolerance" policies as the means to forcefully silence and suppress their ideological opposition of whom they are flagrantly *intolerant* (See Chapter 3: Hypocrisy As a Strategy). Thus, when some bizarre new moral low is inflicted upon society by the leftist counterculture, the demand is first for "tolerance," on the basis that this is the inherently noble response. Eventually however, that precept becomes widely established, at which point any effort to disagree with it is ferociously suppressed amid equal sanctimony, as a result of the leftist "zero tolerance" policy. This is asserted with equal certitude against those boorish heretics who dare to challenge the new orthodoxy.

So it is that, with totally straight faces, leftists can invent a new "gender" definition and demand unquestioned tolerance of it as an inherently "right" thing to do, while in the very next breath they condemn any fealty to the Second Amendment on account of their "zero tolerance" of guns and freedom. In both cases, they have presumed to be on morally unshakable ground, despite exhibiting glaring contradictions in their reasoning. Yet on too many occasions, their duplicity goes completely unquestioned and therefore prevails despite its inherent fragility.

As a telling example of the "Pandora's Box" that this tactic opens, consider the rash of school children (mostly boys) who have been hideously punished and marginalized, based on the notion of school policies of "zero tolerance" of anything related to guns. While students are being thoroughly immersed in every form of countercultural rot, with "tolerance" of it being demanded from them and their parents by the system, any perceived infraction of the anti-gun ideology, no matter how slight, oblique, or even totally fabricated, results in severe repercussions on the student.

The most extreme cases have involved a student holding his hand "like a gun," drawing a picture of a gun, or in that most infamous case, chewing a breakfast pastry into the general shape of a gun. Students with stellar behavioral and academic records are suspended, and even expelled from schools, with their reputations thereafter tainted, for the supposed "violation" of these policies. A major psychological component of the Alinsky strategy is the marginalization and humiliation of those individuals who exhibit any form of "heresy" against the leftist orthodoxy. The injustice is outrageous, but the real goal of such deliberately overblown responses is rarely addressed, which is to make an example of the student, in order to intimidate all onlookers into compliance. The eagerness of leftists to unleash the Alinsky "freeze and isolate" strategy, viciously stigmatizing innocent school children in service to the leftist agenda, is proof of just how malicious and vile leftists really are. Destroying the life and reputation of an innocent child is hardly beneath them. Nothing will stand in the way of their evil "cause." This is another important point to recall, the next time they spew their sanctimony of being "for the children."

> The eagerness of leftists to unleash the Alinsky "freeze and isolate" strategy, viciously stigmatizing innocent school children, is proof of just how malicious and vile leftists really are.

A student who exhibits any affinity towards guns not only represents a potential conservative in the making, but is also likely to share such poisonous ideas with fellow students. By counterattacking with such ferocity, the student becomes a pariah in the eyes of fellow students. Official actions, such as suspensions and expulsions, not only have the same impact on parents, they stand as a stark warning to other students *and their parents* that any departure from the leftist anti-gun "orthodoxy" will be punished swiftly and unmercifully. The lesson here, which is accepted all too frequently, is that the proper course for students and parents to take is one of total, unquestioning acquiescence and compliance.

Politically Correct: Before bypassing this one under the presumption that its meaning and usage is patently obvious, consider it from the perspective of how useful and effective of a weapon it has become to leftists over the past few decades. Like "fairness," the term was a necessary contrivance, in an atmosphere which leftists had diligently rendered devoid of any true moral principle. At the same time, they needed to retain their own ability to establish *"absolutes"* to specifically categorize and control the actions, words, *and thoughts* of their conservative opposition, with supreme authority. And as always, the inherent hypocrisy of liberalism mandates a need for complete flexibility on their part from one situation to the next.

Despite any previous historical or philosophical usage, in the modern context, the term "politically correct" reflects the starkest of absolutes. A good trick from those who initially gained their current status by asserting the non-existence of absolutes. In fact, their mantra "There are *no absolutes*" is itself a statement of absolutism. As such it is a profound contradiction of the "universal truth" it purports to establish. Yet ironies of this nature are foundational to a political movement in which deceit and the perversion of reality are its chief cornerstones. This dichotomy between the leftist assertion of no absolute truth, and the need to promote leftist ideology as inherently virtuous, presented a problem to the godless left, which abhors any mention of traditional morality and its basis in Biblical principle. Furthermore, leftist strategies require that they always dictate their own set of "absolutes." Yet if such concepts remain at all intact, leftists quickly find themselves on the wrong side of their previous edicts, the moment they move on to any new environment or issue. Hence, they seized on the term "politically correct."

On its face, this label actually means *absolutely nothing,* which is completely by design. With "political" as a supposed standard for what is or isn't "correct," its boundaries are so completely arbitrary that liberals can (and do) often define it on the spur of the moment, on a case-by-case basis. Consider the absurdity of something being deemed "correct," according to some fuzzy, nondescript "standard" simply referred to as *politics*. In the minds of most Americans, the inane term might even be derided as an oxymoron. Yet it allows leftists to establish, at their will, an impenetrable boundary on debate and discourse, based on a "standard" that is non-existent on its own merit, and thus can be easily moved and manipulated to suit the issue of the day.

A great example can be observed in how easily leftists can posture from one side to the other of the issue of racial bigotry, depending on the ideology of the individuals in question. It is not "politically correct" we are told, to *ever* accuse minorities of racism, based on the absurd and *irrelevant* premise that they are not a sufficiently large portion of the population. Hence, overt hatred against whites must be accepted, as if even a single incident of hatred from any one person against another can be truly excused in that manner. But certain groups are selectively exempted from any accountability among leftists, so hatred from them is given a mantle of "legitimacy," and proclaimed to be "politically correct." On that basis it is thereafter deemed immune to any mention of the glaring hypocrisy it embodies.

Similarly, the leftist counterculture has marginalized, and even in some cases outlawed such innocuous and worthy acts as wishing someone "Merry Christmas" in government schools, or even on any public property, asserting that it not only violates "politically correct" standards, but according to some of the more unhinged leftist activists, is "unconstitutional" as well! Yet in the next breath, they'll enthusiastically endorse immersion in the Koran, under the guise of "multiculturalism," within the same schools where they insist no Christmas carols can be sung.

By repeating the term with an air of absolute assurance and confidence, leftists have promoted a convoluted and hypocritical worldview replete with "moral" absolutes pertaining to every known topic, with them alone as the sole arbiters of those "absolutes." Yet they are able to engage in such abhorrent behavior with no need for even the most rudimentary levels of consistency in their phony moralizing, since over time their shameless insistence and incessant repetition of such vapid ideology has allowed them to operate with an air of seeming "ironclad" authority that too many moral cowards on the right have grown fearful of challenging.

In the absence of any opposition, "political correctness" has become a means of institutionally marginalizing any individual or idea that does not align with the leftist "orthodoxy" of the day. It is flexible, because leftist "standards" are themselves flexible. Yet it increasingly wields the power to consign non-adherents to the ideological "fringe," while bolstering the most extreme and absurd concepts to a fabricated "mainstream."

> The traditional notion of "bullying" as big kids picking
> on little kids out in the hallway is a phony banner
> under which a leftist agenda is pursued.

Bully/Bullying: As with "hatred," the actual definition of "bullying" in the leftist world is a deliberately broad brush which they readily apply to anyone who dares stand against the presumed "validity" of the leftist position. In recent years, schools have promoted every manner of "anti-bullying" program, with official classroom time devoted to teachings on the subject. Teachers, whose student academic scores are abysmal, attend seminars on the supposed prevention of "bullying" in the classroom. Nevertheless, this effort gains widespread support, because most people presume it to be a means of making schools safer and less frightful places for young, vulnerable students. But the end goal is *not* to make classrooms and playgrounds safe and happy. Rather, something much more sinister is at play.

The traditional notion of "bullying" as big kids picking on little kids out in the hallway is, at best, a phony banner under which an alternative agenda is pursued. And, as is predictable, this agenda is 100% leftist and political. Ultimately, the real "bullies" in the classroom are those leftists who all too frequently hold positions among the faculty and administrative staff. The previously mentioned "zero tolerance" policies are a prime example. When leftists invoke the label of "bully," their accusation is not intended to protect anyone, but to put ideological opponents on the defensive, in the identical manner as their accusations of "hate." In the process, real bullying emanates from these very leftists, on an institutional basis, in the form of the ideological targeting and ostracizing of any under their authority who fail to comply with the liberal orthodoxy.

When such bullying is conducted with sufficient ferocity, others who might have opposed the particular leftist issue in question are not only scared away, but some consider it pragmatic to turn on the main target. By far, these moral cowards are the most pernicious enablers of this leftist onslaught. Having previously claimed to be on our side when it seemed safe to do so, they join the fray alongside leftists, hoping that they can avoid eventually becoming targets themselves. This is the essence of the "freeze/isolate" aspect of the Alinsky strategy, by which supposed "conservatives" all too often strengthen and empower the leftist attack machine, which greatly amplifies its effectiveness and reach. Over time, if this ploy is not strenuously confronted, fewer and fewer can muster the courage to stand virtually alone against the leftist onslaught and firestorm that is sure to come.

The ostensibly "conservative" ranks inside the Beltway and on national media are riddled with such people who, despite occasional professions of devotion to real conservative principle (primarily expressed to constituents back home right before election time) ultimately help entrench the left as "judge, jury, and executioner." Were it not for their spineless betrayals, this scheme would not be nearly so successful.

Controversial: As with "fairness" and so many other deliberately ambiguous terms, leftists employ the term "controversial" as a baseless means of characterizing something to be inherently wrong, in a world where they have, by their own assertions, eliminated any recognition of right and wrong. An issue can be disparaged simply on the basis that it is "controversial," even if the only controversy related to it is the overblown hysterics and hyperbole coming from the left. Time after time, Republican politicians have shown that they will quietly abandon an issue simply because they seek to avoid the "controversy" associated with it. So of course leftists have enjoyed great political leverage, by merely overreacting in feigned outrage, and waiting for the latest interference to their agenda to be decried on the nightly news as "controversial."

Community Organizer: The term "community organizer" has become fairly common and is well known across the political spectrum, especially since Barack Obama's rise to national prominence in 2004. It is worth recalling the actualities of those who were known as "ACORN," the "Association of Community Organizers for Reform Now." The acronym connotes an innocent sapling, that would eventually grow into a stately Oak tree, benevolently providing shade and sustenance to all in its midst. Leftist "community organizers" proudly accepted this characterization prior to ACORN offices being exposed as covens of subversives who had no problems skirting the law. They are still in operation, though they have since ducked out from the limelight and operate under various different names. Though no longer so obvious as a cohesive group, they continue to promote their seditious agenda, with their icon being the noble "community organizer."

Well recognized as this title may be, it needs to be addressed here, since the sheer ugliness of its reality is highly pertinent to combating the left. Ultimately, the term is wholly euphemistic, suggesting images of caring individuals whose primary focus might be the improvement of their neighborhoods. Such people might circulate petitions encouraging the city council to construct bicycle trails and parkways, or oversee gatherings where litter is picked up in housing subdivisions.

The reality, however, is far more grim and dangerous. In truth, these Alinsky acolytes are much more accurately characterized as *mob agitators*. Their methods and goals are the diametric opposite of building more habitable communities or any similar notion. In many cases, their deliberate efforts to gain political advantage actually result in the destruction of those very communities though vandalism and riots.

Saul Alinsky understood the power of the mob, and he diligently honed his efforts to coordinate mob activity in such a way as to maximize the threat it could potentially pose, and wield the fear it could instill on much larger social and political establishments. Doing so required that the boundaries of social decorum, and even legality, not be allowed to hinder the end game of the leaders and agitators. Yet such strategies were potentially risky, if the public became sufficiently aware and outraged over the actualities of the effort. Therefore, the rabble-rousing and inciting were kept clandestine, as much as possible, and the resulting societal chaos and anarchy falsely portrayed as if it had ensued spontaneously.

Labels: It might seem satirical to specifically focus on this term, within a chapter that warns of the use of labels as a political weapon. However, the verbal "gymnastics" of the left are sufficiently convoluted and shameless that the irony of their strategy needs to be mentioned. It is necessary to distinguish between labels which are accurate in their depiction of specific individuals or behavior, as opposed to labels that merely seek to accuse and denigrate.

Of course the practice of labeling neither started nor stopped with Alinsky. But he and his acolytes refined labeling as a "weapon," particularly after institutionalizing and normalizing leftist hypocrisy. Despite the propensity of leftists to engage in venomous name-calling, they are remarkably sensitive to having any label, especially those which are accurate, attached to themselves. They desperately (and hypocritically) seek to dismiss the terms "leftist" and "liberal" as mere "labels." As is the case with their aversion to the mention of the "Democrat Party," leftists run and hide from labels which accurately reflect the malignancy of their tactics and goals. Accusing their opposition of "labeling" is itself a *label* insofar as it suggests some devious behavior, without any tangible basis, especially in the face of labels that provide accurate characterizations of them.

The goal is to *prevent* conservatives from accurately spotlighting the real nature of leftists. This ruse works all too often, since once accused of "labeling," our side is duped into attempting to avoid such criticism. From that point forward it allows itself to be put on the defensive, and is hamstrung from stating the blunt truth of any issue. Consequently, it must be emphasized that not all labels are equal. Despite the immediate cries of "foul" from leftists, there is absolutely nothing wrong with labels which are *accurate*. The term "liar" may describe a dishonest individual with surgical precision.

Despite the propensity of leftists to engage in venomous name-calling, they are remarkably sensitive to having any label, especially those which are accurate, attached to themselves.

On the other hand, reflexively hurling such epithets as "hate-filled bigot" the moment someone disagrees with accepted leftist orthodoxy is wholly unwarranted, and reveals a leftist attempt at manipulation on the basis of race, proving in which political camp the real hate and bigotry lies. The same goes for those other overused and tired out accusations of "sexist," "xenophobe" "nativist," and "homophobe," to name a few of their more popular epithets. All such labels are irrelevant to available evidence, and seek to totally evade facts or proof, while focusing entirely on the presumed motivation *and guilt* of their target. Worst of all, if unchecked, these terms do not function as mere "labels," but as invoked by leftists, are intended as social and political wedges. It is extremely frustrating that a principled opposition can easily turn this transparent tactic back on the left, but so often fails to do so.

At one time, leftists even proudly accepted the title of "liberal," which they believed conferred upon them an image of generosity and benevolence. Eventually, their malicious tactics, moral attacks on America, and ultimately, the disastrous results of their agenda rendered the term a "black eye." At that point they began decrying any mention of the word as a derogatory "label." In its place, they preferred to be called "progressives." Yet that too is becoming synonymous with leftist bullying and lies.

So it is that whenever leftists are properly decried for being who they are, their last desperate effort to deflect criticism is to accuse our side of resorting to "labels." On that basis alone, the accuracy of the particular term being used against them is ostensibly stripped of any validity, and becomes just another baseless and hateful attack. In truth however, this desperation reflects the fragility of their facade. Built upon lies and distortions, it cannot sustain an honest, piercing assessment. And this is a point on which our side should ultimately focus like a laser.

Conspiracy Theory: It is true that many "theories" of immense, nearly omnipotent networks that ostensibly pull every string of government are often unfounded sensationalism. But this is certainly not a good reason to dismiss every assertion of underhanded activity, especially when such behavior is rampant in even the highest levels of government. It is altogether inarguable that seditious forces have sought to infiltrate and manipulate government from the earliest days of the Republic. Yet whenever leftists are suspected of subversive activity, the primary defense is to denigrate any accusations as "conspiracy theories." In so doing, they make their opposition hesitant to speak truth, for fear of being mocked. Here again, the ploy will only work if those aware of the malfeasance lack the spine to face the inevitable derision from the leftist political establishment and its media minions, in which case they'll merely refrain from further discussion and let the matter drop.

However, when the ball is in their court, leftists exercise their "free speech" with no such concern. One of Hillary Clinton's most famous deflections was that Bill was an innocent cherub, who had become the target of a "Vast, right wing conspiracy." On this basis alone, she enjoyed great success, putting conservatives on the defensive in spite of the glaring excesses and abuses committed by her husband. Of course, when the facts were finally made public, and all of the accusations of assaults and abuses of women by Bill Clinton proved to be true, no apology was forthcoming from Hillary. Nor was any sincere remorse ever expected. In the moment, her statement accomplished what it was intended to do.

Dog Whistle: As leftist accusations of hatred, bigotry, and other nefarious motivations by the conservative opposition have become more hysterical and more common, conservatives understandably responded by being more cautious as to the phrasing and choice of words they used, so that their intentions couldn't be deliberately misrepresented by the left. Consequently, in order for leftists to maintain their accusations of inherent evil on the right, they needed to concoct grounds on which to level those charges with zero quantifiable proof. Hence they created the label "dog whistle." According to this premise, conservatives are presumed guilty of any accusation leveled at them, regardless of a total absence of supporting evidence.

For example, since in the leftist alternative reality, all conservatives are evil racists, a totally innocent comment will be deemed "racist" despite the total lack of even an oblique reference to ethnicity. Leftists assert that they "know" the intent of the conservative was to demean others on the basis of race, so they simply claim to see corroborating evidence "between the lines" of a conservative comment to which they take exception. This is deemed a "dog whistle," since it can't be seen or heard by anyone, but leftists know not only that it is there, but that other conservatives pick up on it and agree with its "racist" intent.

It is always a mistake to treat leftist claims of "dog whistle" hate or racism as anything other than ludicrous and desperate efforts to create controversy out of absolutely nothing.

Microaggression: Along the same lines as "dog whistle," leftists vying for the political advantage of "victimhood" have lately resorted to invoking the accusation of "microaggression" as a means of claiming to be attacked in the absence of anything even remotely resembling an attack. Ultimately, this concoction is most appealing to leftist millennials, particularly in the artificially coddling environment of college campuses, where they have been conditioned to engage in the demeaning behavior of throwing tantrums at the slightest provocation. Furthermore, the lengthy nature of this contrived word gives it an air of "sophistication," especially among those who deem themselves to be erudite and "intellectual." In stark contrast, its usage reveals an embarrassingly puerile character trait. By erupting at even the most reasoned disagreement with hysterical accusations that their ideological opponents are engaging in "microaggressions," these intellectual lightweights can then gain that all-important "high ground" as victims of a supposed attack. Of course this imaginary advantage is thereafter treated by the left as an irrefutable moral absolute. If whining leftist millennials "believe" themselves to be victims of imaginary microaggressions, then anyone accused by them must be presumed guilty.

Trigger: Given the contrived hyper-sensitivity of spring-loaded leftists and their pathetically predictable over-reactions to even the most subtle (or even imaginary) opposition, a possibility exists that their tantrums and hyperbole might be invoked against them as evidence that their supposed "tolerance," "open mindedness," and "compassion" aren't such universal "virtues" among them as they piously claim. It has therefore become incumbent upon them to have an escape route if the contravening evidence revealing their hypocrisy becomes too glaringly obvious. Thus the invention of the "trigger" as their supposed justification for the most unhinged and puerile behavior. When the hypocrisy of a morally and intellectually "enlightened" leftist manifests itself in a hate-filled rant, or even physical assault, the excuse is that the individual was "triggered." Thus he/she was incapable of rational behavior, since the word, deed, or even so innocuous an action as a perceived disparaging look, was simply too much for them to endure. As with every other aspect of the entire leftist philosophy, blame for their failures must *always* be assigned to someone or something other than themselves.

Mean Spirited: It would be a vast and difficult task to chronicle the countless nasty and indefensibly ugly statements of leftists, from ranting Democrats on Capitol Hill to their nightly news cohorts, to leftist activists on the street, as they decry and renounce every conservative precept, and seek to politically destroy any on the right who dare to voice such ideals. Suffice to say that entire books could be written on the topic. So, once again, it is almost stunning to realize that accusatory denouncements of supposedly "mean spirited" people and policies overwhelmingly come from leftists, and are used to put conservatives unnecessarily on the defensive. The "brush" with which liberals paint their opposition as "guilty" of this charge is broad, to the point of absurdity. Yet again, this tactic continues to be employed because it continues to work.

The definition of "mean spirited" is, like every leftist label, very fluid and selective. Despite the tangible harm that has resulted from liberal policy, any conservative effort to change course for the better is instantly decried as "mean spirited," with ample "evidence" offered as to the projected (and imaginary) hardships that are guaranteed to befall victims of those callous conservatives. The long-term result of this label has been that Republicans too often abandon any measure that is intended to turn back the evil tide of liberalism, unless it can be implemented with a guarantee of zero pain to anyone under any circumstances, which is a near impossibility. On that basis, any precept of the leftist agenda, once in place, becomes nearly impossible to correct.

Fear Mongering: Historically, the leftist agenda has been a consistent disaster wherever and whenever it was implemented. Behind the facade of benevolence and societal bliss, dire consequences await. Hence, the best defense against it has always been to alert the people of what can be expected in the wake of every empty leftist promise of "utopia." In the vast majority of situations, such blunt warnings of the dismal realities of liberalism are sufficient to thwart its advance.

So of course leftists are compelled to dismiss such warnings without directly addressing their substance. And one of their most reliable and frequently invoked deflections is the accusation that any attempts to alert the people to the lurking dangers are "fear mongering." From this twisted perspective, the actual damage that will ensue is somehow not the "real" problem. Instead, merely discussing the pitfalls of leftist ideology in honest and unambiguous terms is an innate "evil" that needs to be universally opposed. Hence, with sufficient ferocity and venom, truth can be suppressed and ultimately supplanted with lies.

One of the greatest of such leftists successes with this strategy involved the AIDS crisis of recent decades. The most obvious and best method of stalling the spread of the dreaded disease was simply to stop engaging in sexual relationships with multiple partners. Yet the priority of the leftist counterculture was to expand and normalize profligate sex, so any effort to curtail such behavior (and despite the fact that doing so would save lives, including those of countercultural leftists) was loudly and angrily dismissed as "fear mongering." We were told that AIDS was spread by "fear and ignorance," which is clearly a biological and intellectual absurdity. Nevertheless, little was done to curtail behavior that actually helped spread the disease, and its expansion among the population was largely unaddressed until medical advances became effective against it.

Homophobe/Islamophobe: As late as 1987, the American Psychiatric Association classified homosexuality as a "mental disorder." But under intense media and political pressure, the APA was coerced into removing that categorization from its official documentation. Since then, leftist and countercultural activists have relentlessly worked to create the perception that any hint of opposition to the homosexual agenda constitutes its own form of mental illness. Hence, the clinical sounding term "homophobia" was contrived, like all other leftist labels, from thin air.

Nevertheless, the strategy of relentless repetition, with every utterance of the term carrying the weight of vehement clinical certainty from its source, was sufficient to cement a notion of its moral absolutism to a world that lacked the confidence to oppose it. Eventually, even the slightest opposition to the most outlandish actions of the counterculture became sufficient grounds for them to level the accusation of "homophobia," at which point those deemed to be the "homophobes" would almost always recant and retreat. In that manner, virtually all discussion of adverse effects of aberrant sexual conduct on society, and even on unprotected children in classrooms or other unsupervised situations, has been rendered "off limits." From state "family services" agencies to child custody disputes, to the make-up of youth organizations, any consideration of the morality of those in leadership, and their potential to victimize innocent children, has been effectively neutralized.

Islamists, working tirelessly to infiltrate and conform American society and Western Civilization into their own likeness, quickly recognized the value of this strategy, and the success leftists have had forcing their conservative opposition in to a defensive posture with malicious and fraudulent labels. So it was no surprise when they invented the term "Islamophobia," their own version of the "homophobia" brand, to advance their agenda in a virtually identical manner. Exceeding even their wildest expectations, the term was quickly embraced by leftists and globalists, who saw it as yet another effective avenue to stifling their opposition.

Now, Islamists can count on leftists to give them cover, whenever they endeavor to incrementally implement some aspect of sharia, or infiltrate the nation's schools with pro-Islamic curricula or programs, and even in the aftermath of a terrorist attack. Efforts to properly characterize the nature of the incursion or scope of the danger are quickly dismissed by Islamist activists as evidence of "Islamophobia," with their leftist parakeets dutifully repeating the accusation.

It is ironic, or perhaps more accurately, a stinging indictment of the ineptitude and passivity of our side, that such baseless attacks have been allowed to prevail. If any class within our society could be credibly accused of phobias and psychotic irrational fear, it is leftists, particularly on college campuses, who now demand complete dominance of the discourse entirely within the framework of their lies, because truth makes them "feel unsafe." Of course their assertions are phony, and just another excuse to demand the ability to control others. Yet when allowed to operate under an umbrella of total hypocrisy, this is the degree of intellectual dishonesty that quickly becomes inevitable.

> If any class within our society could be credibly accused of phobias and psychotic irrational fear, it is leftists, particularly on college campuses.

Xenophobe/Nativist: Among the more bizarre, but very "useful" concocted verbiage from the left are the terms "xenophobe" and "nativist" and their several derivatives. All are intended to instantly confer irrevocable condemnation on opponents of the leftist ideology, in any situation where race or nationality can be infused into the discourse, on even the most obscure basis. Thus, those who express opposition to open borders, which was once a basic common-sense premise of any nation that hoped to maintain its identity with its own defining culture, are now denounced as "xenophobes" and "nativists." In the current climate, it is the left that increasingly foments selective bigotry, particularly against white America, though in truth it is just as hateful against minorities who uphold our nation's traditional values and heritage. In an effort to put a "virtuous" front on the underlying, anti-American venom it embodies, it hurls the accusation of "xenophobia" against any who dispute its attacks on our national integrity. Those who want America's borders and culture maintained for all, on the historically supportable basis that the overriding benefits of the American ideal redound to the good of *all Americans* of every racial and ethnic background, are vilified and marginalized by virtue of these labels.

Such people are also invariably characterized as "angry" (along with typical insinuations that they are "white males"), merely on the basis that they stridently oppose leftist efforts to dismantle America. Many people of varying backgrounds are unified in their opposition to the leftist onslaught, which portends disaster for all people of all races who love this country. Yet leftist efforts to denigrate specific segments of American society on the basis of physical traits and ethnic backgrounds are somehow exempted from any real consideration of the glaring hypocrisy and bigotry they exhibit.

Nationalist: Not surprisingly, as Americans have increasingly rallied to their country, and against the onslaught of invading foreigners during the past few years, leftist attacks on them as "nativists" and "xenophobes" have proliferated, along with other similar accusatory insinuations of lurking "evil," such as that of being a "nationalist."

Leftists perform a cute trick here, by presuming nationalism to apply on a universal basis throughout all of humanity and all of history.

Though the term is clearly generic in nature, specifically conferring a loyalty to one's own nation and nothing more, leftists selectively identify the worst of circumstances in which "nationalism" supposedly played a part, and then paint all who identify even remotely with it as morally and ethically equal in every possible respect. Thus, Americans who have an affinity for the inherent decency of such figures as George Washington and John Adams, and the great nation they helped birthed, are really no different than the worst monsters of Hitler's Reich.

On many issues, the only criticism invoked by leftists is that the patriotic stand of Americans represents "nationalism," which apparently should be sufficient reason to oppose them, at least from the twisted perspective of the left. In truth, this transparent attack reveals the inherent weakness of the leftist position, with the deflection being a desperate effort to avoid serious discussion of the real issues at hand. The most effective means of comprehending leftist attacks on "nationalism" is to recognize the malignant alternative they seek to promote in its place, which is globalism.

Multiculturalism: In place of the "sin" of nationalism, leftists offer the enlightened view of humanity known as "multiculturalism." The big lie of "multiculturalism" is that, as presented by leftists in academia and elsewhere throughout the leftist cesspool, all cultures are ostensibly equal. This inane supposition is refuted by all of human history, but is an indispensable prerequisite to their advancement of globalism. Clearly, some cultures promote freedom, prosperity, and justice, while others maintain their social structure through brutality and fear. To attempt to concoct any manner of "moral equivalency" among them is the height of absurdity, and presents a looming danger to any culture that embraces such a lie. And if one wants to be really provocative and inflammatory among leftists, it is worth adding that the degree to which a culture either uplifts or oppresses its people can be directly correlated to its alignment with *truly Christian* precepts of right and wrong. Of course leftists will be quick to attempt to refute this by pointing out such events as the inquisition, slavery and the Salem witch trials, which were actually departures from Biblical principles.

> To attempt to concoct any manner
> of "moral equivalency" among the worlds'
> different cultures is the height of absurdity.

Proof of the inane, agenda-driven duplicity of the entire "multicultural" movement is lately evidenced by the new, contravening notion of "cultural appropriation." Leftists who once gained political leverage through accusations of "racism," and "bigotry" were eventually threatened by the fact that ethnic and cultural divides in America were slowly dissipating. Thus, a new "grievance" had to be invented to ensure that the flames of racial discord could continue to be fanned. Now, in some circles, efforts to "build bridges" of commonality among different ethnicities and nationalities are met with angry accusations of "cultural appropriation." The notion is beyond absurd. However, it once again reveals just how important it is to the left to be able to concoct one phony premise or another by which it can claim to be on that vaunted "moral high ground."

In the end, the leftist counterculture can be counted upon to foment as much animosity and lingering resentment among the general population as possible. A citizenry that realizes it need not be mired in such things, and has at its disposal great opportunities for the pursuit of happiness *for all*, is a citizenry that also realizes it doesn't need leftists or their insidious nanny state to survive. And that's a potential threat to the left that it will fanatically oppose.

White Guilt/White Privilege: As a result of the increasing levels of leftist fomented racial discord in America, particularly in the aftermath of Barack Obama having elevated race-baiting to official White House policy throughout his terms, the notion of racial equality is no longer deemed to be a worthy goal in the leftist "vision" for America. A harmonious nation of opportunity for all people, regardless of ethnicity, constitutes a liability to the left and somehow needs to be discarded. At the same time, leftists desperately needed to maintain the political leverage that their race pandering has afforded them over the past several decades. So, as with "Affirmative Action" and all of the other reverse discrimination in which they engaged, the notion of "White Privilege" was concocted, as a means of declaring *all* white citizens culpable for discrimination and suppression of minorities, whether or not any such thing has occurred, or if there is an actual perpetrator at hand.

"White Privilege" is an outgrowth of the toxic combination of racial pandering and white liberal condescension. As such it is the ultimate expression of real bigotry, in that it presumes minorities to be perennial "victims," who can be convinced of this as their inescapable station in life, regardless of their circumstances. By characterizing minorities in this thoroughly demeaning manner, leftists reveal their presumption of them as gullible and easily manipulated.

In short, "white privilege" asserts that the ability to thrive as an American is not attributable to diligence and integrity, but to race, and particularly, to being Caucasian. Thus, minorities who do poorly in school or work are in no way responsible for their actions, nor are they able to better their plight. Instead, they are helpless, hapless "victims." What seems to go largely unnoticed in this assessment of life in America is that it reflects a true contempt for minorities, presuming that their efforts will *inherently* yield inferior results. Sadly, too many have been conditioned to allow themselves to be consigned to such a fate by leftists in power, who are not interested in raising them up, but are only concerned with maintaining them as a reliable electoral power base on account of their presumed dependency. Hence, leftists will resort to any means of convincing minorities that their fate is sealed.

What seems to go largely unnoticed in the left's assessment of life in America is that it reflects a true contempt for minorities, presuming that their efforts will inherently yield inferior results.

Increasingly, such condescension is echoed by white minions, particularly high-school and college students, who seek to be in the good graces of the leftist leadership and their peers by diligently echoing such race pandering. Yet this behavior does not result from any genuine humility. Rather, the best means by which leftists are able to ensure that their minions play their proper roles in this ruse is to prey upon the consuming nature of their *arrogance*. The degree to which these lackeys are vulnerable to such transparent manipulation is a testament to the truly extreme degree of self-absorption of all who ascribe to leftist ideology. As per the previous discussion of this topic, "white guilt" is proclaimed *not* in any actual recognition of one's racial advantage or need to be "humble." Nor does it ever involve real remorse or material sacrifice on the part of those espousing it. But like every leftist claim of "virtue," it is instead a demand for such penance as an expression of contrition *from others*. It would be far more accurate to characterize such shameless self-aggrandizement as "leftist privilege," by which they deem themselves the only people worthy to issue supreme edicts of right and wrong, in the most brazen exhibitions of leftist "moral high ground," issued in this case on the basis of race, since they have nothing else.

Bipartisan/Partisan: Without a doubt, the lowest place on the political ladder is ostensibly held by those politicians accused of being "partisan," which of course also means conservative. In contrast, the most sought-after and treasured label leftists can ever attach to one of their onerous pieces of legislation is that of being a "bipartisan" effort. In this manner, Democrat politicians have often wielded enormous political leverage against needlessly defensive Republicans who will go a long way to avoid being derisively tagged as partisans. Here, in the public spotlight, is a prime example of how the Alinsky strategy has succeeded, simply because spineless Republicans, the designated targets, allow themselves to be manipulated by it.

This need not be the case, since the entire topic can be easily turned back on the left, the moment hapless Republicans recognize their position, and the leverage at their disposal (More on this in Chapter 9). While Republicans of the D.C. "Establishment" are duped into believing that "bipartisanship" is a badge of honor, it is invariably a "lose/lose" for the GOP. A bad bill from the Democrats has a greater chance of advancing if given "bipartisan" cover by Republicans, which means the liberal agenda will advance, to the detriment of everyone. Yet when the actual impact of the bill becomes known, Democrats instantly remind everyone that the effort was "bipartisan," the end result being that disenfranchised voters see the betrayal as coming from both parties, with nobody in Washington being properly held accountable or made to pay a political price. Were Republicans to act in a more "partisan" manner, and steadfastly refuse to support any bad piece of legislation or sanction the appointment of any leftist activist nominee to the courts, the contrast between the two camps in Washington would redound to their benefit. However, whenever the lines are blurred, the GOP bears the brunt of anger from disillusioned voters.

Litmus Test/Single Issue: Not all issues and opinions are created equal. Some issues allow a good deal of latitude for varied perspectives, while others are absolutely morally defining, and illustrative of an individual's entire character. In leftist strategizing, which often succeeds on the perception of "gray areas" to incrementally advance ideas that would initially be considered detestable, real "black and white" determinations of right and wrong are regarded as virtual "poison."

So it is that leftists dismiss any efforts to actually uphold tangible standards, particularly on defining issues of the day (think: abortion), as "litmus tests." The end game is for leftists to convince those ostensibly on *our side* that basic premises of right and wrong are somehow an affront to the political process. A campaigning politician, we are told, cannot be appraised on a "single issue," because that is simply too narrow. For example, one who is adjudged on the basis of his or her stance on abortion is ostensibly denied a fair shake in regards to the other issues of the day.

Yet a genuine understanding of abortion, and the views of any individual in regards to it, prove to be a thoroughly defining reflection of that person's character. As is the case with honesty, a person who can dismiss the sanctity of an innocent human life, simply because that little person is too helpless to defend himself, or herself, is someone who cannot be counted on to truly uphold the rights of *any person.*

Nevertheless, liberals have been very successful in their efforts to undermine the conservative movement with their denigration of "litmus tests," and those steadfast conservatives who refuse to compromise on certain defining principles as being "single issue." Worst of all, politicians claiming to be on the right, but who in reality are primarily looking for what they deem to be politically "safe" ground, are all too willing to hide from taking principled stances with their claims of not wanting to be guilty of "litmus tests" or being "single issue."

Given this, it is no wonder that leftists, who steadfastly enforce *their* litmus tests, not only on abortion but on a wide variety of issues, are all too often successful in implementing their agenda and seeing it upheld by their political operatives and court appointees who are not so easily swayed.

Trickle Down: In a free and unfettered capitalistic society, the goods and services which dominate the marketplace are determined by the needs and desires of the populace, with profits going to those who can best answer the demands. In the process, some entrepreneurs will successfully respond to conditions by providing the things people want, while others will engage in misguided efforts that will ultimately fail. But freedom isn't really freedom, unless it also encompasses the freedom to fail, which still leaves the door open to try again.

According to the leftist worldview, such economic reality is deemed inherently "unfair," and even in the most successful times, is derided as "trickle down economics." The ugly insinuation is that the masses are destined to scrape for a few crumbs, ostensibly dropped on the floor by a few randomly wealthy individuals, who are hopelessly calloused and indifferent to the plight of the "little guy."

However, the historically consistent realities of a truly free society, which by definition must include a free market, as opposed to the true squalor and despair of the collectivist alternative, proves this mantra to be just another lie in the leftist verbal arsenal. That our side should ever be afraid of it is proof of just how effective leftist propagandizing can be, when it remains largely unopposed.

In truth, whenever a corporation or individual in a free society enjoys great business success, the inevitable response is an expansion of the business by which they achieved their wealth. This means building new facilities, hiring more people, shipping more products, and expanding advertisements and other supportive services. Hence, the "rising tide that raises all boats." Successful corporations generate flourishing communities, and if the movement occurs on a sufficiently wide scale basis, the result is thriving and prospering nations where the citizens are able to enjoy expanded freedom to pursue happiness in their own desired methods.

In contrast, the real "trickle down" that deserves scorn and derision, and which is a potential threat to the freedom of all Americans, is that perpetrated by the bloated bureaucratic state. It is no surprise that six of the top ten wealthiest counties in the United States border on the District of Columbia, or lie in close proximity to it. Washington D.C. produces no product, but instead confiscates its wealth from the rest of the nation, by force if necessary. And while its luxury does provide extremely high incomes for those in its vicinity, this is not by any choice of those throughout the rest of the country who ultimately foot the bill. In most cases, the "benefits" redistributed by the D.C. leviathan are meager, and only intended to provide subsistence to recipients sufficient to keep them in a dependent condition, whereby their "loyalty" to the state is assured.

Centrist/Fringe/Extremist/Zealot: With monotonous predictability, the discussion of every political debate in every leftist political speech, every commentary from a liberal columnist, and every report on the "mainstream" (leftist) nightly news will disparagingly reference the supposed "extremism" of those on the right, as opposed to hard-core liberals who are invariably characterized as benign and "centrist." In the same sense, a "zealot" is a person who cares more than leftists think someone should about a topic that leftists oppose. In all cases, the intent is to relegate conservative opponents to the ideological "fringe" as defined by the left, which inherently renders any valid points they might make "off limits" to proper discussion. Such tainted and deceitful labels are offered in a shameless matter-of-fact manner which is intended to convey the notion that everybody recognizes them as unassailable truth. On any given day, leftist "news" reports will characterize a conservative individual or political issue as "extreme" with seemingly dead-pan certainty, as if an objective and universally recognized standard exists somewhere. And all too often, our side neglects to challenge such assertions on their face value, which thereafter allows them an undeserved mantle of "credibility."

It should never be forgotten that by his own words, Alinsky's work was not devoted to the majority, but to *radicals;* the end-game of his strategy being to force the American mainstream to conform to the inherently "superior" leftist agenda. Thus, any leftist assertion of who is in the "middle," and where to draw the boundaries of right-wing "extremism" cannot be credibly defined by *hard-left* ideologues. The moment leftists are able to shift the perception of where their sick ideology lies on the political spectrum, they shift the perception of what constitutes the "center" in their direction as well. At that point, even a mildly conservative perspective can be portrayed as "right wing extremism," since it differs so drastically from the perversity of the leftist counterculture. And as increasing numbers of unprincipled politicians are willing to comply with such baseless dictates, real conservatives are hamstrung in their efforts to prevent the country from listing to the left and falling into the disasters that inevitably ensue.

Settled Science, Settled Law, and the Wrong Side of History: The terms "settled science" and "settled law" are leftist tools to maintain the status quo on a particular issue, as long as it aligns with the thinking of leftists and the counterculture. Otherwise, such premises are totally ignored, and never mentioned by leftists during any discussion or "news" reports on the topic in question. In contrast, the moment leftists seek to upend social standards and traditions for the purpose of supplanting them with the moral bankruptcy of the counterculture, they do a complete "about face" and start warning that those who are determined to maintain the culture as it is (the "status quo") will find themselves on the "wrong side of history." On its face, this term is wholly *baseless* and an absurdity. Yet it has great appeal to the spineless, unprincipled "bandwagon" politician who believes he can find some zone of "safety" by becoming lost in the middle of the perceived "crowd."

Leftists readily tip their collective hand when invoking the term "settled science." Clearly, they do not regard the ideas promoted under this banner as "science," but instead as a dogmatic and tyrannically imposed "religion." Such defining topics as "climate change" are not dealt with on a scientific basis, with open discussion of supporting or contravening evidence. In truth, leftists cannot honestly claim any sincere "scientific" assessment of the issue, given their flagrant selection of doctored "data" on global temperatures and other supposed supporting "evidence," their suppression of readily available information that runs counter to their apocalyptic predictions, and the vicious personal attacks they wage on "heretics" who don't accept their articles of faith. Thus their "settled science" label is far more of a deflection than an indication of logic and reason.

Contrast the phony leftist devotion to climate-change "science" to their completely contradictory behavior regarding human abortion. Having loudly (even hysterically) promoted abortion as the ultimate expression of a "woman's right to choose," they denounce any opposition to it as "religious interference" of a woman's privacy (more on that later). Reality paints a very different picture of abortion than that promoted by leftists. The obvious humanity of the unborn child is clearly *not* a "religious issue," but a biological *fact*. The *settled science* of the unborn child is as a live human being, with fingers, toes, and a heartbeat. This truth presents an enormous obstacle to leftist efforts at painting the entire abortion issue in the rosy, innocuous terms by which they seek to avoid its horrible realities.

At that point they quickly pivot away from real science or any reference to science, and focus entirely on abortion as "settled law." With the judicial abomination of "Roe v. Wade" having occurred back in 1973, the "settled law" rejoinder is deemed effective in preventing any reconsideration of a horrendous constitutional affront by the activist Supreme Court of that era. Furthermore, since the "settled" nature of the law ostensibly elevates the court's decision to the status of being "enshrined," the underlying message is that even the mere questioning of it is an attack on the Constitution and every good thing about America.

> The obvious humanity of the unborn child
> is clearly not a "religious issue,"
> but a biological fact.

Of course the definition of marriage as the legal joining of a man and a woman has been thoroughly established throughout not merely a few decades but for thousands of years. Furthermore, with only the occasional misogynistic exception of polygamy, marriage has been similarly defined throughout the vast majority of cultures in the world. Certainly in America, the matter had been settled law since the nation's founding. And the only reason the founders never specifically addressed it was because they deemed it beyond question by any society with even a shred of morality. But that certainly didn't stop the leftist counterculture, with the assistance of another activist Supreme Court that saw itself not as jurists but as legislators. So they unhesitatingly trashed every law protecting the institution of Holy Matrimony, and supplanted them with so-called same-sex "marriage" to accommodate the agenda of homosexual activists.

In that situation, what had clearly been settled law throughout the entire existence of the United States was jettisoned, and any who opposed the move were disparaged as being on the "wrong side of history." Leftist "prophets" simply proclaimed that the world would be evolving in their desired direction, thus relegating those who attempted to stand on the stabilizing cultural mores of Western Civilization, along with many others, to a newly contrived "fringe." Of course, real history is replete with instances where such thinking rose to prominence, only to lead inexorably to societal collapse. So much for leftist considerations of "history."

Snowflakes, Safe Spaces, and Fake News: In closing this chapter, these seemingly disparate labels need to be discussed in conjunction with each other, not so much because of any direct philosophical commonality between them, but instead because they represent contrasting examples of an ineffective response from our side (in the case of "Snowflakes" and "Safe Spaces"), as opposed to the label of "Fake News" that has proven devastating to the left. The first two stand as an example of how not to confront leftist posturing, while the second is an outstanding example of how the battle can successfully be fought and won.

As leftist indoctrination of college students breached any boundaries of reason and sanity, student claims of "victimhood," on any spurious grounds, reached epidemic proportions. Unfettered from any manner of embarrassment by a leftist counterculture that glorifies puerile self-absorption and weakness, student tantrums erupted and spread over any aspect of human existence to which they objected. Thus was the term "snowflake" birthed, to describe those who were too frail to cope with the realities of life.

Conservatives were quick to latch on to the term and invoke it whenever young leftists engaged in childish tantrums, since they presumed this to be a way to chide them for their insipid and self pitying attitudes. As functioning members of a decent and robust American culture, conservatives expected that those students would recognize the manner in which they were only disgracing themselves with their whining and cowardly demeanor. Surely, anyone realizing the pathetic level to which they had willingly allowed themselves to be degraded would want to take corrective measures and thereafter seek to behave as dignified, mature, functioning young adults.

However, conservatives who believe this have completely underestimated the consuming arrogance of diligently programmed young people, the crippling effects of "political correctness" on their ability to reason, and the thoroughly skewed "morality" that results. The reality of "Snowflake" thinking is that it is so devoid of any aspirations of adulthood that cowardice is actually glorified as a "virtue." Remember, they have no dignity, and *no shame*. The goal is to dominate. A young person whose leftist affinities aren't being immediately accommodated initially makes demands of such, and then collapses into a hysterical fit in order to get his or her way. And among the emotionally and spiritually "castrated" young males who wish to remain in "good standing" in the toxic leftist college environment, any remnant of real manhood is tantamount to mental illness, and so their last vestige of protection against becoming truly pathetic minions of the leftist counterculture has been removed.

Their so-called "safe spaces, which sound like peaceful havens of gentleness and passivity, are actually zones of iron-fisted leftist bullying. The presumed "safety" within them only applies to leftists whose thoughts are in total compliance with the "politically correct" ordinances of the leftist counterculture. Any who dare to deviate, even in the slightest degree, from its twisted orthodoxy are viciously castigated and attacked. Thus, the tendency of weak-minded individuals to seek obscurity within the "herd" drastically increases their willingness to toe the party line. Any attempts at accommodation of the resultant socially dysfunctional behavior by our side only gives it unwarranted legitimacy. Worse yet, "stepping lightly" around their supposed emotional wounds further convinces them that their pathetic exhibitions are reasonable and valid.

In contrast to the disgraceful "Snowflake" debacle, the ongoing conflict over the term "Fake News" spotlights an entirely different scenario; one in which a leftist ruse to destroy the credibility of those on the right completely backfired. Regardless of who actually invented the term, the accusation of "Fake News" was first popularized by the left during the 2016 presidential campaign, specifically as a means of undermining the credibility of then-candidate Donald Trump. Seeking any possible grounds on which to dismiss his hard-hitting statements, the leftist media attempted to trivialize them and ultimately characterize them as complete lies by disparaging them as "Fake News." With media leftists on the major networks and their liberal kindred in the major newspapers essentially marching in "lock-step," the term spread like wildfire.

However, leftist accusations of "Fake News" had one major vulnerability. The term characterized the leftist media and political establishment far too well for them to successfully attach it to anyone else. For years a widespread and simmering anger among the American people burned against deceitful liberal politicians and their media minions, specifically that they had so readily disseminated total lies and suppressed facts in order to derail any opposition to their agenda. Among rational and thinking Americans, the awareness of such rampant bias in liberal "journalism" is beyond dispute, despite leftist anchors and reporters vehemently denying it to this day. Leftists who had become accustomed over the years to "fact checking," merely by contradicting conservatives with liberal opinions, were dismayed to realize that they were no longer the sole arbiters of what could be labeled as "Fake News." All of this portends the end of the unchallenged leftist information monopoly that they had enjoyed in previous decades, and which has always been so essential to their agenda. The initial popularity of the term, which they had proliferated so rapidly among their circles, suddenly evaporated the moment they realized that as a result of their disingenuousness, it was doggedly sticking to them.

What followed has been a panicked and almost comical effort by the left to free itself from the label, like a fly seeking escape from its eventual doom in a spider's web. Leftists loudly decried any use of the term as some sort of attack on the First Amendment, to which they seem to believe they have sole proprietorship. And on one occasion, CNN "reporter" Chris Cuomo desperately attempted to deflect the tenacious label by comparing it to "ethnic disparagement." In other words, accusing a lying leftist "reporter" of fake news was, in Cuomo's convoluted "PC" world, tantamount to racism. Of course Cuomo's contention was itself the *epitome of Fake News,* so despite his transparent attempt to retreat to that overused stronghold of leftist sanctimony, namely the shameless exploitation of the "race card," Cuomo's accusation never gained traction. This last ditch effort to put the "genie back in the bottle" utterly failed.

To this day, leftists sorely regret that they ever attempted to popularize the term. Their misreporting and distortions of the facts are readily and effectively neutralized by conservatives who simply attach the "Fake News" label to them whenever it is appropriate. The lesson learned here will be discussed in greater detail in later chapters.

Chapter Five
Leftist Mantras: Establishing "Truth" by Presumption

In the same manner that leftists preordain the "good guys" and "bad guys" in any debate by the labels they invoke, they establish precepts of their twisted ideology as uncontested "fact" or refute realities they find troublesome with a series of mantras, most which have become well-known over the years *not* because they've ever been proven to be true, but merely because leftists recite them with such an air of absolute certainty. The "irrefutable" status of these mantras is further solidified by the manner in which leftists react with theatrical, coordinated outrage and even violence, the moment anyone dares to question their validity. Such behavior ensures that the spineless members of the "opposition" will run for cover, instead of ever confronting even the most absurd falsehoods, when presented as unimpeachable "truth" by the left. Sadly, too few on our side have been willing to bluntly point out, or even consider, the immense volume of empty platitudes and ludicrous assertions on which leftists build the case for the superiority of their ideology and their agenda.

Admittedly, much of what is addressed here may appear as little more than an attempt to arbitrate squabbling between children in the school yard. But while it appears to be demeaning to deal with things on that level, and it is tempting to sidestep all of it in an effort to elevate the discussion to a level of maturity and reason, these points desperately need to be addressed. Sadly, whether on the nightly "news," in the debates on Capitol Hill, or within academia, so much of the discourse has descended to truly juvenile behavior that cannot be confronted in any other manner. Otherwise, if it is ignored for any reason, it will ultimately prevail.

Whether leftists have all received the same "talking points" memo from some propaganda "group think tank," or they've simply been thoroughly indoctrinated by American academe and their mental processes are so reflexively compartmentalized that they automatically lurch into one mental rut after another, the result is a litany of assertions that ensues with Pavlovian predictability. From their ritualistic denunciation of Fox News, to their attacks on "climate change deniers," to their clarion calls of the looming threat posed by talk radio, in their minds such scripted epithets represent definitive and substantive arguments capable of neutralizing any opposing viewpoint.

> News service "style books" set speech and
> writing codes that are totally driven by their ability
> to support the precepts of the leftist agenda.

Their approved terminology has been meticulously concocted and diligently applied. Words and phrases are studied in depth and established as the only accepted lexicon by liberal politicians and their media minions. News service "style books" set speech and writing codes that are totally driven by their ability to support the precepts of the leftist agenda, and from which no deviation is allowed. From that point forward, approved phrases are casually slipped into every "news" report, every opinion column and every narrative, in order to precisely frame the issue of the day in a manner that unquestioningly promotes the twisted standards of the left, while disparaging those on the right. For example, "news" accounts of terrorist attacks committed by anyone from the middle-east now specifically avoid the word "terrorism." Under no circumstances is the perpetrator's nationality or religion mentioned. However, the moment the issue involves Americans taking a stance against the encroachment of foreigners, the ethnicity and religion of those foreigners will be the only issue on which leftist politicians and "news" reporters focus. None of this is by accident.

In the absence of any opposition, leftists have over time learned to prevail in even the most outrageous and indefensible situations. Throughout his political career, the late Democrat Senator Robert Byrd held such dubious positions as "Exalted Cyclops" in the Ku Klux Klan. He once openly stated that his refusal to serve in the military during World War II was due to his aversion to being "alongside race mongrels." But as a tax and spend liberal with great political clout, Byrd was glowingly recast by fellow Democrats as the "Conscience of the Senate." Such a transformative mantra would never have been conferred on any conservative bearing even the tiniest remnant of similar political baggage, yet liberals repeated their adulation of Byrd with such incessant certitude that few on either side of the aisle ever dared to challenge the notion.

Of course such mantras and slogans have been deftly used by politicians for years. And all too often, the initial impression they generate overwhelms any tendency to seriously consider their real implications and unintended consequences. Consider Franklin Roosevelt's Depression-era promise to provide America with a "chicken in every pot." For a nation suffering in the depths of massive unemployment, foreclosures, and the devastation of the dust bowls, Roosevelt's mantra sounded comforting.

On the surface, the prospect of a "chicken in every pot" could be interpreted as "freedom from want," which was one of Roosevelt's enshrined "Four Freedoms." Yet a serious examination of its figurative and literal implications might have forewarned America of the ensuing wave of nanny-state overreach, and the encroachments on the individual liberties and finances of the American people that it foreshadowed. Rather than any manner of "freedom," it really represented an effort to supplant the pursuit of happiness espoused in the Declaration of Independence with the faux "safety" of meager subsistence.

Too many people who were downtrodden, desperate, and not realizing that their plight was being exploited, were willing to forfeit the opportunities available to them, trading their freedoms for security. Eventually, the notion of bare existence, at the expense of others, became popular to the point that those willing to survive on that basis felt themselves worthy to criticize others who strove for anything higher. Americans who had accepted that metaphorical state-provided "chicken" on their table as their "lot in life," were suddenly filled with venomous sanctimony as they condemned "the greedy rich," who had worked hard to improve their situation to the point of enjoying a steak if they chose to do so.

To a great extent, this set the stage for the biggest leftist ruse of all: liberal "compassion." Alinsky himself invoked such concepts to justify his racialism, lies, and bullying to advance what was ultimately communism. The horrors, genocide, and unfathomable deprivation that occurred under the nightmare of communism have since become well known. But even during the middle of the Twentieth Century, its advocates could not have been unaware of its grim reality. Nevertheless, they advanced their agenda as they still do, under a phony premise that once it is established as an uncontested power in the world, it will suddenly, miraculously, prove to be a blessing to humanity.

Thankfully, despite the temptation, America hasn't yet been totally deceived, and refuses to completely sell its national "soul" for the empty promise of a "chicken in every pot." However, with a long record of unwarranted public-relations successes based on just such shameless and unfounded mantras, it is understandable that leftists would perpetuate the practice, and have enormously expanded it in recent years. In the current climate, incontrovertible facts offered by conservatives are casually dismissed with nothing more than the presumed "truth" of an oft-repeated mantra. A few examples are given here. Once again, this is not in any way intended to be a comprehensive list. Rather, it has been compiled to show the *pattern* of manipulation and deceit, and more importantly, how easily leftist axioms can be dispelled, the moment they are recognized as such, and the truth unabashedly presented in response.

You can't question a person's patriotism: In order to fully grasp the significance of this mantra, a bit of background is necessary. During the leftist "revolution" of the sixties, and even into the post Vietnam era, the concept of patriotism was fiercely and relentlessly attacked by the left. Over the years, patriotism fell into such universal disrepute within leftist circles that the denigration of America and desecration of the flag, even in the most vile and fraudulent of terms, eventually became the liberal "norm." This tendency reached its nadir during the presidency of Bill Clinton who, as a Vietnam War protester and draft dodger, had openly expressed his "loathing" of the United States Military. Leftists in political office and the media eventually became comfortable expressing flagrantly anti-American sentiments and even deriding real patriotism as a potentially dangerous trait that warranted among other things, elevated levels of government scrutiny.

At times, the concept of patriotism was contorted into truly absurd caricatures of its original meaning. In the early years of his first term, President Bill Clinton briefly sought to make the case that patriotism was epitomized by support for the president. His characteristic self-absorption was a little too obvious, so this particular effort backfired and quickly fizzled. Interestingly, barely a dozen years later (after Bill had left office), Hillary Clinton sought to define patriotism in precisely the opposite terms in one of her most infamous screeching rants, asserting that she was "sick and tired" of people saying that disagreement with "any administration" might be regarded as "not patriotic."

In the wake of the September 11, 2001 terrorist attacks however, the nation underwent a significant, albeit somewhat temporary resurgence of genuine patriotism. Flags waved profusely from coast to coast and traditional America, which had never lost its sincere patriotic zeal, was emboldened to openly express love of God and Country. This apparent sudden change in the national temperament had the unanticipated consequence of consigning anti-American leftists to the fringe; a place where they couldn't effectively assert their professed "moral authority."

Consequently, they concocted a means of deflecting derision over their obvious antipathy towards the nation by rebutting such suggestions with the bizarre assertion that every individual could define patriotism in his or her own way, and therefore no individual's "patriotism" could ever be questioned under any circumstances. Once again, this transparent ruse succeeded beyond the left's wildest expectations. Eventually, many on the right acquiesced and conceded that such claims were somehow "legitimate." From that point forward, no action of any leftist, regardless of how treasonous, could be discussed from a perspective of being hostile to America, without leftists squealing that it constituted an "attack" on the individual's "patriotism" and was inherently wrong. The most blatant betrayal of America could thereafter be sidestepped since the far greater "evil," according to leftists, was to dare characterize the act as "unpatriotic."

As is always the case, whenever those on the right surrender any bit of moral high ground, leftists seize upon it and reinvent it in a manner that gives them the unquestioned moral and intellectual advantage. The moment conservatives shied from calling traitorous leftist behavior "unpatriotic," the left was unfettered as it labeled virtually any conservative belief or action in exactly that manner. Former Vice-President Al Gore decried then President George Bush's pursuit of terrorism with claims that Bush had "betrayed America." And on numerous occasions Barack Obama denigrated the actions of his conservative opposition as "un-American." In an only slightly less hypocritical manner, he would disparage actions with which he disagreed as "not who we are." By his words, Obama clearly sought to delineate between the thoughts and deeds of "worthy" Americans, as opposed to those he regarded as an affront to his twisted concept of our national identity. Yet neither Gore nor Obama ever faced backlash for "daring to challenge the patriotism" of their conservative opponents.

You can't say that: It might seem demeaning and distracting to delve into this particularly puerile leftist rejoinder, except that so often, its mere recitation serves to stop conservatives dead in their tracks. In much the same sense that leftists seek to give cover to the most treacherous anti-American activity and sentiments by decrying any criticism as "questioning one's patriotism," they frequently wield an even broader brush with their mantra "You can't say that!" As is the case with their whiny demands for "fairness," this mantra would seem far more reflective of socially dysfunctional fourth graders on the playground than of any serious political discourse. But as leftist politicians and commentators become increasingly puerile in their own lives and their "professional" conduct, such behavior is itself increasingly common. Yet they nonetheless enjoy success with it, merely on account of their vehemence, along with the hesitance of our side to fire back at them. If there was ever a leftist tactic that proves, beyond any doubt, the ultimate flimsiness of their ideology, and indeed the entire manner in which they seek to advance it, this should be it.

However, the moment we are willing to accommodate them (as has historically been the case), they seize the upper hand, and on that basis dominate any further debate. While all of this may seem glaringly obvious, it is apparently a mystery to many supposedly "conservative" politicians and pundits, who are too ready to concede this inane premise as demanded by leftists, for the sake of an "amicable" resolution to the confrontation, which means the leftists win.

When leftists contend that the issue at hand must be dropped on such a basis, it is a sure sign that they are cornered, and feeling very vulnerable. The best rebuttal to their desperate flailing is merely to remind leftists "As conservatives, we speak truth. There's a First Amendment that says we can, and a Bible that says we should!"

You don't know what I'm thinking: Right out of the same fourth-grade debate strategy book as "You can't say that," this mantra is almost too embarrassing to even discuss. Yet leftists are so consumed with arrogance, they are totally devoid of such embarrassment, and thus revert to it with no sense of shame whatsoever. Even the liberal "pundit class" has sunk to it when cornered. The goal is to claim a mantle of "objectivity," despite glaring evidence that leftists are operating from their standard perspective, based on their customary lies and ideological absurdities. In truth, it is often *very easy* to know exactly what leftists are thinking, on account of their reflexive and simplistic devotion to the leftist agenda, which serves as the ultimate and defining "prism" through which they choose to perceive the world around them. While Pavlov's behavioral conditioning experiment with his famous dogs was groundbreaking at the time, it didn't ever really take a genius to know precisely what the dogs were thinking.

Experts across the political spectrum agree: This was one of Barack Obama's favorite ploys. With no qualifying information, he simply asserted that "everyone" held to the viewpoint he sought to promote, which in reality was almost always a twisted precept taken directly from the playbook of the leftist fringe. Nevertheless, it relied on a basic component of the Alinsky strategy, which is to marginalize those who deviate from the professed conclusion of the "experts." Once again, its success is totally dependent on the tacit "cooperation" of those who might stridently disagree with a particular point, but do not possess the necessary backbone to stand alone, or face the inevitable leftist arsenal of scorn and derision that will be unloaded on them if they dare to say so.

However, in the face of a vocal and unwavering opposition, this mantra can be instantly shattered, merely by requesting the identity of those "experts" and legitimately questioning their motives.

Our diversity is our strength: Among the most profound examples of an empty slogan eventually gaining traction as seemingly irrefutable truth, is the mantra "Our diversity is our strength." The success of this ruse relies on the expectation that without any supporting evidence, people have heard this platitude repeated so often and with such certainty, it simply "must" be true. The supposed historical evidence, invoked to "prove" the point, is that America is a great nation, and has been made up of many diverse cultures. Case closed.

In reality, nothing could be further from the truth. It is not our "diversity," but our *Americanism*, that provided such opportunity for those arriving from foreign lands to achieve their greatest potential. Our *Americanism* is the defining pillar of our societal and cultural strength. And that quality is a direct result of the Judeo-Christian principles on which our nation was founded. Leftists would gladly see America abandon those ideals and descend into the chaos of Balkanism, a term which describes a region where society totally fractured among disparate warring cultures. In truth, the growing strife and animosity among different demographics throughout America stands as grim testimony to the degree that leftist "diversity" has taken root, as it supplants our culture and divides Americans from each other, ultimately separating many from the founding principles that once promoted national cohesion and unity.

In contrast to the looming danger of a fractured culture, it was our *Americanism* that, in the aftermath of the Revolutionary War, enabled the founders to forge a government devoted to the preservation and protection of the rights of the individual, rather than empowering itself and thus replacing one form of despotism with another. It was our *Americanism* by which we tamed a continent, defeated the Axis Powers, landed a man on the moon, prevailed against the Soviet Union in the Cold War, and rose to the pinnacle of the world economy.

America is a nation of immigrants: One of the most transparent leftist efforts to destroy America's national identity is this overused rejoinder which asserts that since a major portion of our population descended at some point from immigrants, we as a nation have no right to turn away *any* outsiders under any circumstances. In many respects, this is merely a reiteration of the "Our diversity is our strength" mantra. Of course it studiously ignores the other aspects of the immigration debate which absolutely define it. For several reasons, immigration in recent years is a far different situation from what it ever was in the past. Thus, it is imperative that our side does not ignore the decisive factors that frame any objective discussion of immigration, lest we allow it to be redirected onto totally meaningless premises, which of course is the entire goal of the left.

Perhaps most importantly, as a result of the pathological absurdities of "Political Correctness," our country has largely been hamstrung in its ability to assert defining character traits of Americanism. Back when Americans were unashamed to be Americans, incoming foreigners recognized a need to assimilate, which was the essence of those references to our country as "*E Pluribus Unum*" and the "melting pot."

As a result of the pathological absurdities of "Political Correctness," our country has been hamstrung in its ability to assert defining character traits of Americanism.

But the days of foreigners coming to our shores, to symbolically or even literally kiss the ground in gratitude, and from that point forward proudly wave the *American Flag*, appear to be a thing of the past. The nihilism of the leftist counterculture has been very successful in destroying that concept, whereupon invading foreigners are no longer the least bit embarrassed to flee third-world oppression and destitution, only to come to our shores and immediately start demanding that

Americans conform to their preferences, customs and creeds, in an effort to recreate the mess from which they fled.

A President should be given his choice of judges: Like so many other popular pronouncements from the political establishment, the exact source of this one is not known, nor is it really relevant. However, in its current form, it became very popular during the 1990s, as Bill Clinton nominated one agenda-driven leftist after another to the nation's highest courts. Clearly, the Democrats saw this as their best means of neutralizing opposition to Clinton's hard-left picks for the nation's high courts, especially after Republicans gained a Senate majority in 1994. Worse yet, the Republican "Establishment" also embraced the notion and shamefully hid behind it as the best hope of avoiding contentious nomination hearings and rejections, while maintaining a facade of opposition to the Clinton agenda. By their assent, spineless Republicans could claim to be doing their civic duty, for the good of the nation, as they rubber stamped Clinton judicial political hacks Stephen Breyer and Ruth Ginsburg for the Supreme Court, along with a host of leftist federal judges who universally despised the precepts of the Constitution and would readily concoct ways to bypass it. Thus was this despicable and indefensible platitude thoroughly established as "conventional wisdom," at least whenever a Democrat was in the White House.

Yet despite its widespread acceptance, it has absolutely no basis in truth, and in fact it stands in diametric opposition to the actual purpose of the Constitution's "advise and consent" clause. Far from the nomination and confirmation circus of the modern day, the Framers intended the process to be the best means of ensuring both the good faith and judgment of the Executive Branch, where the nomination originated, as well as that of the Senate, where a nominee would be either confirmed or denied. The criteria for doing so was presumed to be a genuine devotion, by members of both branches, to their respective oaths of office. The possibility of a Senate rejection of a nominee was predicated on that nominee's unfitness to uphold the law and the Constitution, based not on party affiliation or political agenda, but on the lack of competence, sincerity, and integrity of that individual as a guardian of our nation's founding charter.

Having acquiesced to the leftist position, Republicans have abhorrently allowed modern courts to establish themselves as unaccountable alternatives to the legislative process, where Democrat minions hold positions of power in spite of their open hostility to the rule of law and the nation's founding principles. And of course, when the tables are turned, those same hapless Republicans are completely blindsided. Having granted so much latitude for leftist abuses of power with the naive expectation of reciprocity, they continue to presume some mutual deference, once their side is back in power. Yet at that point they are shocked to see leftists pull out every despicable accusation and ploy to undermine and hopefully destroy any nominee who might seriously endeavor to pursue justice and constitutional impartiality. Thus, as a result of Republican cowardice and incompetence, leftists have all-too-often been successful at easily confirming nominees whose track records of anti-constitutional ideology are flagrant and indefensible. Meanwhile, constitutional originalist nominees from the GOP face an uphill battle, amid unconscionable objections from a shameless left that hurls lies and venom from its supposed perch on the "moral high ground."

A far more effective case can be made by a president who intends to restore the primacy of the Constitution in U.S. law, and who is unafraid to say so. By unabashedly asserting the critical importance of re-establishing the integrity of constitutional law, and by only nominating individuals to the bench who have *provable* records of faithfulness to this principle, a virtually "air-tight" case can be made that *only* such nominees are inherently and unquestionably fit for office. The only proper course is to assess and approve the nomination on that basis, or to oppose it if the nominee is indeed unfit. Once this truth is cemented in the minds of the American people, it is the leftists who would thereafter be put totally on the defensive, both during the tenure of Republican presidents and by future Republican opposition to any anti-constitutional Democrat nominee. If our side remains steadfast, leftists would then be forced into the position of attempting to make a case with the American people that they have as much "right" to undermine the Constitution as conservatives have to uphold its integrity. Let leftists squall that supporting only a constitutional originalist somehow represents Republican "partisanship." Doing so would effectively be an admission that their agenda is to undermine and eradicate our Constitution as the cornerstone of American law, and the guarantor of freedom and justice that it has been for over two centuries.

One Person, one vote: Leftists have an enormous stake in this mantra, because it is used on so many fronts to undermine the real foundation of our nation, which was very deliberately *not* established as a "democracy," but as a representative republic. This isn't a mere debate point for civics class. The underlying issue here is a defining characteristic of how our nation was structured, and on what basis it has thrived and prospered in the two and a half centuries since independence was declared.

In a democracy, any abhorrent action can occur at any given moment and be deemed completely "legal," as long as fifty-one percent of the population endorses it. In such an environment, the suppression of individual rights becomes inevitable, the moment a majority reaches the consensus that it doesn't want to hear from the minority. And the situation only degenerates from there. Thus the Founders studiously instituted a system that would require a vast shift in public sentiments in order to bypass such safeguards for the powerless. And while admittedly, no system is foolproof if societal morality is sufficiently corrupted, the founding principles of our American Republic have overwhelmingly promoted respect for the rights and property of the individual for most of its existence.

Clearly, such national institutions as the United States Senate and the Electoral College were specifically designed to promote the virtues of a representative republic over the pitfalls of total democracy, which itself is barely elevated from the inevitable atrocities of mob rule. As such, our governing institutions are the antithesis of "one person, one vote." And for icing on the cake, consider the role of the Judiciary Branch of American Government. A tiny panel of judges wields influence on the people far exceeding that of any average individual. The Constitution is inarguably clear on this issue. Yet the principles in our national charter are totally and deliberately ignored by those who defer to the "one person, one vote" mantra.

The corrosive effects of "one person, one vote" have been to elevate the concept of rule by any angry mob, as long as it can even momentarily get large enough to dominate its opposition. Activist judges have even overturned state constitutions, on the basis that legislative chambers did not comply with this concept. Of course leftists are waiting in the wings to invoke "one person one vote" as the catalyst to give votes to illegal aliens, on the empty presumption that they "deserve representation." State sovereignty, and the real ability of Americans to chart their course within their chosen locale have been subordinated to a notion of "equality" that has no constitutional basis, and ultimately undermines their freedom, their independence, and in the long run, that very "equality" which leftists claim to endorse.

We need to end the rancor: Every so often, conservatives are roused to anger at the outrages being committed by the left, which are either passively accepted by the Republican party, or too often are actively enabled by it. At that point, a significant groundswell of resistance arises from the Heartland, which reverberates throughout the nation and is eventually felt inside the Beltway. The liberal agenda cannot withstand such opposition, because it directly undermines the notion that leftists represent the "mainstream" of society. Furthermore, it has the potential of energizing Republicans to pay attention to the sentiments of their constituents, and actually stand for the principles which their party claims to uphold. If that happens, the contrast between the guiding philosophies of the two parties becomes glaringly evident. Historically, that spells electoral disaster for the left.

So in order to prevent this scenario from reaching its end game, liberals concocted the mantra of "Ending the Rancor" as a creative means of totally deflecting from the actual issue at hand, and focusing instead on an irrelevancy that sounds "virtuous" to the perennially gullible as well as the moral cowards who are supposedly on the "right" side of the aisle. For those who were elected to uphold conservative principles, but are either fainthearted or totally duplicitous, this mantra provides an alluring escape route from the political pressure cooker they fear and revile.

Rather than spotlighting contentious issues as critical in nature and thus worth the fight, leftists can suddenly sound "reasonable" and ostensibly "concerned" with finding real and amicable solutions to the nation's problems, as opposed to those mean, nasty conservatives who refuse to get along. The strategy is tantamount to issuing a demand for conservatives to "move to the center" in order to find that mythical "common ground" with the left, which means leftists are back at the reins of power. Of course such posturing can easily be proven as transparent and empty, if one merely takes a moment to consider where the *real* bile, venom, and hateful slander originates in current political discourse. The countless examples of truly hateful, racist, and threatening behavior among leftists can easily be chronicled. Predictably, doing so is dismissed by the left as an escalation of the "hate" it ostensibly abhors, and is now seeking to diffuse. And on that shameless and flimsy basis, conservatives frequently back down, and leftists are able to neutralize the momentum of conservative opposition.

Democrats are the party of the little guy: As with so many topics mentioned here, an entire chapter, if not an entire book, could be written on this mantra. So, for the sake of simplicity and clarity three basic issues will be discussed in order to make the relevant point: family, income, and education. Though this is by no means comprehensive, it does make the case of who the Democrats really are, and how they flourish as a political party.

A host of social and political analyses unequivocally prove that intact families are the best means of achieving a good living standard in America. Along with that, a truly worthwhile education is enormously significant in determining a person's living standard. And of course, a diminished income puts an enormous burden on one's ability to achieve either.

So why is it that, in spite of their incessantly repeated mantra of being "The party of the little guy," Democrats in office obsessively do their utmost to undermine the American people in all three areas? Of course they vehemently deny this. Yet with even a cursory examination of their political track record, the causes they embrace, as well as those they oppose, this conclusion becomes inescapable.

Real families, in which a father and a mother are readily available to raise their children, to ensure that they conduct themselves in a civil manner, and to guide them into productive adulthood, are by far the best means of maintaining a thriving American culture, as has been the case with all cultures throughout human history. Yet it is patently obvious that leftists regard intact families as an obstacle to their agenda. From their efforts to redefine "family" in the most bizarre and convoluted terms, to their relentless expansion of the nanny state with its tacit promotion of "deadbeat dads," to their denigration of the time-honored concept of family as outdated and naive in media, in the "education" establishment, and among the liberal punditry, the goal is obviously to eradicate the traditional "nuclear" family. Why is it that something which is so beneficial to individuals would be derided so cruelly and callously? The answer to this is as alarming as it is simple. A shattered society is far more accepting of leftists, with their flowery but empty promises of fixing everything, once they are in total control.

In a similar sense, a valid education in which the pupil learns to read, write, and achieve functionality in mathematics could only be regarded as a worthwhile foundation on which to move forward in life with the likelihood of eventual success in the professional world. Yet here again, the leftist agenda throws every possible stumbling block in the way. Failing government schools, particularly in the inner cities, regularly crank out an assembly line of illiterate and inept "graduates" who are clueless as to even the most rudimentary premises of math, science and real history. But of course they're all totally "aware" of America's inherently racist culture, as well as being experts on "global warming" and a host of other leftist causes, none of which will actually help them function in the real world. Worst of all, this travesty occurs at enormous expense to the taxpaying public.

Any efforts to actually address the problem of failing schools are instantly rejected by the left, who then go on to tag them as being "anti-child." School vouchers are a perfect example of a truly workable solution that has shown great results wherever they are implemented, yet are vehemently detested by liberals, on the most transparent and flimsy grounds. Some claim that because voucher recipients might use them to enroll children in religious schools, this somehow threatens their venerated "separation of Church and state." Yet on those grounds, any food-stamp or welfare recipient who purchases a Bible or buys Kosher food is every bit the threat to the First Amendment (or a least to leftists' deliberate misinterpretation of it). Al Sharpton, who claims to be the supreme advocate of downtrodden minorities (and who should thus be a champion of vouchers), is instead a vehement opponent of them. On one occasion, he attempted to excuse his opposition to vouchers by asserting that since they aren't available to *all* urban students, it was wrong for *any* to benefit from them. On that basis, we must assume that he also opposed Harriet Tubman, who ran the Underground Railroad in the antebellum South. She couldn't free all of the slaves, so it was apparently wrong, according to Sharpton's twisted logic, that she was able to free any slave. Clearly, Sharpton's real goal was to invent any rejoinder, no matter how weak, in order to maintain support for the status quo of America's leftist dominated "educational" wasteland. In this, Sharpton proved himself to be entirely in lockstep with the left, at the expense of minority children.

Along with their relentless attacks on the family, and maniacal determination to keep underprivileged children in failing government schools, the most direct leftist attack on the citizenry is to undermine the pursuit of personal financial gain. From their obsessive efforts to continually raise taxes, to their equally malicious onslaught against the big and small businesses that fuel the economy and create prosperity, leftists do their utmost to prevent common citizens from achieving any manner of self-sufficiency. During the entire eight years that Obama occupied the White House, the economy choked and struggled. Wages stagnated and real employment plummeted. Yet nightly news broadcasts were unceasingly "rosy," with headlines regularly trumpeting over a dozen iterations of the latest "economic recovery." Of course their propagandizing never addressed the obvious question: If there was only one recession, why were so many "recoveries" needed? Furthermore, why were wages stagnant and the economy still struggling at the end of it all?

Despite this being an extremely condensed presentation of the Democrat "vision" for America, the underlying pattern should be inescapably evident. Democrats seek to supplant the Founders' hope of securing the rights of "life, liberty and the pursuit of happiness" with an empty promise of bare subsistence, if the public will forfeit its freedom, and lay aspirations of anything higher than that at the feet of the Democrat political machine. Still, Democrats shamelessly claim to be "the party of the little guy." Yet their moral bankruptcy over the years has put them in a place where their very existence is contingent upon a society that is chaotic and failing. Thus, they work tirelessly to guarantee that the "little guy" remains little, and thoroughly dependent on them.

> Democrats seek to supplant the Founders' hope of securing
> the rights of "life, liberty and the pursuit of happiness"
> by substituting empty promises of bare subsistence.

Liberals only want to keep abortion safe and legal: In all respects, this leftist mantra is a total lie. For starters, abortion is anything but "safe," especially for the helpless, innocent unborn child who will be brutally and mercilessly slaughtered in every case. And the toll paid by the mothers, both emotionally and physically, is also enormous. Nevertheless, leftists have successfully used their support of abortion to bolster a facade of "compassion" for women, despite mountains of evidence to the contrary.

Having demagogued the possibility of "back alley abortions" in their initial efforts to achieve legal status for the killing of unborn children, the leftist counterculture has since worked obsessively to paint a mantle of "virtue" on the abortion holocaust. The sheer ugliness of the reality of abortion nearly defies description. As a procedure that represents a total abomination to the Hippocratic Oath, no ethical member of the medical profession can be expected to support it. So those who do engage in the procedure are, by definition, the antithesis of the nurturing and caring that is presumed to be the role of doctors and nurses. And the evidence of this is as glaring as it is unspeakably ugly.

The virtual media blackout of the trial and conviction of "Dr." Kermit Gosnell, who ran a nightmarish abortion mill in Philadelphia, stands as a textbook example of the lies and deceit enshrouding the abortion issue. In 2013, Gosnell was finally convicted of murdering live-born children in his "clinic" by snipping their spinal cords with scissors. But that was only part of the horror. An FBI and Pennsylvania Department of Health investigation described Gosnell's facility this way: "There was blood on the floor. A stench of urine filled the air. A flea-infested cat was wandering through the facility, and there were cat feces on the stairs. Semi-conscious women scheduled for abortions were moaning in the waiting room or the recovery room, where they sat on dirty recliners covered with blood-stained blankets." Elsewhere, it was learned that the facility had not been inspected since 1993. Even the most overblown dramatization of a "back alley abortion" would pale in comparison to the real filth and squalor of Gosnell's facility, a circumstance that was apparently just fine with the pro-aborts.

Were the leftist counterculture serious about the plight of women, and even if it still resorted to such a flimsy excuse to sanction the killing of unborn babies, it would seem reasonable that the Gosnell situation and others like it would concern them. However, being driven solely by the advancement of the leftist/feminist agenda, it was deemed more important to the leftist political apparatus to simply suppress the Gosnell nightmare as thoroughly as possible, since the only real concern was avoiding adverse publicity.

In the leftist and counterculture worldview, the "sacred" nature of abortion is worth any risk and any lie, in order to maintain its facade of legitimacy.

Furthermore, given the location of Gosnell's "clinic," it is certain that the vast majority of his "patients" were inner city minorities. Once again, any genuine interest in the plight of hapless, victimized young black women would warrant serious reconsideration of how the abortion industry operates. Yet this is clearly not the case. Instead, the left obsessively guards every aspect of the abortion industry from even cursory scrutiny. In the leftist and counterculture worldview, the "sacred" nature of abortion is worth any risk and any lie, in order to maintain its facade of legitimacy.

It must be understood that while the Gosnell horror story is among the most well known, the standard practices of an industry that makes merchandise of innocent humanity *cannot* be both unfathomably exploitative while "virtuous" or "compassionate." Elsewhere across the nation, any effort to bring a reasonable degree of accountability to the abortion business, or to properly inform victims as to the liabilities and dangers the procedures pose, are stridently opposed by leftists. The pattern of abuse is not confined to Gosnell. Otherwise, abortion proponents would not be nearly so virulent in their determination to avoid any serious oversight.

Abortion is a bedroom issue: This effort to sanitize the real motives of those who promote abortion is based in the premise that the issue is not about the life of an innocent unborn child, but rather is a matter of the mother's "privacy." By deflecting from the realities of abortion in this manner, the grimness of it can be side-stepped, and focus shifted instead to something much more benign, such as the constitutionally protected sanctity of one's home.

Of course this is a ruse in many respects. For starters, while the prohibition against "unreasonable search and seizure" is a constitutionally enshrined right, this does not suggest that any and every illicit action is immune to the law, as long as it occurs within the boundaries of one's personal property. Surely, child molesting or any other violent crime would not be deemed "off limits" to law enforcement if it occurs within the walls of a private residence. Secondly, it is a well-established fact that abortionists *do not* make "house calls."

The procedure is conducted in publicly accessible locales, though (per the previous topic) such places frequently operate in filth and squalor that couldn't meet the minimum standards of a food inspector evaluating a butcher shop.

Every aspect of the abortion issue is likewise cloaked in deceit and deflection. For example, leftist "news" accounts on those who oppose abortion *never* use the term "pro-life," but instead strictly characterize that viewpoint as "anti-abortion." The term "pro-abortion" is likewise never applied to those promoting the slaughter of unborn children, who are instead diligently identified as "pro-choice." In recent times pro-aborts and their publicity minions have engaged in even more ludicrous verbal gymnastics, euphemistically claiming to be noble supporters of "reproductive rights," which is a total deflection as well as an almost laughable absurdity. People have the right to reproduce *any way they want to*, and nobody ever tries to stop them. Pro-lifers only object to killing the child that results from that reproduction.

In closing this segment, it must be reiterated that neither of these compilations, either from this chapter or the previous one, are meant to be comprehensive. Hopefully, an awareness of the pattern of deceit they represent has been established in the reader so as to be able to proficiently recognize the manipulative and duplicitous nature of leftists as they attempt to expand their reach. When confined to facts, persuasion of the supposed "worthiness" of the leftist agenda becomes a virtual impossibility for all but the most dogmatically committed minions. So the task facing them is how to make their case while deftly sidestepping the facts. It should be understood that this effort thoroughly permeates every venue in which they can establish an inroad, and is not just confined to the political realm, the nightly news, or the classroom. In the current climate they have successfully influenced a broad portion of the exchange of information, including manufacturers and their advertising.

Some corporations, such as the cadre of Silicon Valley giants, already have a thoroughly deserved reputation for leftist propaganda and distortion in their products, while others who may not genuinely share their ideology are still coerced into playing along with it, out of fear of the repercussions. In the long run, the effect has been an ongoing corrosion of reasoned thought, that has been replaced with such canned talking points that will prevail and be ever further solidified as truth, *unless* they are diligently identified, assessed, and refuted wherever the situation warrants. And that is the job of those who recognize the liberating power of truth, and endeavor to see it prevail.

CHAPTER SIX
THE STRATEGIC IMPORTANCE OF
DESTROYING OUR MORAL CERTITUDE

After gaining an understanding of who leftists are, the blinding arrogance that motivates them, and the total duplicity by which they advance their agenda, it becomes inescapably obvious that their concept of "morality" is irredeemably and *deliberately* skewed, and therefore thoroughly incompatible with the values of traditional America. It is imperative to gain a clear recognition of how leftists tirelessly work to undermine and eradicate fundamental premises of real morality and truth, for the purpose of completely and irrevocably supplanting those principles with their own twisted ideology. From that point forward, it is presented as undeniable fact. Consequently, any attempts at finding "common ground" with leftists on any matter of morality are, at best, an exercise in futility. At worst, such efforts give them a "toehold" of unwarranted credibility and momentum, which translates into ideological leverage.

The Alinsky strategy can only succeed against those who allow it. As a cornerstone of this effort, it is *absolutely crucial* for leftists to perch on their contrived "moral high ground" that they claim, first by flatly declaring real moral principles and societal norms as "invalid," and then by aggressively promoting their own perverse "moral code" as a substitute. Once they've sufficiently accomplished this, they issue defining proclamations of "right and wrong" on every facet of life, thwarting all opposition by sanctimoniously dictating what is and isn't "permissible" behavior or debate, according to their edicts.

It is crucial to understand that, regardless of any cause they claim to champion, when leftists attack conservatives on ideological grounds, their *singular goal* is to seize this "moral high ground" by any means, and on any premise, no matter how twisted or absurd it might be. And always, this is done with the sole consideration being their political agenda. The brazen hypocrisy of their attacks is key to establishing the double standards by which they continually issue edicts to hamstring our side, while granting themselves unfettered "license" to selectively proclaim the guilt and innocence of each side on a situational basis as they see fit. However, the essential element of their ability to prevail is that our side tacitly allows such double standards to stand, which suggests they are "legitimate." Predictably, such acceptance is thereafter played as an irrefutable seal of credibility and "approval." Any leftist double-standard that goes unchallenged, no matter how baseless or ridiculous, will eventually be heralded as inarguable "truth." Thus the compliant and conciliatory nature of too many on our side proves to be a great asset to the left, which is frequently wielded as a weapon against us with dangerous effectiveness, as leftists demand that we "moderate" our stance in an effort to work with them.

On a host of topics, leftists now brazenly proclaim their twisted and morally bankrupt belief system as self-evident truth, daring anyone to be so inexcusably "hateful" or "ignorant" as to dispute a single letter of it. Among the intellectually honest, the self-righteousness of such proclamations would be embarrassing, and sufficient reason in itself to question their logic and motives. Yet for leftists, the extreme nature of their sheer arrogance actually constitutes the ultimate evidence of their irrefutable "virtue." It is appalling to consider how many issues are deemed "settled," and thereafter immune to any reconsideration, simply because leftists so adamantly declare them as such.

Evidence of this can be seen on a daily basis in leftist "news" reports. In the wake of any calamity which leftists believe they can exploit, they instantly get to the front of the line, declaring with absolute certainty who has unassailable "standing and expertise" to define the issue at hand.

And without fail, this always lines up with leftist ideology. In order to shield their edicts from serious consideration, they will loudly and venomously decry even the slightest expression of doubt as to their validity on the predictable grounds that doing so constitutes "hate," "ignorance," or "insensitivity."

Out among the general populace, those "Coexist" bumper stickers and t-shirts are great examples of this trait. In the leftist mindset, merely claiming to have no animus against any fellow human being, regardless of any conflicting viewpoints or religious dogma (Obama's Brandenburg Gate "citizen of the world" drivel comes immediately to mind), renders the bearer a superior member of the human race who holds the key to societal bliss and human happiness. And this they exuberantly assert, despite the reality that untold numbers of Americans have sacrificed and died in major wars, in order to protect the freedom of self-absorbed leftists to spew such baseless platitudes. But facts and history are irrelevant to them. They just "know" that their views on life and the human condition are inherently superior, so they loudly and shamelessly proclaim as much. Therefore no countervailing opinion can be allowed to stand. Yet the moment anyone attempts to disrupt leftist utopianism by introducing an element of reality into it, their "coexist" sanctimony vanishes, and they attack with a vindictiveness that stands in stark contrast to the "love and peace" they claimed, revealing the real ugliness of their inner souls.

Still, the most dangerous consequence of this scenario by far is that, in the face of blind and raging leftist self-assurance, conservatives so often lose their moral certitude and become hesitant to contradict the inane assertions of the left. This has been among the greatest failures on the part of conservatives, which sadly explains so many of the unwarranted successes and advances in the leftist onslaught against America and Western Civilization.

A classic episode involving this insidious tendency was the May 1, 2003 carrier landing by then President George W. Bush on the USS Abraham Lincoln, which had just returned from combat operations in the Persian Gulf. With the United States in the midst of its post 9-11 "War on Terror," the event was clearly an effort to boost the morale of American troops, while sending a message of courage and resolve to the enemy. America and its president were ready and able to fight this war, and to triumph. American Democrats and leftists, with their typical fixation on their self-serving political agenda above all else, regarded President Bush's action as a potential political benefit to him. With the 2004 presidential election looming, they put Democrat Party interests above those of the nation, and did their best to demean the event.

Their primary criticism was concocted on the basis that as President Bush gave his speech on the deck of the carrier, a banner behind him declared "Mission Accomplished." Leftists asserted that this was false, because the "War on Terror" was still being waged and, aside from the USS Abraham Lincoln, American troops were still in the field. Worst of all however, was that instead of those on the right stridently confronting the leftists over their blatant effort to undermine American morale, while giving direct "aid and comfort" to America's enemies (See: The definition of treason in the U.S. Constitution), major "conservative" voices allowed themselves to be dragged into a rambling debate on the real definition of "Mission Accomplished," and whether or not President Bush was "guilty" of uttering the phrase or implying its validity. What could have been a rousing patriotic moment to rally the nation and strike fear into the hearts of our enemies, instead degenerated into just more "back and forth" between left and right. Meanwhile, the corrosive effect of such criticism on America and the morale of its military forces was easily sidestepped by those leftists who should have been called to account for their seditious behavior.

In contrast to all of the leftist "second guessing" of President Bush and his visit to the USS Abraham Lincoln, their reaction is entirely different, and vastly beneath any standard of intellectual honesty, when it is any of their icons who might be called into question. Leftists were unrestrained in their "righteous" indignation, as they viciously attacked any who dared criticize those students at Marjory Stoneman Douglas High School, in Parkland Florida, who jumped in front of the cameras, and onto the anti-Second Amendment bandwagon in the wake of the February 14, 2018 mass shooting at their school. Yet here, as well as in the case of the USS Abraham Lincoln, leftists prevailed because our side went totally on the defensive, essentially accepting leftist certitude in its characterization of each situation.

Consider a few other glaring examples of psychologically unbalanced leftist "moralizing," and more specifically, how these absurdities are specifically tailored to give the leftist counterculture a political upper hand, which they exploit with their crafted exhibitions of total moral and ethical certitude. An enshrined axiom in the alternative universe of the leftist counterculture is that because in certain cases, an inarguable concrete boundary between right and wrong cannot be defined, it is thereafter presumed and declared that *no* boundary exists. Nevertheless, many legal situations are concretely determined without an exact defining point where a breach of that legality occurs. One may not know at exactly what speed an icy road becomes unsafe. Yet if a driver on an icy road goes into a skid and has an accident, the fault will be deemed as "excessive speed" for existing road conditions.

Despite such realities, the ruse continues to work for the left. For example, in their world, if one can't define exactly where "art" becomes obscene, then no image or object, regardless of how vile and demeaning it might be, can be prohibited from public display despite being obviously obscene. It must be allowed as an expression of "art." Or so we are told. The political "sleight of hand" here is that nowhere in any legal document was the notion established that the banner of "art" gives blanket license to brazen obscenity. Yet in landmark cases of lewd public displays, the First Amendment has been tortured and contorted into a form that "legalizes" anything which can be deemed "art," allowing perpetrators to walk free solely because their obscenities had been classified as such.

Similarly, the evil of abortion has been legally expanded to the point that fully developed children are being butchered, moments away from live delivery, simply because leftists have contended that no exact event can be defined to their liking as the moment when an unborn child transforms from being a mass of cells into a human life. Of course, the defining moment that begins human existence is conception. And this is not religious ideology, but *biological fact.* Yet even if that scientific proof is ignored, it is obvious beyond any possible argument that long before a baby reaches nine months of gestation, he/she is a fully alive and kicking *human being.*

Nevertheless, on their totally contrived "moral" grounds, leftists have studiously maintained a cold-blooded indifference towards the plight of the unborn, since any recognition of the humanity of an unborn child interferes with their anti-Christian, anti-family agenda. Proving themselves to be an ugly mockery of their professed "compassion," they callously ignore the hideous pain suffered by unborn children that are dismembered and slaughtered in the womb by abortionists. Meanwhile, with equal authority, leftists laud themselves as great humanitarians, sanctimoniously lecturing us on the notion that pain can ostensibly be felt by *lobsters* headed for the steamer, whose plight they champion. In both cases, the *only* basis on which their inane, inverted, and morally bankrupt positions are advanced is the vehemence with which they are asserted, and the inevitable rage visited upon any who dare to disagree with them.

Again, with equal authority, the moment a child survives gestation and is born, leftists suddenly become his or her most devoted "advocates," and the loudest chorus of what must be done or prohibited, in order to "properly" raise that child. This they accomplish in their consistently warped and perverse manner, which invariably makes a total mess of things. The same people who were indifferent to an unborn child being violently ripped apart in the womb suddenly decry any sort of discipline, including mere scolding or exhortations to succeed, as unbearable abuse. Punishing children for bad behavior, or encouraging them to strive for excellence, whether academically or in athletics, is tantamount to brutality and therefore deemed "unacceptable." Actually, in both cases, the goal of the leftist counterculture is served, first by completely abominating the natural instincts of motherhood in the case of abortion. Then, if a child survives beyond that, by imposing a thoroughly warped and ineffective version of "parenthood" that ensures the child will grow up to be socially dysfunctional and totally irresponsible, thereby "needing" the trappings of liberal government, not to thrive, but just to survive. And this, of course, further empowers the left.

Countless other examples exist. Since leftists are so defined and consumed by their sanctimony, they never hesitate to delve into any area of life with their supposedly superior perspective. The goal is always the same; to portray themselves on that "moral high ground," not just among their own, but in the eyes of gullible conservatives who may occasionally stumble in a moment of self-doubt. If leftists can accomplish this maneuver through any means, the tendency of conservatives to become introspective and conciliatory gives leftists a *decisive* advantage. Nor does it matter that leftist premises for claiming the high ground are totally bogus and would be easily debunked if they had been confronted with diligence and resolve. The only consideration is whether or not the left can convince the general populace, and maybe some conservatives, to accept, or at least acquiesce, to their sanctimony.

At that point, control of the discourse has effectively been yielded to them, which almost invariably means that they win.

Consider the unspeakable evil and horror of Planned Parenthood dissecting live unborn children and selling the body parts on a nightmarish "black market" (a practice which continues to this day). Yet leftists never backed away from their endorsement of such atrocities, or those committing them. Instead, when this vile practice was exposed, the left merely deflected attention onto the fact that those who had obtained evidence of the abhorrent practice did so while presenting false identification to the monsters at Planned Parenthood. Callously ignoring the hideous abuses, exploitation, and ghoulish murders of the unborn, leftist public officials and their media parakeets squalled that the real transgression against nature and humanity was the presentation of false identification to obtain the needed proof of what was transpiring inside the doors of Planned Parenthood "clinics." And this was the *only* "crime" that leftist public officials and their lackeys in law enforcement saw fit to aggressively pursue.

Of course, First Amendment protections of free speech (even freedom to speak the truth) don't apply here, or in any circumstance where a stronghold of the leftist counterculture might be called into question. Leftists contend that the various "causes" they claim to serve are so critically important to the fate of humanity, they are above any accountability. Without exception, their duplicity and hypocrisy must always be given a pass, regardless of the particular topic at hand. For example, their advocacy of "environmental issues," and specifically "climate change," are deemed to be life and death matters for humanity. This gives them unchallenged authority to selectively declare individuals, lifestyles, and societal norms as threats to the human race, and to foment any manner of retribution, including violence, against those they deem "guilty" of crimes against mother earth.

The hypocrisy they exhibit as they *selectively* "moralize" is beyond any standard of absurdity, and would be truly comical, were its consequences not so dire. Leftists assert that brutally killing a child in the womb is OK, but that discussing it with blunt honesty is "abusive" and even constitutes "terrorism." Leftists assert that a man can become a woman with some plastic surgery and unnatural hormone treatments, and that a deranged man can go into a public restroom with your daughter just because he "feels" he belongs there. Meanwhile, refusing to allow such an affront and threat to an innocent child is decried as "hate." Furthermore, according to leftists, it is thoroughly "moral" to demand, under penalty of law, that society assents to the notion, and that it is a crime against nature to dispute or even question such claims.

The result of our acceptance of leftist hypocrisy is that eventually we have, *in our own eyes*, no standing to oppose any moral or ethical outrage perpetrated by the left.

In every case where leftist hypocrisy prevails, it is we on the right who bear the final guilt for tacitly allowing it to stand, by our refusal to stridently call it out and cease any further discourse with leftists until their flawed premises and duplicity are properly addressed and corrected. Consequently, bizarre moral edicts are essentially "validated" and immediately turned back on us to destroy *our moral certitude* on the sole basis that leftists claim their beliefs *and behavior* are "above reproach." In contrast, according to their selective "moralizing," it is we on the right who are deemed unfit to identify anything as being wrong or right, because we are unable live up to our own standards with the absolute fidelity, which *they* insist is a non-negotiable prerequisite to our side having *any* credibility. The result is that eventually we have, *in our own eyes*, no standing to oppose *any* moral or ethical outrage perpetrated by the left. So leftist hypocrisy and our willingness to overlook it makes them virtually immune to any similar backlash from us. On the other hand, our lack of total perfection ostensibly grants them "license" to say or do *anything*, on any occasion, and no matter how heinous, while still deeming themselves perfectly "justified."

Whether it is opposition to Christianity, accommodating Islamists and Sharia, or the criminal brutality and lawlessness of "Antifa" and "Black Lives Matter," leftists assert their "moral authority" with unbridled sanctimony under the comically absurd banners of "compassion" and "sensitivity." The same can be said of the embarrassing glorified cowardice and sniveling of the "snowflake" movement of whiny leftist youths on college campuses with their backdoor approach to bullying. In every case, the leftist goal is to stay in control, by structuring their "moral high ground" in any absurd, convoluted manner by which they can make a claim of dominance. In truth, those who have been confronted either by "snowflakes" or the Antifa/Black Lives Matter crowd find the same virulence, the same bullying, the same intimidation, and in many cases the same faces. The players just wear different masks at different times for public relations purposes, as situations warrant. Nevertheless, on every occasion, leftists will assert the inherent "worthiness" of such groups with an absolute certitude that literally dares anyone to challenge its legitimacy. Unfortunately, on that basis alone, their faux "credibility" frequently prevails.

Even in those rare instances where leftists appear to be espousing valid moral principles, it is a certainty that their underlying motives are thoroughly disingenuous, and that their end game is something other than any seemingly "noble cause" which they claim to endorse at the moment. A couple of glaring examples of this are their pious denunciations of racism and the exploitation of women. These particular issues epitomize the manner in which leftists shamelessly spew undiluted sanctimony one moment in supposed deference to women and minorities, while knowingly enabling actual abuses against those same demographics in the very next breath, the moment doing so helps to advance the leftist agenda.

As explained in the chapters dealing with leftist hypocrisy, they have absolutely no pangs of conscience engaging in the vilest of sexual or racial denigration when politically expedient. Leftists unhesitatingly invoke the most despicable racial and gender slurs against their opponents, the moment any opportunity presents itself, and particularly if their targets happen to be *conservative* women and/or minorities. Here again, failing to fully grasp the extent of leftist moral duplicity puts them at a distinct advantage; one which they have skillfully exploited over the years.

In stark contrast to the left, our side seeks to arrive at truth and promote our ideology in a manner we deem to be "right," as determined by its alignment with the morals and principles we strive to uphold. The moment we believe we may be acting contrary to those ideals, we reevaluate our stances and if necessary, modify them, all of which is the essence of moral and ethical consistency. Being sure we are on the "right track" and absolutely morally consistent is the primary strength of conservative momentum. For our moral certitude to be worth anything, it must be thoroughly genuine, which means it must be maintained on true and legitimate principles. But it is beyond foolhardy to accept leftist definitions of those principles or to ever expect leftists to operate in any similar manner with the only difference being the particular precepts they seek to advance. Instead, it must be understood that their goal is simply to gain uncontested dominance of every situation by any possible means, in order to amass and wield greater social and political power and control. And that is precisely why our moral certitude is a primary target of leftist countercultural attacks that, despite being cloaked in glowing sanctimony, are *never* intended to improve real morality and decency, but are specifically designed to undermine them.

It is entirely relevant to take note of how exuberant and energized leftists become, the moment they think they have any excuse to exert moral "superiority," which is itself just more proof of how essential that presumption of the "moral high ground" is to their agenda. In truth, they can't claim such a position based on any provable track record of actually addressing problems or instituting any substantive "fix." Rather, they deem themselves "better" than the rest of us merely because they are able to prolifically spew empty claims of caring and compassion on a far more expansive, shameless, and self-aggrandizing basis than we do. And this behavior highlights one of the biggest advantages of their strategy, which is that it is a "one way street." Leftists feel no similar compunction to ever concede their stance on any issue, merely because their contentions are proven to be totally baseless and disingenuous. When leftists are confronted with facts which reveal them to be hypocritical and intellectually dishonest, their response is *never* to admit as much or reevaluate their ideological paradigm, but rather to deflect in one manner or another, so as to be able to continue undeterred on their chosen path.

Such counterfeit "moralizing" takes on some truly bizarre forms. Yet all that really matters to them is that their scams work. On college campuses in recent years, it has become increasingly common for leftists to "weaponize" cowardice and degrading self-absorption; traits that used to be cause for embarrassment and shame, but are now upheld among their ranks as virtues. Leftist minions have actually been conditioned to believe that if they can concoct any excuse to claim "offense," or that they are supposedly "afraid" of opposition from those on our side, they are fully justified to throw tantrums, which in their minds actually constitutes being on that vaunted "moral high ground." From this point forward, they deem themselves immune to any reasoned response. Caterwauling students claim to be unable to cope with conservative opposition out of "fear" and what they hysterically decry as "unfairness," even over the most benign effort to present any view that differs from leftist orthodoxy.

It requires a truly perverse alternative reality to make these "snowflakes" believe that their disgraceful and pitiable sniveling and whining are actually the traits of heroic and righteous "warriors." However, that is the nature of the current situation. Leftist activists have accomplished this neat trick because they and their dutiful minions are thoroughly morally and ethically bankrupt, and have been completely stripped of self-respect on any basis other than their compliance with the perverse dogma of the left. Unfortunately, the allure of "victimhood" has a strong influence on the weak minded, who have lost any sense of human dignity. Instead of being dismissed as cowards or derided for the childishness of their antics, they are enshrined, and their puerile demands for "safe spaces" deemed to be among the most basic human "rights" needing to be indulged and protected, which in actuality means the systematic and often brutal suppression of opposing points of view.

> Unfortunately, the allure of "victimhood"
> has a strong influence on the weak minded,
> who have lost any sense of human dignity.

This is simply who they are and, as leftists, who they will always be. Expecting any fundamental change in their guiding philosophy is dangerously naive. That is why it is futile and counterproductive to "pull punches" in any misguided effort to avoid "offending" them, in vain hopes of maintaining imaginary "lines of communication" with them. As with any psychosis, pandering to them will only solidify the belief in the "validity" of their delusions. Regardless of how transparent, despicable, and spiritually suicidal their mindset might be, its greatest potential for harm to the nation lies in the fact that it is ever allowed to affect how *our side* reacts to them. Too often, conservatives respond by stepping lightly around glaring issues of the social and political landscape with undue delicacy, for fear of inciting their phony hysterics. Our unwillingness to bluntly and unhesitatingly characterize both their agenda and their behavior as reprehensible and childish frequently weakens our proper response to it and in so doing, actually serves to strengthen their abominable "worldview."

As always, intellectual honesty, and the courage to unabashedly express it, are essential to effectively contending with the leftist onslaught. It is inarguable that leftists are obsessed with the destruction of traditional America, and they intend to accomplish this goal by disparaging, marginalizing, and eventually eradicating the Judeo-Christian principles on which the nation was founded. In their relentless efforts, leftists have developed a pernicious yet finite "bag of tricks." Some, but not all, are taken directly from Alinsky's *"Rules."* And it must be conceded that even with such a limited and predictable "repertoire," leftists have enjoyed tremendous successes as they work tirelessly to dismantle America's moral and ethical moorings. Some attacks are blatantly obvious, while others are more insidious and subtle, which makes them much harder to directly confront.

For example, as they seek to force our side to accommodate their ongoing attacks on American culture and morality, leftists have successfully promoted their agenda under the auspices of "tolerance," which on occasion they assert as the ultimate human virtue. To buttress their case for tolerance, they invariably point to the Nazi Holocaust as an example of "intolerance." On this basis, they relentlessly infiltrate and poison the culture and the dialogue on issues that bear no relation whatsoever to the horrors of the Reich. Eventually, under the guise of "tolerance," the most perverse leftist "mores" effectively supplant reality and stifle the ability to honestly discuss a host of social topics, whereby leftist dogma eventually become accepted societal "standards" by default.

Yet even the notion that the Holocaust resulted from "intolerance" of the Jewish race is a total absurdity. Sadly, the world has been virulently intolerant of Jewish people throughout most of history, going back to the time of Isaac and Ishmael. But the nightmare of the Holocaust was only able to ensue once the German culture reached a point of being *tolerant* of the Reich and the depravity it embodied. "Tolerance" as the left defines it, is *not* a "virtue." It is the enabling passivity that turns a blind eye while evil metastasizes.

Under a constant onslaught of such skewed premises, leftist attacks on the defining institutions and standards of Western Civilization have progressed with amazing ease, owing to society's misconception of the real agenda of leftists preaching "tolerance," and the general aversion of most people to being labeled and condemned as "intolerant." So a thorough understanding of where and how these attacks are conducted, and the threat they truly represent, will provide the best means of recognizing them with as much advanced warning as possible, and thereby not falling so easily into their snares.

From its founding, America was lauded both by its citizens and foreigners as a "beacon" to the world, not of perfection, but of the hope of a people who would continue to aspire to perfection. To the degree that America deserved such accolades, credit can be given to the founding principles of our nation, its Declaration of Independence, and its Constitution, all of which were overwhelmingly Biblical in their origins. But this point is crucial: America itself was *never* deemed to be "perfect." Nor did any of its Founding Fathers or their proponents throughout history ever claim its validity on that basis.

The American experiment was indeed a vast improvement over other cultures, which typically exhibited a predisposition towards tyranny and brutal oppression of individual rights. As such, America offered the hope of liberty and justice for the common man, with the promise of improving its deficiencies and correcting its flaws. Even the blight of slavery, which had been an entrenched part of the nation and its culture since long before its founding, was subject to reassessment. And it is altogether significant that the task of abolishing slavery began in earnest in the immediate aftermath of the Revolution and ratification of the Constitution.

Yet the left has long played the game of using its own supposed standard of "perfection" as reason to proclaim the unworthiness of America. Since that standard can never be achieved, leftists with their selective "moralizing" incessantly remind us *only* of our nation's flaws, both past and present. But here's where their real scam commences. Based on the fact that America never met that standard of perfection, leftists deem themselves justified thereafter to engage in *any* form of malice and sedition, with no limits on them, as our side is ostensibly stripped of all moral standing to oppose the onslaught. Because those who uphold the values of traditional America aren't absolutely unassailable in every respect and at all times, leftists suddenly have license to engage in the most vile and anti-social behavior, from lies to intimidation to violence, in order to supplant our flawed America with their empty promises of leftist "utopia." And in their twisted worldview, nobody has any right to criticize them. Once again, as with every other Alinsky tactic, this transparent scam only works when our side tacitly accepts its bogus premises and thus allows it to ensue. Sadly, leftists have achieved enormous gains on that dubious and flimsy basis.

This pattern of weighing the utopian but empty promises of the left against the real world, and thereafter claiming unassailable superiority, is textbook leftist "moralizing." Because inadequacies and flaws can always be identified in actual daily life, the reality of the day can always be deemed "inferior" to that mythical leftist "utopia" that only exists in the platitudes they spew. If accurately appraised on its face value, this is a worthless argument. Yet leftists have become very adept at the technique, and with it have all too often successfully bluffed their way onto that all-important "moral high ground."

Consider how the entire Obamacare ruse was implemented, and more significantly, how leftist "moralizing" with yet another empty promise, in this case supposedly "free" healthcare for everyone, has made Republicans truly intimidated at the prospect of repeal. In a huge exercise of intellectual dishonesty, Democrats bogusly equated the notion of Obamacare "coverage" (on paper) to actual quality care. Since the Obamacare nightmare is "available" to virtually anyone foolish enough to want it, Democrats can thereafter claim to offer such "care" to everybody. Once this lying premise is established, any effort to extricate American medical care from the leftist bureaucratic morass of Obamacare amounts to "taking coverage away" from people. Hence, Americans are diverted from the nightmarish realities of Obamacare, including canceled policies, exorbitant premiums, astronomical deductibles, and minimal care for health issues that really matter. Instead they are warned in hysterical terms of everything they don't actually have, but will ostensibly "lose," if those mean-spirited Republicans are ever able to steal their "coverage."

Of course, leftists can be counted on to engage in such shameless moral posturing at election time more than at any other. One of the best political examples of how leftists gained an unwarranted advantage and eventually triumphed at the ballot box, based on an unfounded claim to the "moral high ground," was the 2012 Missouri Senate race in which Republican Congressman Todd Akin challenged incumbent Democrat Claire McCaskill. Akin was running significantly ahead of McCaskill in the polls until he made a single thoughtless, offhanded comment about the possibility of a woman becoming pregnant during a rape. Akin's unpardonable sin, for which he stands condemned to this day, was that he chose the word "legitimate," rather than something more fitting, such as "actual," to distinguish between real episodes of rape as opposed to phony accusations of such. However, the word combination was quickly seized upon by opportunistic leftists, who then contended that Akin used the phrase "legitimate rape," to assert that in certain situations, rape was somehow "legitimate" and apparently justified.

In accordance with Alinsky's rules, the leftist onslaught was immediate, fierce, and orchestrated, with every liberal news anchor and pandering politician weighing in on Akin's supposed callous disregard for women in horrific circumstances. Not surprisingly, Barack Obama was quick to join the grandstanding, piously admonishing that "No rape is legitimate." Worst of all, Republicans seeking to avoid Akin's fate quickly distanced themselves from him by accepting the sanctimony of attacking leftists as sincere, and joining in the blanket condemnation of him. Many of them went a step further, calling for him to drop out of the race. As a result, Akin's lead vanished and he was handily defeated by McCaskill in November of that year.

Throughout this episode some of the most thoroughly vile and *deliberately hateful* statements from the left were essentially deemed acceptable, owing to "bipartisan" agreement that Akin had committed an egregious crime against humanity. Hard-core leftist commentator Reza Aslan, who hosted a show on CNN (Though CNN insisted that his capacity there somehow did *not* make him an employee), posted on Twitter "Just to be clear, I was indeed wishing someone would rape Congressman Akin. I'd hate to be misunderstood." Given all of the leftist sanctimony about "ending the rancor" and "restoring civility" to the political discourse, one might expect that Aslan's screed would be deemed horribly inappropriate, regardless of the circumstances which he claimed had spawned it. Yet as a result of depraved leftist "moral certitude," and more importantly, the total lack of any push-back from conservatives (owing to the absence of any steadfast sense of real morality among them), Aslan's ugly comment was met with tacit approval.

In textbook Alinsky fashion, Akin had been targeted, frozen, and isolated by the raging leftist attack machine. Worst of all, as a result of the morally rudderless Republican "Establishment" and even some conservatives who were willing to aid and abet the effort, essentially becoming a "cheerleading section" for the vastly overblown Democrat indignation, the onslaught gained a wholly undeserved mantle of "validity." Once again, with a thoroughly manufactured outcry, the left had seized a significant portion of the "moral high ground" as self-proclaimed advocates of the nation's women.

> In every case, leftists attack and undermine our moral certitude, with the intent to convince us we have no inherent right to criticize *any* of their aberrant behaviors or policies.

Of course reality paints a completely different picture. As previously discussed, the appalling and callous disregard for truly victimized women resides entirely among those on the left. In a despicable train of events that both preceded and followed the Akin ruckus, real and verifiable assaults on women, committed by Democrat assailants, have been universally met with mockery, derision, and dismissive comments against the *women*, from the same leftists who were shameless in their grandstanding as they sought to thoroughly destroy Akin for the mere misuse of a word.

In every case, leftists attack and undermine our moral certitude, with the intent to convince us we have no inherent right to criticize *any* of their aberrant behaviors or policies, while they alone are in the position of moral and ethical clarity to pass judgment on us. Consider, in contrast to Todd Akin's single episode of what was at worst, momentary carelessness, this vile but clearly premeditated and intentional statement of Barack Obama, which would have ended the career of any Republican uttering a similar thing. Speaking at a 2008 Philadelphia political fundraiser, Obama exhorted leftists to respond to conservatives with "If they bring a knife to the fight, we bring a gun!" Obama's reprehensible declaration was never deemed as the endorsement of violence that it clearly was. Nor was this appalling statement anything out of the ordinary for Obama, who has a long track record of such belligerent and incendiary rhetoric. And given the marked uptick of leftist violence that beset America throughout Obama's time in office (and some of which continues to this day), the effects of his incitement are undeniable.

Yet simply because the left was so flagrantly dismissive of all of it (which was another thoroughly coordinated effort), conservatives have been hesitant, and even "delicate" in their criticism of Obama's ugly rhetoric. In this manner, a horrendous double standard exists, not only in the minds of leftists, but worst of all, among far too many on the right who, by their silence, essentially accept such venom and hypocrisy, once again giving it unwarranted credence and power. Obama was easily able to walk away from indefensible and deliberately inflammatory statements, and the Democrats were never seriously held to account for the venom of their leader which they refused to denounce, thus proving their agreement with it. Meanwhile, on more than one occasion, the GOP has allowed itself to be significantly defined and condemned by a *single* misspoken word from a minor player.

If leftists are allowed to continue their onslaught under such absurd and skewed premises, they will always be able to concoct grounds to target and "neutralize" conservatives, while declaring even the most buffoonish and detestable leftist players to be great statesmen and humanitarians who are exempt from criticism. Yet the choice to concede to such absurdity does *not* ultimately lie with them. Rather, it is a direct consequence of whether or not *our side* deems it worthwhile to face the phony backlash and confront their fraud and duplicity. Sadly, too many on the right assume a role similar to "battered wives," and have essentially been conditioned to accept baseless assertions of "moral high ground" from the left. And as long as this despicable status quo goes uncontested, leftists will continue to press their advantage and expand their reach. Their goal in all of this is to thoroughly *morally* redefine America.

In a December 2017 speech, President Donald Trump stated "A nation that is not certain of its values cannot summon the will to defend them." With those few words, he explained why leftists are so obsessive in their efforts to sabotage America's moral certitude on every defining issue of our culture. Like clockwork, the time-honored parables and proverbs of American history are targeted and undermined, to be torn down like great historical statues that have been deemed repugnant. The intent is to prove that since nothing about this nation was ever as noble as it may have previously been portrayed, every worthy aspect of it must be abandoned in order to make way for the new, ostensibly pure and virtuous leftist order.

Yet those who wish to preserve and protect America from the leftist/Alinsky onslaught need not continue as sitting ducks. Instead, they must be able to recognize the true nature and motivation of every attack on a conservative, every incursion on traditional morality and every effort at destroying our culture. The leftist goal is never to actually hone or improve America's moral guideposts, but rather to undermine and eventually supplant them with the perverse and arbitrary precepts of leftist ideology. So, despite any seemingly well packaged arguments, no accommodation can be given to the wholly perverse leftist ideology under any circumstances. And for this to be the case, the various baseless leftist attacks on the moral certitude of the right, and indeed America itself, must be identified and recognized in their true light.

Hence, the "elephant in the room," which leftists studiously camouflage, is that every aspect of their agenda and its Marxist and Alinskyite roots is consistently abhorrent and the consequences inevitably tragic. By any standard, the worst failings of America and Western Civilization pale in comparison to the horrors and calamity of leftist governing, wherever and whenever leftists gain uncontested dominance. Leftist attacks on our flawed nation continue on a relentless, and invariably dishonest basis. So they must be just as consistently and bluntly characterized as such. Otherwise, they eventually attain a presumption of "normality" that will quickly be seized upon by leftists as faux "credence" with which they eagerly expand their domain and bludgeon all opposition.

This aspect of the Alinsky strategy is no mere matter of semantics. On a disturbingly widespread basis, Americans are no longer certain that they have the "right" to stand for anything worthwhile, or against any moral threat facing them. And this is totally by design. It was the destruction of our moral certitude, and the moral "vacuum" that followed, which opened the floodgates for every pernicious leftist encroachment on the greatness of our nation, whether from its now corrupted and perverse "academic" institutions, its propagandizing "news" media apparatus, or the mindless droning of its agenda-driven "entertainment" industry. Even in something as seemingly innocuous as advertising and supermarket product labels, or the cartoons viewed by our children, the patterns of leftist "moralizing" are not hard to spot. Currently, this leftist "moralizing" is pervasive in virtually every aspect of American life. For one example, white males have virtually gone extinct as the "hero" of any advertisement, whether pertaining to the banks we use, the beverages we drink, or any other topic by which the left claims to address a relevant moral issue. But in truth, this attack is not specifically limited to white males. Rather, it is part of a much broader effort to eradicate the principles and institutions they represent in the eyes of leftists, including those of the nation's founding.

Despite the consistently devastating results the nation has reaped from every manifestation of the leftist ideology, Americans are increasingly hesitant to assert any aspect of traditional morality and the American culture in response, including the worthiness of their own country, or their duty to stand for its national integrity. This pattern has resulted in grave moral vulnerability, not only to domestic maladies but even in the face of an invasion of ambivalent and frequently hostile foreigners. For most of the nation's history, Americans were proud to trumpet their patriotism and steadfast commitment to the American ideal. As a result, arriving foreigners recognized that their ability to resettle in America was contingent on their willingness to assimilate and embrace this nation's defining principles. Only in this manner could they make it their home and call Americans their neighbors and eventually, their friends.

> Americans are no longer certain that they have the "right" to stand for anything worthwhile, or against any moral threat facing them.

However, as a result of leftist attacks on the moral certitude of America, even the necessity for assimilation into the American way of life has been stalled on the basis that we ostensibly have no moral authority to impose American values on people of other cultures as a condition of allowing them into "E Pluribus Unum." Leftist "multiculturalism" contends that Americans must be increasingly accommodating to disparate, and often antithetical foreign cultures who share no historical or philosophical common ground with us and have no intention of adopting our way of life, but instead seek to force Americans to comply with their cultural sentiments and religious edicts. The end result is a dangerous fracturing of our society, with regions increasingly divided over creeds and ideology. The "melting pot" has become a cauldron, made up of disparate subcultures that no longer have any love of country to serve as a unifying "glue" among the people living within these shores.

During World War II, a walk down Main Street in any town across America would find people of differing ethnic backgrounds. Yet if the question was asked "Who is the enemy we're fighting?" virtually everyone would answer with absolute certainty. That moral certitude was the single most important factor in maintaining American cohesion throughout the difficult years of the War. It stood in stark contrast to the current leftist disdain and denigration of our nation, much of which originates from among the sixties "retreads" who currently infect and poison academia. Now, in the face of foreign attacks, their response is to begin by presuming that our enemies have a legitimate gripe against us, and that it is America which must engage in intense soul-searching, in order to figure out what sins we committed to make our enemies hate us and wish to destroy us.

Throughout the Cold War, the monstrous abuses and crimes against humanity committed by the Soviet Union were overlooked by leftists, who insisted that America needed to follow the "model" for societal utopia promoted in Soviet propaganda. The vast swaths of citizenry under the failed communist system who lived in deprivation and squalor, along with literally millions who were consigned to the gulag, or exterminated in unspeakable pogroms, were of no consequence to the left, since America had only recently forsaken segregated lunch counters. To this day, horrendous abuses of human rights by foreign governments devoted to failed ideologies and brutish religions are irrelevant to the left, and any mention of them will only be deflected with some example, whether real, grossly exaggerated, or totally concocted, of an ethical lapse that occurred within our nation or somewhere in Western Culture at some point during the past millennium. Among the most valuable pawns of leftists who engage in this ploy are those "conservatives" who respond by verbally hamstringing themselves (which is, in reality, undermining the rest of *us*) with concessions to such duplicity under the phony banner of "humility."

Since women didn't have the right to vote for a major portion of our nation's history, and until recent decades have suffered discrimination and unequal pay, we are made to believe by the left that we have no standing to oppose or even criticize the growing number of Islamists worldwide, and even in this country, who advocate Sharia and its brutal institutionalized oppression of women and exploitation of young girls. A similar mindset has proven particularly noxious in Europe and the United Kingdom, where the leverage of leftists in government is far greater than it is in America. Those regions are being virtually overrun by invading Islamists who increasingly wield control of the enforcement of laws, which they bend to their advantage. It must be understood that this onslaught is being directly aided and abetted by leftists in key positions of the governments of Britain and the European Union, who are mired in a belief that Western Civilization's imperfections throughout history nullify any possible objections to encroaching evil and animosity from hostile foreign cultures.

The dire straits in which Europe currently finds itself do not result from some recent upsurge in the strength of Islam, which is essentially the same as it has been throughout the past fourteen centuries. Rather, the single factor which has significantly changed in the social and political landscape of Europe during recent decades is that it has lost its own sense of moral certitude at the hands of leftists who have supplanted justice, decency, and truth with their sick, nihilistic ideology of "political correctness." Thus Europe has totally forfeited its previous cultural strength. And as a result, any effort to stand against an incursion of such a drastically incompatible nature is now virtually incapacitated. Sadly, America is not far behind.

As conservatives attempt to preserve the morals and societal norms of America, they face a constant game of leftist "bobbing and weaving," whereupon the underlying factors that define any situation suddenly change, in order to accommodate arbitrary and shifting leftist "principles." By this duplicitous means, leftists remain busily on "offense," denigrating and marginalizing those of the right, while escaping any diligent scrutiny of their real goals. They simply declare a "cause" to be virtuous, and give it a noble sounding name. "Income equality" and "social justice" immediately come to mind. Both "justice" and "equality" sound appealing, and are asserted with such unfettered confidence that few among the leftist "rank and file" ever question their legitimacy. In reality they are flimsy veneers created to put a seemingly worthy face on the nightmare of Marxism, the most oppressive and destructive ideology the world has ever known. But under such banners of contrived "beneficence," neither "social justice," "income equality," nor the damage they portend to society can be called into question without critics facing a waiting firestorm of denigration and mockery. Hence, they are too often allowed to assume a place of "worthiness" in the discourse.

Similarly, the inclusion of undiluted Islamist propagandizing in public school classrooms is deemed a noble exercise in "multiculturalism," while singing Silent Night has been virtually banned, on the basis that it poses a mortal threat to the Constitution and the Bill of Rights. Conservatives, who are either too timid or too hapless to remain fixed on the real issues at hand, fail to stand resolutely against such duplicity, and are eventually forced not only to accept these appalling premises, but also to pay for them with their tax dollars.

Our nation has already reaped horrendous consequences from this onslaught, including a growing number of terrorist attacks occurring within the American homeland. Leftists dodge accountability for the dangerous situation they've helped create, by flippantly asserting that nothing can be done to protect innocent citizens from hostile foreigners living among us, and that terrorist attacks are now an "inevitability" of American life. Terrorism, we are told, must be accepted as an inescapable aspect of modern living, and deemed "normal" on that basis. In contrast, plenty can be done to suppress and eliminate "Islamophobia," which suddenly supersedes actual brutality and slaughter visited upon innocent Americans, as the "real" moral issue and "mortal danger" to our nation's future that absolutely must be confronted. In truth, leftists are wholly indifferent to any Islamist attack that doesn't directly affect them on a personal basis. Their real concern is contriving a way to make as much political "hay" out of the situation as possible, and preventing any of their "politically correct" absolutes from being breached, or even questioned. As a result, their enabling behavior amounts to tacit "collaboration" with the terrorists, and is second only to the deeds of the terrorists themselves in assuring that further mayhem and slaughter will eventuate.

During political campaigns and investigations of the rampant corruption of the Clinton White House, Bill Clinton claimed a mantle of faux "righteousness" with such rebuttals to his critics as "No attack ever fed a hungry child," and his pious condemnation of "the politics of personal destruction." In both cases, his self-proclaimed "virtue" only actually exalted his own interests, which were to be reelected and to avoid accountability for the rampant corruption of his administration. Yet he shamelessly disguised his totally self-serving goal as the height of altruism on behalf of hungry children, and skillfully pitted it against the need for justice in the American political system as if the two were mutually exclusive. Of course no funding was ever withheld from the billions of dollars spent by the government on such programs as food stamps, in order to pay for the investigations of Clinton crimes, numerous though they were. Nor were any of the efforts to uncover rampant Clinton corruption motivated by a desire to engage in "personal destruction," but rather were deemed crucial to the restoration of integrity in government. Yet by fraudulently recasting the issues in such a manner, Clinton was successful in putting his opposition totally on the defensive and weakening it so severely that he eventually evaded any accountability for his actions.

Despite the transparent sanctimony of Bill Clinton and others like him, leftists continue to engage in the most venomous attacks on

RULES FOR DEFEATING RADICALS

politicians with whom they disagree. Moreover, they rule with an iron fist the moment they gain dominance of any situation, while demanding concessions in the name of "collegiality" whenever they find themselves in the minority. In both situations, they insist that they are on the "moral high ground," solely because of the inherently virtuous agenda that they seek to advance. Sadly, too many on the right reflexively surrender to their antics, thus giving them credence for sincerity, thereafter operating from a totally disadvantaged position by attempting to play according to the constantly shifting leftist rules.

When Barack Obama won his election in 2008, he didn't exhibit the slightest intention of "finding common ground" with Republicans. Rather, in a 2009 meeting on Obama's deficit-busting, government-bloating "stimulus," he flatly informed participating Republicans "I won," as sufficient reason to completely reject any input from them. Yet the moment the Republicans retook the House in 2010, he was immediately among those loudly decrying their "obstructionism" and "partisanship" for standing against his agenda. The orchestrated condemnation and grandstanding against the Republicans reached such a fevered pitch that House Speaker John Boehner essentially surrendered to Obama, giving in to every budget excess and policy abuse of the Democrats, as if the GOP had never received a charge from the American people to oppose the Obama onslaught. Boehner's infamous excuse was that the GOP only controlled "one half of one third of the government."

The pattern continued in 2014, when the Republicans also achieved majority status in the Senate, as Majority Leader Mitch McConnell allowed himself to be hamstrung by the same calls for "bipartisanship." Ultimately, he became the Republican lame duck "figurehead" in that body. In truth neither Boehner nor McConnell regarded the conservative agenda as being sufficiently important to the future of

America to fight the leftist Democrats in the Congress and the White House.

When dealing with leftist efforts to confuse and undermine basic morality, it is necessary to examine a leftist "moral certitude" scam that has gained prominence in recent years, which is the construction of phony "moral equivalencies" that attempt to justify leftist outrages on the grounds that they can ostensibly be likened to events and ideologies of the right. In truth, this requires extreme verbal gymnastics and distortions of reality. Yet leftists are sufficiently shameless that they eagerly engage in such ideological "sleights of hand," if their deceitful ethical contortions are not identified and stridently confronted as the total fraud that they are. So on those occasions when leftists find it difficult to simply claim their "moral high ground" with a blanket deflection from the facts, they regroup and accomplish the same end by offering another counterfeit.

With one oblique excuse or another, leftists will predictably assert their glowing "virtue" as embodied by any actions they intend to justify, asserting their "moral equivalency" when they find themselves in tight spaces by comparing their pet issues on a purely arbitrary basis to conservative words and deeds. This, despite their strident condemnation of those very beliefs and actions when it is expedient to do so. Such a transparent effort to cloud the defining moral issues of the day should be immediately recognized for the ruse that it is. Sadly, that doesn't happen as often as it should, and leftists are able to play their moral equivalency games with impunity.

Thus, leftists can engage in their partisan efforts to nominate and appoint activist judges to the nation's high courts because conservatives are just as "partisan" when they appoint jurists devoted to upholding the integrity of the Constitution. Leftists who promote the slaughter of children in the nation's abortion mills are "morally equivalent" to conservatives who seek to end the barbaric practice. They're just on the opposite side of the issue. If they succeed in presenting their case from the perspective that "both points of view are equally valid," they win. Leftists know that upholding both a high and low standard on any issue means that only the low standard will prevail.

"Multiculturalism" plays perfectly into this strategy. The glaring flaw of "multiculturalism," which has been expertly side-stepped by leftist propagandists, is that not all cultures are created equal. In a similar sense, not all "religions" are conducive to the "life, liberty and pursuit of happiness" enshrined in our Declaration of Independence and upheld by the protective tenets of the Constitution and Bill of Rights. The presence of these timeless principles in the nation's founding documents directly resulted from the Biblical tenets on which the ideology of those documents, and the nation they established, were based. Throughout history, the degree to which justice, liberty, and freedom have been able to thrive in any society can be directly tied to the steadfastness with which those societies endeavored to uphold *truly* Biblical principles. In contrast, some creeds and religions are vehemently antithetical to such ideals. Therefore, merely declaring all religions equally "valid" opens the door to the oppression of one faith by another in a manner that rejects the concept of respect for the weak and defenseless.

> The glaring flaw of "multiculturalism," which has been expertly side-stepped by leftist propagandists, is that not all cultures are created equal.

Leftists invoke empty platitudes such as "multiculturalism" to invalidate a host of time honored principles that have been essential to America's greatness, on the flimsy basis that some cultures just don't uphold them. A frequent rejoinder leftists use to give credence to this assault is their assertion that "You can't legislate morality." Originally, this principle merely contended that a person would not become "righteous" in his heart and soul by legally banning illicit activity. It eventually mutated into the leftist "axiom" that any societal standard based in "morality" (and more specifically, *Biblical* morality), was a violation of the "separation of Church and state," and thus unconstitutional. Hence, one standard of decency after another was attacked, dismantled, and eradicated.

These assaults have been perpetrated and expanded methodically, and with a specific goal in mind. The institutions of a great America are an obstacle to the left, which must be systematically undermined. Can anyone doubt that United States Senators showing up for work dressed like the price-club sale rack, or Obama's "paint by numbers" White House portrait, are efforts aimed at demeaning those institutions? And the same is true of the real motivations to destroy not only statues of great historical figures in American history, and not only those from the Civil War, but any who reflect the character and traditions of our nation.

At every grade from K through 12, and into higher education, American "history" is now taught from a perspective that specifically accentuates its flaws and trivializes its accomplishments. The same goes for the history of all of Western Civilization, while the dangers of its ideological enemies are minimized or ignored. In the process, those who come to America, seeking to infiltrate and overtake it are elevated to "victim" status as "refugees" which, in the eyes of "PC" leftists, gives them heightened "standing" to wage their attacks on Western Culture.

However, it is critically important to recognize just how selectively (and hypocritically) this leftist "moralizing" is applied. As true concepts of morality are successfully marginalized and erased, they are predictably and systematically supplanted by perverse leftist counterfeits, which are then enforced with an iron fist. Hence, classrooms where the *Lord's Prayer* was once recited but is now banned, have since become stages for every twisted "moral" teaching including pedophilia, presented not as the leftist countercultural dogma that they are, but as "normality" and universally recognized "fact." Thus leftists, the proponents of corrupt and detestable moral decay, somehow have sufficient latitude to declare themselves as moral champions, even of innocent children, as they fill young minds with every form of perversion.

This pattern continues into the workplace where the leftist ideology has thoroughly infiltrated corporate personnel departments. Under the banner of "sensitivity training," employees are bludgeoned with leftist orthodoxy, including every aberrant sexual doctrine of the counterculture, imposed on them in a bullying and coercive manner. With tactics that increasingly reflect Communist "retraining camps," leftists bombard workers with their views on every imaginable subject, from human sexuality to the environment to "religion" itself, presented as inarguable truth. In the process, they shamelessly promote and elevate themselves to the point of being its unassailable high priests.

Consider this example of how such a duplicitous feat is typically accomplished. In June of 2017, while castigating President Trump for his rejection of the Paris "Climate Accords," House Minority Leader Nancy Pelosi asserted "To ignore these needs is to dishonor God." In recent years, Pelosi's Democrat Party has established itself as the vehemently anti-God party, increasingly embracing every godless precept of the counterculture from abortion to same-sex "marriage" to perverse and sacrilegious, publicly funded "art." This blasphemous denigration of every genuinely Christian principle has been deliberate and unrelenting. Yet, on the basis of advancing the leftist "climate change" agenda, Pelosi is suddenly transfigured into the resident "expert" of what it means to honor God. So in Pelosi's world, refusing to be ensnared by this pillar of the leftist agenda is tantamount to the murder of millions of unborn children or the official ridicule of Christian morality in government schools and every other public venue. On such a specious basis, the ultra-liberal Pelosi suddenly elevates herself and the leftist agenda to ostensibly equal status with the issues of concern among the Christian right. Moreover, Pelosi is then free to engage in this absurd assertion totally without fear of the ACLU hysterically decrying her words as a dangerous affront to the "separation of Church and state."

The ACLU, Nancy Pelosi, and their kind are free to behave in this manner because intellectual honesty simply does not exist on the left, *and* because too few on the right are willing to call them out on it. Any efforts to ensure leftists actually uphold the standards they occasionally profess to believe are casually dismissed with such puerile rejoinders as "whataboutism," a fairly recent concoction of the left that is intended to totally deflect any recognition of leftist duplicity, on the sole grounds that leftists simply deem it irrelevant to the current discourse.

That is why "ending the rancor" is such a transparent ploy and should be flatly dismissed, right along with every other leftist attempt to claim their phony "moral high ground." It presumes moral equivalency between the leftist agenda, with all the harm it portends for the nation, as contrasted against the sincere and fervent efforts of those on the right who oppose it. Both sides, we are told, bear equal guilt for the hostility and discord that exists, while the specifics over which they contend are, when the occasion warrants, deemed irrelevant. But this is only the case when leftists dominate the Congress or hold the White House, because the goal at that point is solely to force the Republicans to cease any opposition to the leftist agenda. Once the tables are turned, and Republicans are in the majority, then the rancor of leftist opposition suddenly becomes the highest embodiment of "patriotism," and the essence of principled, constitutional governing.

Despite their shameless professions of virtue and intellect, leftists have always made their case with lies and hate, which is the real root cause of any repugnant rancor inside the Beltway. Yet if conservatives call out their rhetoric as lies and hate, they're presumed to be guilty of "coarsening the political discourse" with such accusations, and thus, from the leftist perspective, are equally as bad. Here's where the "moral equivalency" ruse kicks in. Both sides are complicit because they've both uttered uncomplimentary viewpoints of their opposition. Thus, strenuously opposing evil suddenly becomes just as "wrong" and "hateful" as the evil itself.

As conservatives have gained an ever more significant voice among the general public through alternative media, leftists are increasingly forced to reinvent their image, in order to dispel any widespread realization of their steady drift towards the extremes of Marxist radicalism, and to maintain their claims of being "mainstream." This is largely accomplished within political circles by deliberately clouding the ideological boundaries between left and right, with their "moral equivalency" ruse. Still, in the current era, the two ideological camps can easily be identified as "right and left" and, given the tenets of their agenda, they can be even more accurately characterized simply as "good and evil." Of course doing so effectively consigns leftists to being out on the "fringe," which is a difficult position for them to defend in the eyes of the general populace. So, when convenient, they promote their ideology, and any contention over it, under the seemingly equivalent banners of "Democrat versus Republican." In that manner, each side is most likely to be presumed as operating on a morally "level" playing field, with equally worthwhile goals. Of course all of that changes, the moment the Democrats believe they can gain more political traction by declaring the Republicans as the embodiment of "evil." Unfortunately, this ploy finds ready assistance from those "Republicans" who are so anxious to "reach across the aisle" and "rise above the rancor," that they happily collaborate with the Democrats. Eager to receive credit for their part in accomplishing that most noble inside-the-Beltway goal of "getting things done," they are perfectly comfortable betraying their party, and their voting base.

Under the cloak of moral equivalency, leftists deflect from the flagrant lies and bias of their politicians, which are echoed on the nightly news, on the basis that those on the right are equally biased. In an effort to make this case, they cite news and information sources which present points of view that aren't necessarily incorrect in any manner, but may merely run counter to leftist orthodoxy. However, given that the leftist agenda is built on lies, and thus can only be advanced through lies, intellectual honesty automatically refutes liberalism. By definition, reporting that is factual and *unbiased* is inherently "anti-leftist." So leftists will predictably accuse honest, conservative voices of being "partisan and biased." In truth, when leftists revert to this diversion, it is evidence that they are getting desperate, and are in an inherently weak position. The fact that they've frequently been able to turn the tables on their Republican opposition from such a weak position proves the fecklessness, and worse, the *treacherous complicity* of so many within the inner circles of the GOP. More on that in the next chapter.

CHAPTER SEVEN
RINOs: The Essential Alinsky Fifth Column

This examination of the treachery of RINOs (*Republicans In Name Only*) might be the single most important chapter in this entire book. Given that the Alinsky strategy can only work on those who allow it, the likelihood of either tacit or sometimes *deliberate* collaboration of RINOs with any leftist attack can become the determining factor in whether the attack fails or succeeds. Often, a leftist onslaught is on the verge of collapsing or even backfiring on its perpetrators on account of its transparent dishonesty and lack of substance, when suddenly a prominent complicit RINO steps in to rescue it by asserting that its premises are somehow "legitimate." When the motivation behind such behavior is questioned, this manner of RINO treachery is typically defended with the sanctimony of "putting principle above party." Not surprisingly, in these circumstances the "principles" being advanced are invariably those of the Democrat party. Therefore, a thorough understanding of the RINO phenomenon is essential to effectively combating this "flank attack" variation of the leftist/Alinsky onslaught.

For the sake of this discussion, a certain point must first be clarified. It has proven to be unnecessarily distracting to initially identify which specific Republican politicians and commentators may or may not qualify as RINOs. While a few notorious players, such as Arizona Senator John McCain, have well established reputations as such, many Republican politicians, despite their long track records of double-dealing and consistent betrayals of the conservative agenda, still manage to maintain devotees among their voting base. This occurs for several reasons, from personal relationships, to the standard RINO tactic of campaigning as the "Second coming of Ronald Reagan" when on their home turf. Such individuals know how to put on a good front for their constituents, which somehow overshadows their real pattern of disparaging and deliberately undermining genuine conservatism once they are back inside the Beltway.

Moreover, a large number of Republican voters at the "grassroots" continue to feel a deep sense of loyalty to the party, and are wholly unwilling to be critical of it, as if opposition to its increasing duplicity is somehow tantamount to disloyalty to conservatism itself. This longstanding emotional connection to the "Grand Old Party" has been deftly exploited by those at its inner circles, who shamelessly and disingenuously tout the former ideals of the party, such as the traditional values (Judeo-Christian morality) on which the nation was founded, while actually devoting party resources and political capital to an agenda that is much further to the left, aligning much more closely with the Democrats. In the process, the benefits of a healthy society, such as limited government, maximized freedom, and economic prosperity, are dealt major setbacks by the very people who loudly claim to champion those ideals, especially while on the campaign trail. Nevertheless, they are able to maintain a loyal following solely on the basis of empty words, and their claims of embodying the ideals of the Republican Party. Consequently, the ideological foundation of the party continues to erode and decay.

Such posturing and political tap-dancing takes on many forms. Some Republicans strategically vote to undermine defining conservative principles, while loudly touting other "hot button" issues that are either inconsequential or are assured losers for which politicians can voice support while knowing all along that nothing of any significance will ever result from their grandstanding. The disgraceful abundance of votes held in the House and Senate, ostensibly to repeal Obamacare prior to the inauguration of President Trump, proved to be just so much pandering, since repeal was a popular rallying cry among the conservative grassroots. However, the Republican leadership was absolutely confident that Obama would veto every such bill. Therefore, RINOs could fund-raise and grandstand off of their "opposition" to Obamacare, while being fully assured that they'd never have to face any actual repercussions from their loud demands for its repeal.

Yet once they were under a Trump presidency, the Republican Congress and Senate were suddenly adverse to any such effort, since a vote to rid the nation of the nightmare of Obamacare might now actually succeed. A fulfillment of this previously "promised" action would surely reap the inevitable media backlash, with possible political consequences. So once again, at a critical moment when the Republicans could have significantly changed the nation's direction, they waffled and offered excuses, while deliberately leaving the Democrat agenda intact. Clearly, a major portion of the congressional GOP caucus is not interested in advancing any real conservative principles, but is instead intent on preserving the Washington "establishment" as it is, which ensures re-election for most, and perks for all.

Nevertheless, actually identifying the RINO tendencies of a specific politician, particularly on the national scene, will all too frequently result in further fractures and arguments among the conservative movement as to the validity of the accusation. Thus, for the purpose of establishing RINO behavioral patterns and the effects of their treachery without being distracted and dragged off into arguments as to who does or doesn't personally qualify, the immediate focus will instead be on understanding how RINOs operate, and the appalling consequences of their actions. Hopefully, as this case is laid out, the deeds and motivations of particular politicians will become self-evident, whereupon they can then be accurately judged on their own merits. Despite their flowery orating, pandering, or any other political skill they may possess, the overall assessment of specific Republican politicians must result solely from an objective and *ongoing* appraisal of which direction they actually "move the ball down the field." It may take a bit more effort to get beyond the rhetoric and platitudes in order to substantively judge them, but once a sincere determination is made to do so in this manner, their real character becomes inescapably evident.

RINOs can be divided into a few general categories. Their motivations for betraying conservatism are varied, and therefore each must be dealt with differently. In any case, it is safe to assume that none of them can be trusted. The first are the political cowards, who may in fact actually believe in the validity of the conservatism they espouse back home. However, once they become immersed in the political pressure cooker inside the Beltway, they live in fear of the inevitable firestorm of criticism they are sure to receive from leftist politicians and their media minions, the moment they dare undertake any real effort at promoting a conservative agenda. These people would be happy to see real conservatism prevail, but only if they can somehow accomplish the feat while remaining on politically "safe" ground, thus avoiding any missteps that might anger the left. Of course such a premise is impossible to achieve, and thus these RINOs invariably end up waving the white flag and allowing the leftist agenda to proceed undeterred, regardless of which party has a majority in the Congress or holds the White House. Political cowards are easy to manipulate through fear; a trait which the left diligently exploits.

Similarly, Republicans who personally lack the moral certitude of their party's guiding principles are easily thrown off course by any well-crafted leftist argument against it. These morally rudderless Republicans are among the first to jump onto the bandwagon of "bipartisanship," believing that by their capitulation, they are acting in the best interests of the citizenry. It somehow escapes them that their leftist and Democrat opponents *never* find themselves in any similar position, but always manage to rally to the wishes of their leaders, who are thoroughly and unshakably devoted to the leftist agenda.

Among these morally rudderless RINOs, a certain "subset" can also be found, who are equally devoid of any guiding principle, but who believe themselves to be a bit more crafty in their ethical obfuscations. These are the "fiscal conservatives," who claim this mantle as a means of asserting that they hold to the GOP philosophy of smaller and less expensive government, while studiously sidestepping the so-called "social issues." In essence, they endorse the same moral degradation of society promoted by the leftist counterculture, but somehow think they can do so at a lower cost to everyone. In the end, they invariably embrace the entire leftist agenda, including the inescapable costs of government intervention to deal with all of the squalor and tragedy that are the inevitable consequences of a broken, morally dysfunctional nation.

In the wake of any major catastrophe or any other significant occurrence in which people suffer and lives are lost, the transparent and reflexive response of leftists is to seize the limelight, then twist and pervert the actualities of the event in order to lay blame at the feet of their political enemies. The proper response would be to confront these leftists for their callous grandstanding, refusing to give any further credence to the sanctimony they spew, which would effectively shut them down. Such a principled stance could also spotlight the self-serving coldness of the leftists in front of the general public who need to know what they are really about. Unfortunately, the predictable RINO faces are eager to line up behind the leftists like quails, loudly and piously agreeing with their every bogus premise. The primary motivation of these pandering RINOs is to make sure they are perceived as being on the "correct" side of the issue at hand. Thus, they give wholly unwarranted "credibility" to the shameless opportunism of leftists. As with "bipartisan" legislating, the left can thereafter cite these RINOs as a "unified" coalition of great statesmen who "put principle above politics," to support the invariably leftist spin on the incident in question.

The last, and most pernicious group of RINOs are the closet liberals, who secretly embrace the Democrat agenda, but must maintain a facade of "conservatism" in order to continue to be re-elected in districts where being "Republican" is equated to being conservative. This group is particularly noxious, owing to their underlying malicious intent to derail conservatism at every opportunity. The political *mission* of these RINOs is to give credibility and cover to *every* despicable and absurd leftist premise, by publicly applauding it with the highest of accolades in the face of conservative opposition. In like manner, these RINOs can be counted on to instantly jump to the defense of any scandal plagued leftist politician whose behavior might be cause for controversy. The cases have been all too common, when liberal Democrat politicians come briefly under fire for their abominable moral lapses or their partisan venom, yet they escape any real accountability because the predictable RINO collaborators are ready and waiting to publicly endorse them with assertions of their irrefutable honor and decency. In precisely this manner, attacks from hyper-partisan leftist politicians, which might have been dispelled on the basis of their glaring hypocrisy, are nevertheless given unwarranted "weight," as a direct result of the accolades they enjoy from their RINO accomplices.

> The political mission of these RINOs
> is to give credibility and cover to
> every despicable and absurd leftist premise.

It is also these RINOs who are the quickest to very publicly laud themselves for their defiance of those nasty conservatives, shamelessly grandstanding with their platitudes of "reaching across the aisle" and embracing "bipartisanship," while decrying the "rancor" and "divisiveness" of true conservatism. With such treachery, they deliberately hamstring legitimate efforts to oppose the leftist onslaught. There is a reason that, in a time of war, enemy spies are regarded as the gravest of threats, and face the harshest consequences of any combatant. Similarly, whether or not the story of the Trojan Horse is deemed history or myth, its lesson is profoundly significant. A few key players who are able to successfully worm their way into strategically valuable positions behind enemy lines can accomplish what an entire army across the field cannot. And on this basis, the last group of RINOs is fully aware of the clout they wield with their duplicitous ways, as long as they can continue to engage in their treachery under a phony mantle of actually being "Republican."

The summation of these circumstances is that an infuriating pattern of capitulation and deceit has increasingly characterized the entire GOP in recent years. And this has too often been the deciding factor in whether or not leftist policy prevails, while conservative opposition is undercut. In virtually every case, the net result is a "win/win" for the left, because its leaders and base are "energized" by their victory, while Republican "leaders" are left empty-handed, and offering lame excuses to a thoroughly disenfranchised base. It is therefore no understatement to assert that the successful reversal of the leftist/Alinsky onslaught against America, or the failure to achieve this goal (which means the *failure of America*), is contingent on effectively dealing with the treachery of RINO politicians.

Moreover, it is crucial to understand that the treachery of closet liberals masquerading as "conservatives" is not confined to the realm of elected office holders. The RINO phenomenon is particularly pernicious when it occurs among professed and acclaimed members of the "conservative" commentariat. It is likely to be taken far more seriously than it deserves, not as leftist propaganda but as reasoned analysis, offered in the best interests of conservatism and the Republican Party, while it specifically and deliberately erodes those very principles. Damaging statements, ostensibly from the "right," but which bolster leftist ideology, are immediately seized upon by the left and heralded as "proof" of the worthiness of their agenda among reasonable and right thinking "conservatives."

Many among this group, who do not hold elected positions, are able to dodge accusations of their duplicity by specifically denying official party affiliation. But despite their lack of GOP membership cards, they are RINOs in every sense of the word. While claiming to be all-knowing voices of "conservatism," they selectively subordinate real conservative principle to one misbegotten liberal premise or another that invariably undercuts the validity of conservatism and discourages any substantive action to implement it. Of course this puts leftists and their twisted ideology back in the "driver's seat." And whether these RINOs are dupes or traitors, when they achieve their intended goal of eroding the moral certitude of conservatives, the loss of cohesion on our side the results from their treachery is always and *only* beneficial to the left.

Frequently, when Democrat leaders become aware of conservatives who may be gaining an alarming degree of momentum, they mobilize against such individuals by employing the Alinsky tactic of declaring them to be "pariahs" on some spurious basis, such as rumors of a past scandal, or a former misstatement that can be blown vastly out of proportion. The most valuable addition to this transparent ploy is the predictable RINO who is always on hand and, hoping to be grouped among the sanctimonious leftists, is quick to join in and agree with the premises of their criticism. Thus the ploy gains unwarranted credence, and is perceived as being elevated from political posturing and grandstanding to seeming "validity." This scenario typically has a cascading effect. As the situation gains prominence on the nightly news, the condemnation from every colluding RINO makes it ever more difficult to defend the individual in question, or to re-establish a proper sense of proportion to the "scandal" that is certain to have been vastly overblown.

Here again is the essence of the Alinsky "freeze/isolate" strategy, which becomes far more effective the moment a willing RINO joins the Democrats. Instead of the onslaught being dismissed as it should be, it suddenly gains credence, allowing leftists to attack more boldly and with seemingly greater assurance of appearing justified and thus holding their phony "moral high ground." The more conservatives are hesitant thereafter to be associated with the targeted individual, the more they aid and abet the attack. From that point forward the individual appears increasingly isolated and marginalized, and is often dealt a politically fatal blow as a result.

Since RINOs ultimately empower the political left, and given that some RINOs actually are closet liberals, it should be no surprise that they often operate in the same, deceitful manner and employ the same underhanded tactics, the same selective "moralizing," and ultimately, *the same hypocrisy* as the left. This goes for both the active political office-holders, as well as the political "consultant" class and the punditry. The game plan is to boldly assert their "conservatism" on the basis of credentials or pedigree, and then promote an agenda that is essentially liberal, under the banner of being "mainstream," or some similar platitude. Truth and facts are subordinated to the party line, which is then asserted as "conventional wisdom." And this is all proclaimed with the pretense of unquestioned intellectual, and even *moral* authority.

> Sincere conservatives who defy RINO opposition
> and manage to be elected are often thoroughly
> damaged and hamstrung once they assume office.

Consequently, real conservatism is increasingly marginalized and dismissed by these RINOs as "extreme," and therefore "nonviable." Truly conservative candidates are deemed "unelectable," and, we are told, should be rejected in lieu of more "moderate" candidates who will readily embrace the wishes of the party's inner circle, which of course puts the Democrats back in control of the agenda. Aspiring politicians who are legitimately conservative face a savage but predictable onslaught from both parties on this basis, which has sadly proven to be extremely effective at neutralizing many worthy "rising stars" on the right. Those sincere conservatives who still manage to be elected are often thoroughly damaged and hamstrung once they assume office, and thereafter find it a difficult and endlessly uphill battle to impact the "business as usual" climate that predominates inside the Beltway. It is imperative to recognize that this despicable pattern is RINO standard operating procedure, and is perhaps the greatest obstacle facing any real conservative ascendancy in the political realm. It should also be noted here that those Republicans who engage in such treachery, despite their ability to eloquently espouse the conservative philosophy when pragmatic to do so, reveal themselves as the real manifestation of liberal subversion within the GOP.

When engaged grassroots "Tea Party" conservatives in Delaware chose Christine O'Donnell in that state's 2010 Senate primary and rejected Mike Castle, who was the predetermined choice of the Delaware Republican Party (which itself was answering to the wishes of the Washington political establishment), GOP insiders at every level reacted openly and angrily, denouncing O'Donnell in the most vicious and demeaning of terms, insisting that Castle was the only right choice and that he was "most electable." Many among the supposedly "conservative" punditry were quick to join the chorus, thoroughly disparaging and undermining O'Donnell in virtual collaboration with the Democrats, thus destroying her political momentum and dooming her candidacy. Predictably, the moment she lost her race, they were quick to get in front of the cameras, loudly and sanctimoniously claiming that her race had been a lost cause from the start, not on account of their treachery, but as a result of her "unelectable" nature. In that manner, their back-stabbing accomplished *two* important goals. First, they prevented a real conservative from taking a seat in the United

States Senate. Secondly, and perhaps more importantly, they could thereafter hold her up as an example of the supposed futility of grassroots involvement that doesn't align with the wishes of the party establishment. Real conservatives need not apply.

Such RINO treachery was equally evident in Mississippi when conservative state Senator Chris McDaniel challenged incumbent Thad Cochran in the 2014 Senate Primary. Cochran, an "establishment" Republican with a long track record of unfaithfulness to conservatism, actually called on Democrats to cross over party lines and support him, in order to prevent McDaniel from winning the primary. This ploy, abetted by the usual suspects among a complicit media, was sufficient to derail McDaniel's momentum, whereupon we were told, once again, that it had been a foolish mistake to challenge Cochran, since McDaniel was obviously "unelectable." It was with Democrat help at the ballot box that Cochran managed to maintain his seat by an extremely slim margin. But it was also with the support of those at the inner circles of the GOP. Most significant of all however, is that nowhere among the Republican Party "mainstream" was there any mention of "circular firing squads," or the obvious devastation to "party unity" resulting from Cochran's outreach to the left, which he undertook in order to prevail over a genuine conservative. Instead, the Cochran debacle proved that in the minds of the GOP elite, it's perfectly fine to run candidates who are preferred by the Democrats.

Other examples abound, and in every case the pattern is identical. Frustrated with "business as usual" inside the Beltway, conservatives stray from the reservation and rally around a political "outsider" who holds the potential to actually confront the abhorrent status quo. The GOP "establishment" unleashes its attack dogs, who coordinate their efforts *with the Democrat opposition* to derail the candidacy. Once these collaborating members of the "ruling class" achieve their goal of preventing a real conservative from gaining office, they sternly and piously lecture grassroots activists on the foolishness of interfering with their political elitist club. The proper course, we are told, is to allow party insiders to decide in advance who among their ranks should be the nominee. They alone will dictate who is "most electable," which is how they describe their own, once they've sufficiently railroaded and undercut any outsider candidates to the point of rendering them "unelectable." And this is how the ruling class maintains its "business as usual." Over time, what this portends is that liberal supporters get results from their elected officials, while our side gets excuses and obfuscations from the Republican "leadership," who insist that they are diligently working to fix the mess inside the Beltway, but on one premise or another are simply unable to ever accomplish anything of significance.

Eventually, frustrated conservatives rally to return fire at this ongoing pattern of RINO duplicity. Yet the moment the tables are turned on them, RINOs respond with fraud, hypocrisy and sanctimony that is indistinguishable from that of the Democrats. Let a liberal Republican win a primary, and any criticism of them from conservatives is immediately met with angry accusations and denunciations that the conservatives are "eating their own," engaging in a "circular firing squad" and violating "Reagan's 11th Commandment" (Thou shalt not criticize a fellow Republican). Ronald Reagan's "Big Tent" is loudly trumpeted as the only proper response to the party's chosen candidate. Yet somehow, neither the political class nor its ostensibly "conservative" cheering section in the alternative media ever feel compelled to rally around conservative candidates who are targeted and undercut by the RINO "establishment."

In particular, the "circular firing squad" and "Big Tent" metaphors warrant further examination. From the RINO/liberal perspective, the "circular firing squad" connotes a bunch of hapless conservatives who surround an ostensibly worthwhile candidate, whom they deem as less than ideologically pure. After prolonged RINO treachery, conservative patience finally wears thin, and they decide to respond in kind, whereupon they are immediately condemned as engaging in a "circular firing squad," thus constituting a threat to "party unity." Their efforts to attack the individual are supposedly misdirected and thus end up inflicting damage on fellow Republicans, to the detriment of all. Of course the preferred arrangement, according to the RINOs, is for conservatives to simply stand around and accept malicious potshots from the RINO establishment.

RINOs also love claiming to embrace Ronald Reagan's "Big Tent," though their version of it is deliberately contorted into something that bears no similarity to Reagan's real intent. In truth, Reagan's "Big Tent" was an outgrowth of his leadership. It was a means of inviting others, who might not totally agree with him, to put aside *their* petty differences and join with his overall vision for America and the worthy goals he sought. They were free to disagree on some particulars, but could nevertheless get behind his agenda, based on its overall appeal and merits. The alternative "Big Tent," promoted by the RINOs, contends that the GOP should stand for anything and everything, in order to make any individual of any personal or political persuasion feel "welcome." Rather than being an expression of leadership, it is a pitiful example of pandering and following. In claiming to embrace any ideology, it reveals that it ultimately stands for none, other than its own self-promotion. A party that claims to embrace high standards and low standards (right and left) on an equal basis, is a party that will only ever uphold the low standards. Ultimately, the party will be totally defined by the lowest standards it accepts. And this is the essence of the modern GOP establishment. As such it has a consistent track record of failure.

The identical hypocrisy and duplicity of RINOs is rampant not only when campaigning or in front of the cameras, but also within the legislative process, and during any hotly contested issue, such as consideration of judicial or cabinet nominees. Any efforts to insist on upholding true conservatism or ensuring that a nominee actually embraces such principles are instantly dismissed as "litmus tests," and the supporters of such standards tagged as "single issue" which, in the eyes of the political elite, somehow relegates the concerns of conservatives to irrelevancy. In truth, a litmus test merely connotes an immutable defining standard from which an office holder cannot deviate without proving himself/herself to be antithetical to conservative ideology. Certain issues are absolutely defining, and cannot be compromised or trivialized without wholly conceding an entire political platform.

Failing to steadfastly uphold such standards is the surest route to passing laws and impaneling individuals that are guaranteed to undermine and abandon the conservative agenda. This is, of course, the ultimate goal of the "establishment," the moment it starts hurling accusations of "litmus tests" and being "single issue," or some other characterization of conservatives as extreme. It must be recognized that this ploy is used just as readily by RINOs as it is by the Democrats, and always in a manner that specifically disparages conservative principle as overly rigid and inflexible. In stark contrast to those on the right, Democrats and liberal Republicans who are unbending and obsessive in their devotion to liberal ideology, and unwavering in their opposition to conservatives, are *never* accused of holding to leftist "litmus tests." Democrats in particular, who won't bend or compromise, are lauded as the "conscience" or "lion" of their respective legislative bodies, connoting courage and heroism.

> Failing to steadfastly uphold standards is the surest route to passing laws and impaneling individuals that are guaranteed to undermine the conservative agenda.

The RINO phenomenon is significantly bolstered by so-called Republican "political strategists," whose abysmal track record of failed candidacies so often proves they are neither Republican, nor are they strategically astute. These individuals have over time played right into the hands of the Democrats to the point of becoming hapless dupes, if not outright collaborators. For example, leftists fully understand that they must cloak their real intentions, particularly at election time, in order to fool enough of the electorate to achieve victory. Consequently, far-left candidates invariably posture to the right, and portray themselves as "centrist," because the political middle ground is far less threatening to citizens on Main Street than the ugly realities and failed policies of the left. However, this does not mean that the political "spectrum" reaches its peak of appeal to the general public at the insipid and uninspiring "middle ground." The rightward shift of liberal posturing is totally misconstrued by GOP "strategists," who believe that a *leftward* shift on the part of their candidates constitutes a similarly pragmatic move.

What they fail to understand (if they are indeed attempting to truly understand anything) is that although leftists must cloak their real ideology and agenda in order to gain acceptance from the public in all but the most left-leaning regions, Republican candidates are far more often bolstered by an unabashed conservative stance, while waffling and "moderating" seriously erodes their credibility. Thus, attempting to play the political game in the same manner as the left is a guaranteed loser for conservatives. And while some Republican politicians are hapless and gullible enough to fall for this scam, a disturbingly large contingency of RINOs is fully aware of the political quagmire that it represents and how it ultimately benefits the liberal agenda, yet they happily promote it for that very reason.

The results of such political posturing are predictably bleak. A telling case study of the fate of political chameleons within the GOP was the meteoric rise, and subsequent implosion, of Scott Brown of Massachusetts. Elected in the January 2010 special election to replace Senator Ted Kennedy after his death, Brown campaigned as a strident opponent of Obama's socialist onslaught, and in particular, the looming threat of Obamacare. With major Tea Party support, Brown became the first Republican Senator to be elected from Massachusetts since 1972, triumphing over enormous coordinated Democrat opposition, both from within Massachusetts and from across the nation. Unfortunately, the moment Brown found himself among the elites in D.C. the limelight proved to be too much for him and he embraced the self-serving mindset of Beltway insiders. Rather than remaining fixed on the ideas by which he gained victory, he began posturing to the center, and pursued inane and futile efforts to broaden his base of support, by adopting ever more liberal stances on major issues. As per usual, this totally alienated those who had supported him, while completely failing (as it always does) to make him more palatable to leftists who will never accept such a candidate. In the next election, he was soundly defeated by the hard-left Elizabeth Warren.

Unfortunately, the damage from such self-serving behavior isn't confined to those who engage in it. In the long run, the overall impact of RINO treachery has been devastating, to the point of possibly being the single most significant factor contributing to liberal successes. The result is that the political landscape has been drastically altered. Conservatives now find it far more difficult to contend with the absurdities and disasters of leftist policy, which were once relatively easy to shoot down in all but the most hardcore leftist regions. Owing to RINO collaboration with the leftist ploy of shifting the perception of where "centrism" and "right wing extremism" exist on the political spectrum, conservatives who attempt any engagement with their leftist opposition are now forced to begin from a gravely disadvantaged position, where any reasonable idea that deviates from leftist dogma is automatically deemed extreme. Not surprisingly, among the political establishment, left wing extremism doesn't exist. Consequently, abhorrently illegal and even unconstitutional leftist policy is allowed to prevail, while efforts to uphold any vestige of traditional law and established precedent of the Constitution are excoriated in the most severe and alarmist of terms.

The duplicity, political fecklessness, and ideological timidity of Republicans was never more evident than in the aftermath of the 2000 presidential election "cliff hanger" in Florida, in which George W. Bush barely eked out an Electoral College victory over Democrat Al Gore. After several weeks of recount chicanery, in which the Democrat Party resorted to every trick and scam it could muster including the infamous "dimpled chads" in hopes of garnering enough votes to swing the election to Gore, the United States Supreme Court finally shut down the circus, and deemed the original Florida election results valid, in favor of Bush. Yet if the Republicans ever "snatched defeat from the jaws of victory," it was in the months following that decision. Democrats proceeded to stir discord and anger among their base, primarily for the purpose of maximizing campaign contributions from outraged supporters. In the Congress and Senate, they displayed their hysterics by pushing hard-left, as a supposed neutralizing response to the election which they contended was "stolen" from them.

To their initial surprise, instead of the GOP hitting back with vigor and resolve, it reacted to leftist tantrums by attempting to placate and mollify them, "reaching across the aisle" and acquiescing to as many absurdities of liberal policy as possible. In the new Congress of 2001, Trent Lott of Mississippi presided over a fifty-fifty Senate in which his claim to the position of Majority Leader rested in the tie-breaking vote of Vice-President Dick Cheney. Lott became ensnared in an unprecedented ruse whereby Republicans would essentially forfeit the traditional majority status granted them by Senate rules, allowing committees to be made up of equal numbers of Republicans and Democrats, as well as being funded on an equal basis. In this manner, Lott and the Republicans sought to show the Democrats that they weren't going to be unreasonable, vainly hoping to assuage the hyped

Democrat "anger" over the Florida recount. According to Lott, everyone would benefit from the arrangement, as he asserted "I don't think it's bad. I think this is a framework for *bipartisanship*."

Of course everything changed a few months later when RINO Senator Jim Jeffords of Vermont switched his party affiliation to "Independent," which of course meant that he would be siding with the Democrats, essentially giving them a one-vote majority. Suddenly South Dakota Democrat Tom Daschle superseded Lott as Majority Leader, whereupon he proceeded to rule with the iron fisted *partisanship* that is standard operating procedure for the Democrats.

Meanwhile, during that same era, President George W. Bush, proclaiming his "new tone" of bipartisanship and collegiality, was busily conceding and capitulating his way into historical irrelevancy, which likely would have been his legacy, were it not for the terrorist attacks of September 11, 2001. The very notion of Bush's "new tone" as a supposed fix for the problems plaguing Washington was itself a presumption that the rancor and discord resulted from a previously existing contentiousness among conservatives. Thus did Bush's pandering validate leftist accusations of Republican "extremism" as the source of problems in Washington and America. It further put enormous pressure on conservatives to "moderate" (which means to abandon conservatism), or else face accusations of creating and aggravating the political divide in the Congress. Over time however, the only thing Bush's inane outreach actually accomplished was to allow Democrats on Capitol Hill the latitude to move even further left, while increasing their political clout to totally set the agenda; an opportunity which they readily seized.

Democrats realized that the more stridently they pulled to the left, the more Republicans would slither along behind them, in vain hopes of "ending the rancor" by working together. So Democrats became even more shrill, more venomous, and more deceitful in their accusations, while feckless Republicans overwhelmingly responded with further concessions and timidity. The current day hysteria and lies of leftist Democrat politicians would once have relegated them to an embarrassing fringe, except that post 2001, the GOP simply refused to call them out on their despicable behavior, opting instead to pretend all was well, and that America could somehow benefit from a Republican Party that "reached across the aisle" to ranting and sputtering Democrats.

The RINO betrayal continues to this day, and it portends not only a stalled conservative agenda and short term losses, but long term damage to the electoral landscape. And that's entirely by design. In the 2013 Virginia governor's race, conservative Ken Cucinelli lost to Terry McAuliffe, a well known liberal Democrat and long-time lackey of Bill and Hillary Clinton. McAuliffe's margin of victory was less than three percent. Several factors point to the corrosive effects of high level Republican Party treachery on Cucinelli's effort, and how it not only doomed his immediate political fortunes, but also inflicted lingering harm on the conservative movement in general. In stark contrast to the 2009 Virginia Governor's race, in which the Republican National Committee gave then candidate Bob McDonnell nine million dollars, Cucinelli received barely a third of that amount, thus severely limiting his ability to run an effective campaign. GOP insiders were adverse to supporting Cucinelli, owing to his conservative stances on abortion and marriage. The same crowd of establishment "Republicans" that so fervently decries conservative "litmus tests" supportive of traditional morality and the Constitution, was perfectly willing to abide by litmus tests dictated by the leftist counterculture, as it worked insidiously to undermine Cucinelli on that basis.

Clearly, with only a bit more financial help, Cucinelli could have made up his tiny vote deficit that instead delivered a victory to the Democrats. Yet even more flagrant RINO intrigues surfaced. Boyd

Marcus, the former Chief of Staff to Virginia Republican Congressman and former House Minority Whip Eric Cantor, jumped onto the McAuliffe team. So much for Republican Party "unity," or any real deference to Reagan's 11th Commandment, the moment GOP liberals train their sights on a conservative.

Yet the full scope of this Virginia race, all of the RINO treachery, and its damaging effect on the GOP and America is even more far reaching. As Governor, McAuliffe proceeded to give voting rights to sixty thousand convicted felons. Not surprisingly, the criminal vote in Virginia and elsewhere is solidly Democrat. McAuliffe's flagrant abuse of executive power was a violation of the law, which was initially reined in by the Virginia Supreme Court. Yet in textbook Obama fashion, McAuliffe soon found a way to sidestep the court's decision, so he proceeded on his course in blatant defiance of it. With schemes and chicanery (standard operating procedure for leftists) that flout the law, Virginia was driven significantly further into the liberal Democrat camp. In the end however, it should never be forgotten that McAuliffe might never have gained such a position of power and influence were it not for the tacit *and active* collaboration of RINOs who helped him get elected in the first place.

No discussion of RINO culpability in the long term erosion of our constitutional republic would be complete without a further mention of their complicity in undermining the judiciary. As discussed in greater detail in Chapter 5, it was the willingness of RINOs to assent to the absurd notion that "A president should be given his choice of judicial nominees," which enabled the Democrats to fill America's courts with hard left activists, masquerading as "jurists," who are openly hostile to the Constitution and the rule of law. This was ostensibly perpetrated in a hapless effort to make the confirmation process less rancorous. Clearly, it has had entirely the opposite effect. In the process, Democrats were afforded the latitude to turn nomination battles into purely political contests, with the fate of the Constitution as the basis for American law and jurisprudence being relegated to partisan posturing. Confirmation hearings for Democrat appointees focus almost entirely on the academic "pedigree" of the nominee, since few if any could survive scrutiny of their track record of support or opposition to the Constitution.

It is appalling, but not surprising, that the Clinton and Obama appointees to the Supreme Court behave not as jurists or guardians of the integrity of the Constitution, but as unaccountable leftist activists, whose "decisions" are completely predictable before a single word of any argument in any case before the court is ever heard. Worst of all, this is how the entire Washington political establishment, which includes members of both parties, prefers the courts to operate, since it regards the Constitution as an obstacle needing to be circumvented. As a result of RINO treachery and eagerness to endorse leftist premises, a wholly winnable battle to safeguard the freedoms and rights of Americans, as enshrined in our nation's founding documents, has been needlessly forfeited.

Imagine how much stronger the conservative position would be, if the real goal of the GOP was to diligently and steadfastly promote the integrity of the Constitution as its standard for supporting or opposing the confirmation of any judicial nominee. Instead of fearing leftist accusations of "partisanship," Republicans could completely turn such attacks back on their Democrat accusers. Let those Democrats, characterize the supremacy of our Constitution as "partisan." So be it, since at that point the Democrats would be tacitly admitting that as a defining precept of their ideology, they *do not* seek to uphold the integrity of the Constitution in law and jurisprudence. Such is the potential that awaits the nation, whenever the Republican Party can be rid of its liberal impostors, and brought back to the principles of the nation's founding, where it belongs.

As America increasingly decries the rampant corruption and disregard for constitutional principle that has overtaken Washington, the degree of RINO complicity in these abhorrent circumstances must be clearly understood. In the GOP "establishment" worldview, the pursuit of crimes and scandal does not reflect a duty to uphold justice and the law for the good of the country, or any loyalty of politicians to their sworn oaths of office. Rather, it is solely a matter of political gain or loss for the party. Maintaining the integrity of government, so essential for a free and just society, has degenerated into a question of having the "political will" to take on the issues of high crimes and misdemeanors. And doing so on that basis will always eventually require support from a leftist media, in order to be deemed palatable to the disengaged public. As long as politicians operate from this perspective, nothing of substance will ever be done to address real crimes or other excesses that the political "establishment" intends to sweep under the rug.

Worst of all, while such GOP fecklessness has enabled every vile abuse of public office by corrupt liberal Democrats to go unaddressed, Republicans are increasingly forced to walk an impossible tightrope. Amazingly, this abhorrent situation has transpired specifically because the GOP vainly seeks to gain the approval of a hostile leftist media and its minions who blindly place their faith in the propaganda they hear on the nightly "news." Yet it is the very refusal of the GOP to hold Democrat crimes accountable that is the overriding reason for seeming "disinterest."

RINOs allow Democrat criminality to go uncontested, the moment upholding the law is demeaned by leftist politicians and the media as "partisan."

It is the inevitable outgrowth of the disillusionment and disenfranchisement that results when the entire political system allows flagrant crimes against America to go unpunished. These are winnable battles, both in the political realm and in the pursuit of justice for the inherent good of the nation. Unfortunately, RINOs quickly abandon them and allow Democrat criminality to go uncontested, the moment upholding the law is demeaned by leftist politicians and the media as "partisan."

So, given the monumental scope and appalling nature of the current political landscape, it may seem overwhelming or even impossible to actually ever fix things. But while the looming task is vast and difficult, fixing it is far from impossible, if certain realities are recognized and accepted. And having the intellectual honesty and courage to face those realities has proven, over time, to be where the greatest difficulty lies.

In the beginning of this chapter, it was mentioned that the moment specific individuals are identified as RINOs, heated disputes break out *among conservatives* over the validity of the accusation. Yet as the case is laid out through the remainder of the chapter, evidence mounts as to the widespread nature of the RINO phenomenon, and the grave damage to conservatism that has resulted from it. Throughout the conservative movement, it is widely understood that such a treacherous liberal undercurrent does indeed exist within the GOP. But on a case-by-case basis, duplicitous Republican politicians are too often granted a "pass" by those who ought to be holding them accountable. Being accurately identified as a RINO should be a politically fatal blow to any aspiring politician. Otherwise, the party in its entirety will eventually sink to the lowest standard its leaders *and its base* will tolerate. Sadly, too few on our side have been willing to recognize specific individuals engaging in RINO duplicity and deal decisively with them. In this sense, it is recalcitrant conservatives at the grassroots who are the ultimate enablers of RINO treachery.

It does no good to become aware of a festering problem with one's own representatives, but to then respond with passivity or indifference, while lamenting the existence of identical problems in other districts throughout the country. RINO behavior is easily identifiable and quantifiable. And the deftness with which RINO politicians deflect criticism, or glibly justify their ongoing betrayals, is a testament to their duplicity as skilled and self-serving, but ethically bankrupt individuals. Despite their frequently eloquent claims of wishing they could do the right thing, excepting the latest set of extenuating circumstances of course, their pandering and posturing is *not* evidence of any suppressed underlying devotion to conservatism. In fact, it is precisely the opposite.

Americans who are sincere in their intentions to rebuff the leftist Alinsky onslaught that ravages our nation must begin by recognizing that this battle has been waged against America for quite some time, and on numerous fronts, most often insidiously and fraudulently. And if political and ideological ground which has been ceded over the years is ever to be reclaimed, the enemy must be identified and engaged wherever it lurks.

CHAPTER EIGHT
THE RULES, PART I

The insidious leftist/Alinsky onslaught against America has ensued on an orchestrated basis for nearly half a century, and the left certainly has some profound and disturbing accomplishments to show for its efforts. The present day boundaries of right and wrong are a grotesque and inverted caricature of what they once were, back when the streets of most American communities were safe, healthy families could be held up as role models for the next generation, and the majority of the population wasn't afraid to explain such things in rational, common sense terms.

The intent of this book so far has been to thoroughly unmask leftists, by showing who they are, how they operate, and how they camouflage the havoc they wreak by packaging it as a supposedly great "gift" to humanity. It is imperative that leftists be properly characterized as the malignancy on American society that they are, since failing to do so allows them to engage in their most strategically indispensable ploy, which is to claim to be on the supposed "moral high ground." Once they've accomplished this maneuver, they are able to completely side-step the ugly but predictable consequences of their policies, presuming to dictate who is right, who is wrong, which arguments are permissible by way of being supportive, which ones cannot be presented in opposition to them, and ultimately why any deviation from their ideology is thoroughly and unquestionably immoral.

Step one of their plan is to convince sufficient numbers of the gullible to embrace their countercultural worldview and empty promises of socialist "utopia," at least until they can gain enough of a foothold to claim something resembling "normalcy." At that point leftists go onto the offensive, seeking to completely silence their opposition through intimidation and, if possible, ideologically-driven legislation. Once such ground is taken by the left, the task of restoring decency and common sense to any former definition of truth becomes extremely difficult. Clearly, their end game is to continually shift such boundaries in their favor in order to eventually reach uncontested dominance of both the political and social landscape; a condition better known as despotism.

It is crucial that our side thoroughly understands the significance of this scenario to their success, because it represents the sum total of their efforts to persuade Americans to accept their unfounded claims of "virtue" long enough to allow them the latitude to implement their sordid agenda with minimal resistance. It also represents a critical juncture, since until they establish their position as being beyond any possible question or criticism, they are vulnerable to an informed public that is capable of seeing through their posturing and scheming, at which point their efforts collapse. However, despite the ferocity and seeming "invincibility" of the leftist onslaught, it is built on such fraudulent premises, and is so fundamentally flawed that it is inherently vulnerable, *if* our side is truly willing to take up the cause of effectively opposing it. The Alinsky strategy only works on those who allow it. Principled and unabashed opposition to it can effectively neutralize the attack in short order. But for this effort to be successful, the restoration of conservative principle must be the genuine and only acceptable goal. Otherwise, push-back from the right is perfunctory, tepid, and ultimately ineffective. Worst of all, a half-hearted resistance, followed by surrender, always serves to strengthen the standing of the enemy. Like all bullies, leftists are thoroughly energized by a weak rebuttal which they are able to quickly crush.

So despite increasing calls for violence from leftist activists, and the "deafening silence" from their enablers in official positions (think: Democrat politicians) who, were they as thoroughly drenched in the "virtues" of open mindedness and tolerance as they profess, would be loudly condemning such behavior, the leftist onslaught can still be beaten back even at this late date. An astute and principled conservative opposition can actually do so while remaining within the boundaries of public discourse, though the strenuous nature of the effort will predictably be decried as the epitome of "rancor," "incivility," and of course, "hate" by leftists who instantly cry foul in the face of any opposition. Yet if the prospect of such accusations is too heavy of a burden for our side to bear, the only alternative is surrender.

It must be clearly understood that leftists do not constitute anything approaching a majority of the American population. They must therefore disguise both their numbers and their actual agenda in order to create the impression that they represent the mindset of the American "mainstream." If they were actually in the majority, they would simply declare their true intentions and win elections on that basis, having no need to aggressively denigrate and silence their opposition. Alinsky was acutely aware of this, despite his sanctimonious claims of representing the universal hopes and dreams of humanity. He knew full well that he was motivating a *fringe* to achieve goals that far outweighed either its size, or any moral "validity" of its cause. And the inarguable proof of this is the devious and manipulative manner in which he saw fit to advance the leftist agenda, as outlined in *"Rules for Radicals."*

> Alinsky knew full well that he was motivating a *fringe* to achieve goals that far outweighed either its size, or any moral "validity" of its cause.

When boiled down to its basics, the core of the Alinsky strategy involves the few distinct elements of "picking a target, freezing it and isolating it." First, leftists coordinate a fierce and vocal attack on a specific individual who either poses an immediate threat to them, or appears particularly vulnerable. This is accomplished by framing the discourse in a manner that allows leftists to claim their phony but all important "moral high ground," and declaring the person or issue they've targeted to be in violation of the *artificial* boundaries they've so vehemently asserted. What follows is an immediate and orchestrated attack of surprising fury. By thoroughly humiliating and discrediting their target in this manner, leftists ensure that others who might have been sympathetic or allied with the targeted individual become intimidated at the prospect of being dragged into the firestorm. At this point many supposed conservatives distance themselves from the entire situation. Some even voice their agreement with the "validity" of the attacks, which is the vilest of betrayals by faux conservatives and RINOs, in that it provides an invaluable boost to the credibility of the leftist onslaught. Then, once the political isolation and destruction of the targeted individual is complete, leftists relentlessly continue their castigation and humiliation, brazenly holding their thoroughly bludgeoned "quarry" up as an example and a warning to others, threatening the prospect of a similar fate to anyone who dares to cross paths with the leftists and their agenda.

Though diabolically effective, this strategy is far from invincible. Thwarting any of its basic components will neutralize the entire attack, and may in fact cause it to backfire on its originators. Consequently, the actual methods for dealing with the Alinsky onslaught are themselves relatively simple. Since Alinsky plays off of the basest behavioral patterns of juvenile bullying, the thrust of any effort to rebut coordinated leftist attacks amounts to standing firm against such bullying. But while the principles of dealing with leftists are easily understood, remaining steadfast in them requires a vigilance and discernment to quickly recognize them, followed by an unwavering refusal to be easily distracted or unnerved by the deviousness and ferocity of leftist counterattacks. For starters, several frequently fatal leftist snares must be avoided. Only then can our side go on "offense" and successfully prevail over the leftist onslaught.

Rule No. 1: Never apologize unless an actual wrong has been committed. And then, if an apology is truly warranted, remain very specific as to the issue that is actually being addressed.

The saddest day ever to be visited upon the American political scene was when a public official first felt compelled to "apologize" for speaking the truth. From that day forward, the flagrant and provable lies of the leftist orthodoxy could take on a seemingly equal "moral standing" with truth, based simply on the vehemence with which leftists would proclaim them, and the intensity of contrived outrage and indignation they would spew toward any who dared to disagree. Hysterical leftist claims of being egregiously "wronged," with no other basis than that they are "offended," need to be dismissed as totally devoid of substance, and unworthy of even the slightest accommodation. Graciousness, when misapplied, only serves to "validate" their false accusations and pretense of having suffered unspeakable emotional wounds.

In the vast majority of cases, leftist claims of taking "offense," and subsequent demands for "apology" are not predicated on any hurt feelings, but are strictly an effort to force recantation of truths that are damaging to their fragile ideological constructs, and which leftists cannot otherwise refute. Therefore, any attempt at apologizing only bolsters their ability to dodge the facts and further advance their agenda, armed with their falsehoods which now bear unwarranted "credibility."

> Hysterical leftist claims of being egregiously "wronged,"
> with no other basis than that they are "offended,"
> need to be dismissed as totally devoid of substance.

The *worst* trap for conservatives in the face of a baseless and contrived leftist "firestorm" is to try to smooth things over by offering any manner of apology. It is appalling how often certain Republicans, who should know better, continue to fall into this snare, seeking to "end the rancor" with conciliatory rhetoric. Yet regardless of their motive, such misbegotten attempts to apologize, whether for "giving offense," or "not being sufficiently clear" when making a point, are never accepted as "conciliatory," but instead are touted as admissions of guilt. And from that point forward, any effort to get the discourse back into the realm of reality will be met with leftists reverting to those misbegotten "apologies," which they invoke as justification for their "righteous" rage against anyone who isn't totally in line with them.

This pattern is particularly counterproductive for our side, since its success only inspires grandstanding leftists to increase the intensity of their feigned indignation on every possible occasion where they can concoct even the most absurd grounds to claim "offense." And in the leftist world, *only they* have a "right" to claim to be offended. Failure to call them out on their duplicity at this point is the primary reason their ruse works. It must be firmly understood that their goal is never to find the truth or to offer real solutions to problems, but rather to exploit the latest contrived controversy as a means of solidifying their position in the eyes of the public and leveraging it for maximum political gain.

The proper response to leftists over a truth which they seek to suppress through phony indignation and hysterics is not to be intimidated or embarrassed by their theatrics, but to use the spotlight generated by their overwrought behavior as an *opportunity* to reiterate the original premise, stressing its validity and expounding on the real reasons why leftists are so venomously opposed to it. At that point, the facts begin to speak for themselves, and the true nature of the latest leftist tantrum becomes apparent, whereupon it frequently backfires, or simply vanishes into thin air once leftist politicians and their media minions realize that subsequent attention will only mean more publicity for those speaking the truth.

Conservatives should never retreat from truth. It is the single greatest weapon they have at their disposal, and accordingly it is the left's greatest "enemy." Failing to properly and honestly couch a situation or frame an argument, out of fear of leftist "outrage," is the best way to give the left an undeserved advantage with it. Recall that "Phase One" of the Alinsky strategy is for leftists to "freeze" the individual they've chosen to attack. An unabashedly truthful concurrence from conservatives at this point ensures that any continuation of leftist tantrums will result in the conservative viewpoint being given further emphasis and publicity, making it nearly impossible for leftists to accomplish this phase of their strategy, which means the likely nullification of their entire effort.

Conversely, if a principled stand is initially taken by prominent conservatives, which then results in a leftist firestorm, the *worst* possible response is to begin back pedaling from it, even in the face of imminent defeat. Doing so never appeases the opposition, but instead "validates" them, while dispiriting those who have stood on worthy principle. The likelihood that those on the right, who courageously took a stand only to be abandoned by fellow conservatives, will enter the fray in the future is diminished. In the process, accusations from the leftist opposition, no matter how ridiculous or vile, gain unwarranted credence in the eyes of those in the "middle" who are attempting to observe and learn.

This is among the chief reasons why the treachery of the RINOs, in particular, is so insidious. From the time that the Democrat Party was overtaken by leftists in the Congress and Senate, hapless Republicans responded by working to "build bridges" with them. Yet as a result of Republican willingness to accommodate such behavior, the discourse from Democrats has only shifted further left, to become more strident, more venomous, and more fraught with deceit. Meanwhile, the perception of where the political "center" should reside has also shifted significantly left. Those Republicans who are overly eager to "apologize" and otherwise appease are either underhandedly working for the opposition, or are clueless as to the real consequences of their actions. And no Republican who has reached such high office as the United

States Senate or House of Representatives has any excuse for being so gullible or naive. Yet whether it is incompetence or treachery, their behavior in such positions represents the "lifeblood" of the Alinsky onslaught. Without their cooperation, many leftist attacks would dissipate and fail, and the leftist agenda would be completely stalled on that particular front. It is no wonder that on every occasion where instead of standing fast, the GOP attempts to move beyond some political impasse by "reaching across the aisle," Americans are the ultimate losers in the deal.

It is safe to assume that leftists are *never* sincerely interested in any cause which they claim to champion. The examples are numerous. Leftist assertions of being "pro-woman" have proven to be overwhelmingly selective and situational, based not on the actual circumstances of any assault or harassment, but on the politics of the parties in question. Leftist grandstanding over the Anita Hill/Clarence Thomas debacle was always and only about preventing a staunch pro-Constitution jurist from being appointed to the Supreme Court. Charges of "sexual harassment" against Thomas were flimsy and unsubstantiated. Yet the left ranted incessantly that Thomas's confirmation was an affront to women everywhere.

Only a few years later, when the many assaults and abuses of women by Bill Clinton began to be known, leftists resorted to the most absurd and embarrassing contortions of reason, in efforts to exonerate Clinton and claim that his thoroughly established record of attacking women somehow didn't constitute "harassment." In neither situation was their concern about the actual behavior, or protecting women from harm. It was always about the agenda. Yet in many such instances, leftists are able to maintain their narrative simply because conservatives aren't sufficiently steadfast in identifying their intellectual dishonesty, and calling them out on it.

On a host of other issues, such as their supposed concern for the education of children and the plight of minorities or the state of the environment, the same shameless "moralizing" can be observed, which is always selective and therefore totally hypocritical and agenda driven. For their part, when leftists are caught in blatant lies or criminal corruption, no actual apologies are ever forthcoming. Instead, they respond with more lies and deflections, along with accusations and character assassinations against those who dared to identify them, who are frequently cited as the real root cause of the problem. Invariably, the sole purpose of such antics is to side-step the untenable hypocrisy of their position. Leftists only "apologize" in the abstract, when no real action to make amends is required, and their "moralizing" carries with it a blanket claim of superior virtue for offering such platitudes. And if they need to totally contradict themselves and recant their "remorse" in the very next sentence, or in the next ensuing debate, they will effortlessly do so.

In contrast, the slightest misstep by a conservative is treated by the left as an irredeemable crime against humanity, and a defining moment in history, followed by a broad brush condemnation of the entire conservative movement as being indelibly tainted by it. Any acquiescence to this ploy only strengthens its credibility and its effects. So in order to effectively confront such shamelessness and duplicity, conservatives need to loudly and unequivocally reject the phony leftist characterization of the situation. On the rare occasion that an actual wrong has been committed, an apology must be very diligently directed at *only* the event in question, and *never* at leftist assertions of what it ostensibly represents as an inherent flaw in conservative ideology, for example when viewed through the thoroughly warped lens of "political correctness." While substantive mistakes or erroneous information need to be rectified, this effort should never be undertaken over inconsequential details, particularly amid leftist demands, since they are only interested in using any "specks in our eyes" as leverage to presume their "moral high ground." It is as a result of just such hapless acquiescence from the right that the actual hypocrisy and duplicity of leftists will often be rendered immune to challenge.

Any reasonable sense of proportion is missing from such discourse. The moment leftists seek to magnify the scope and significance of the accused conservative "infraction" (Which is their inevitable reaction when given any opportunity to grandstand), their lies must be loudly refuted, and the duplicity of their accusations highlighted as the *real* issue at hand, and as evidence of the total fraudulence of their original bone of contention.

Rule No.2: Never engage leftist leaders and activists for the purpose of persuading them with the truth.

It is imperative to understand that the leaders and activists at the forefront of the leftist onslaught are devout *ideologues*. As ideologues, they *begin* with a conclusion which aligns with their twisted belief system, and then selectively embrace "facts" while dismissing contrary concepts, not with any intellectual honesty, but only on the basis of whether or not those "facts" support their predetermined conclusions.

Persuasion only works with those who seek truth. In many cases, leftist ringleaders are already fully aware of contravening facts, but choose to ignore them, either out of shameless opportunism, or from a belief that their ideology is so overflowing with virtue that it will somehow prevail, even in the absence of any supporting evidence. And yes, the mind-bending nature of their ideology is entirely capable of such an absurdity. Their devotion to the leftist orthodoxy is nothing short of religious fanaticism, and therefore devoid of any reason or sense. Among this kind, the presumed worthiness of "the cause" is so consuming that they have no intention of ever allowing even a momentary consideration of the possibility that other viewpoints might rightfully exist. Those in leadership are entirely given over to mindlessly advancing their orthodoxy. Meanwhile, their most zealous minions are themselves in various stages of descent to this same state. Consequently, they will never discuss their dogmatic stances for *any* purpose other than to persuade, or at least confuse their conservative opponents. And when that effort fails, the singular focus from that point forward is to silence any contravening viewpoint.

So when such leftists claim that "we must have a conversation," or that we should work to "find common ground" with them, what they are really demanding is our unilateral ideological surrender. Since conservatism is advanced by honestly assessing information and determining the truth, some on the right naively believe that by merely articulating the facts and realities of conservatism with sufficient power and eloquence, leftist activists will eventually "see the light" and forswear their ways. Among the leftist ideologues, this is rarely the case. In actuality, many of them are already fully aware that they are promoting their agenda under a banner of lies. Their goal has never been to deal in facts or reality, but to stoke the egos of a sufficient number of their minions with the supposed "worthiness" and "virtue" of their cause to incite them to blindly follow. The obedient loyalty of these underlings is compounded by an instilled "need" to remain in good standing with the leftist "herd" by accepting and professing leftist dogma with the zeal of the "faithful." It is in this manner that leftist minions are conditioned to studiously ignore the ugly truths and dire consequences of their twisted ideology, while deeming themselves to be the most "virtuous" of people for doing so.

It is important to understand that leftists have gotten to where they are, not due to any lack of truth or facts, but as a result of their corporate and willful *rejection* of facts, which is reflected in their obsessive efforts to suppress facts and truth among others who disagree with them. So instead of leftist leaders wasting time attempting to persuade informed and *engaged* conservatives of the supposed worthiness of their cause (since both they and their conservative opponents know they are lying), their efforts are directed at buying off a sufficient portion of the populace which they regard as the gullible and disengaged "center" with platitudes and empty promises, delivered with enough flagrancy and force that many will reflexively accept the "virtue" they claim to embody. Seeking to convince such leftists, particularly those in leadership, of the errant nature of their ways, by offering them real world evidence, is an exercise in futility.

It is important to understand that leftists have gotten to where they are, not due to any lack of truth or facts refuting them, but as a result of their corporate and willful *rejection* of facts.

It must be thoroughly understood that when leftists attempt to debate the issues by demanding facts and specifics, they don't really want information. Their sole purpose is to make a case that their conservative opposition doesn't really have facts to back up its stance. That's why it's a total waste of time and energy to do the research to find them the pertinent information. They'll always concoct some grounds on which to dismiss it and reiterate their original premise. And while conservatives too often waste precious time and energy in this effort, leftists are busily mopping up many in the "middle" with their phony moralizing and shameless sanctimony. Our side is dangerously naive to believe "bridges" can be built with the left in this manner. Such efforts only further enable the left.

Our case must be structured *not* to convince leftists, but to be presented to the population at large, spotlighting the ugly reality of the leftist agenda and its consistently disastrous results when applicable. Instead of spending time and resources to convince leftists who are determined to reject the truth under *any* premise, the energy needs to be devoted to identifying both the nature of leftists in the current era, as well as their long and abysmal track record of failed past policies, and the damage they've done to society in every area of life and in every region of the country where they were ever able to gain a foot-hold. This case must then be vigorously presented to those Americans who aren't necessarily involved in political activism, but who have become increasingly aware that our nation faces some dire problems that need to be addressed. Many among this group have remained disengaged and therefore casually assume that some manner of moral and intellectual "equivalency" exists between the two camps. However, once the ugly realities of the leftist agenda are unmasked, leftist players become virtually "hamstrung" in their attempts to persuade anything approaching a majority of the people to embrace their twisted worldview or support their proposed "solutions."

By focusing on the stark contrasts between the leftist agenda and the realities of conservatism, and by unabashedly presenting the grim and inevitable consequences of leftist policies to the Americans on "Main Street" who fight the wars, plant the crops, build the factories and produce the goods that make the country thrive, conservatives can drive leftists back into a totally defensive position from which it is difficult for them to advance. But the effort must be to take this message to those Americans who desire to know the truth, and not to attempt to repackage it in any manner that might seem more palatable to leftists who have no intention of ever embracing truth.

If we gear our words and actions towards getting a "good" response from the left, we will always lose. If we measure our success or the worthiness of our message by gaining their approval, we will always lose. The goal must not be to gain appreciation or affection from the avowed enemies of everything we hold dear, but rather to present the undiluted truth to the American people who deserve to know it. Doing so will reach the worthwhile ones among them, and that is the real definition of victory.

Rule No.3: Never allow leftists to move past their hypocrisy and lies.

In misbegotten attempts to engage in "meaningful discourse," conservatives frequently allow leftist lies and hypocrisy to go unchallenged or, after briefly mentioning them, an effort is made to move the discourse forward by shifting to topics and issues which are wrongly presumed to be more relevant and substantive. This behavior pattern results from a futile belief in the supposed benefits of reaching "common ground" with leftists on a particular matter, along with the hapless desire to not be mired down in trading accusations or quibbling over seemingly inconsequential "details," but to return instead to the "important" issues at hand. However, any phony leftist premise that goes unchallenged, and fails to be brought completely back to reality, will be deemed "valid" and presented as such from that point forward, which means the discourse is hopelessly slanted in its direction. Failing to confront the intellectual dishonesty of the left, for fear of the predictable backlash, is tantamount to ceding the issue in its entirety. Leftists bank on this likelihood.

Like every science-fiction or fantasy movie, a seemingly plausible plot can be developed from sheer nonsense, once a bogus premise is tacitly accepted. For example, leftists have enjoyed enormous success implementing their statist agenda, because they shamelessly characterize their intentions as being pro-family, and ultimately "for the children." However, every sanctimonious contention from the leftist counterculture that it professes any concern whatsoever for the well-being of children can and *should* be immediately stopped in its tracks with two words: "*Planned Parenthood.*" Leftists cannot credibly "care" about the plight of children, while enabling their wanton slaughter, by the millions, in America's abortion mills. So no further discourse with them should ever be undertaken that doesn't call them out on their abject hypocrisy regarding their supposed concern for "the children." And if pursued with sufficient focus and intensity, this retort can instead beg the question of just what their real intentions are when advocating anything else ostensibly in the interests of "the children." Responding to them in this manner can devastate the credibility of any of their agenda items that exploit the plight of children for their own political gain. Of course, doing so will inevitably generate raucous protests and hysterical indignation, with none of it carrying any weight beyond that which our side is willing to accept. Yet in the process, the onlooking general public has an opportunity to see just how transparent and disingenuous leftist compassion for "the children," or anyone else, really is.

On a host of other issues, the same glaring hypocrisy is readily apparent. When leftist climate alarmists seek to curtail the use of fossil fuels by the common people, under the guise of "saving the planet," while they fly around the country in private jets, stay at lavish hotels, and live in opulent estates, they make it abundantly clear that they have no concern for the "carbon footprint" created by humanity. Otherwise they wouldn't be so wasteful and self-indulgent as they maximize their own carbon footprints, with zero concern for the supposed negative impact on the planet.

So, instead of those on the right taking the bait, accepting their bogus premise, and trying to get on the bandwagon by insisting that we too care about the latest contrived "crisis," the proper response is to continually re-affix any discourse back onto what their real intention must be, since it is clearly not what they claim that it is.

> Like every science-fiction or fantasy movie, a seemingly plausible plot can be developed from sheer nonsense, once a bogus premise is tacitly accepted.

Over the years, the left has, by force and persistence, succeeded in creating an alternative universe from where it issues its moral edicts. Somehow, it accomplishes this in the face of a glaring reality that

RULES FOR *DEFEATING* RADICALS

contradicts its every premise. Yet on the basis of its sheer arrogance and willingness to shamelessly attack all who disagree, the left has reached a point where it can contend, with virtually no opposition, that any attempt to properly ensure the identity of voters is "racism." Muslim men who show up in hordes demanding asylum while attacking our nation's institutions and traditions are "refugees," and foreigners who cross the border illegally are "undocumented Americans" and "dreamers," ostensibly here for the betterment of the country. Meanwhile, American citizens who desire honesty and accountability at the ballot box, or who have been displaced from their homeland and their jobs and had to face organized (and sometimes violent) demonstrations of intimidation and pressure to acquiesce to foreigners and their customs, are accused of "hate," and derided as "nativists."

Despite being thoroughly warped and absurd, the moment such premises are sidestepped, they are presumed to be reality, and any subsequent effort to engage the left, with hopes of arriving at the truth, become hopelessly crippled. The misbegotten desires to get back "on topic" (defined as what leftists wish to discuss) and pursue "common ground" are total futility. The best means of avoiding such an unnecessary impasse is to recognize that whenever leftists seek to invoke lies and fraud in order to prevail in the debate of any issue, those lies and fraud become *the issue* that needs to be confronted. The willingness of leftists to engage in such behavior and brush past glaring inconsistencies proves that from the start, congenial and intellectually honest discourse was never their intent. However, if their moral and ethical inconsistencies are allowed to stand, leftists quickly assume the role of "judge, jury, and executioner," according to standards they arbitrarily set. Our failure to dismiss their edicts as hypocrisy gives them a seeming mantle of legitimacy.

Nor should *any* ground be ceded to them simply because they respond with overblown indignation and revert to mocking the conservative premise. Mockery is a fundamental precept of the Alinsky strategy, so it is fully to be expected. Leftists have gotten so adept at it, and our side has over time become so reflexively defensive in the face of it, that leftists are frequently able to totally bury an inarguable truth, just by loudly and shamelessly mocking anyone who dares mention it. And all too often, our side responds by dutifully abandoning the issue.

However, if we instead stand firm with an unshakable confidence in the truth and refuse to be moved from it even though the volume and shrillness of their derision and feigned hysteria doubles, their efforts to evade truth are effectively neutralized. Furthermore, it should be noted that if leftists can ever refute a point of debate with facts, they most certainly will do so. In light of this, their reversion to mockery proves that they have no factual standing, and their premise should be treated as such. But here again, it is imperative to recognize that they will concede *nothing* at this juncture. Attempting to bring them to an admission of the truth is invariably an exercise in futility. The goal must instead be to spotlight the emptiness of their arguments and the wholesale dishonesty of their tactics and antics in a manner that thoroughly clarifies things for those people on "Main Street" whose support or opposition will hold ultimate sway in advancing or thwarting the leftist agenda.

Whether leftists prevail over conservatives by dragging them into phony collegiality that hamstrings them, or by demeaning them with venomous attacks (A tactic to which they'll instantly revert when expedient, despite it being the diametric opposite of the "collegiality" they initially profess), the end game is the same. The triumph of the leftist agenda was their singular goal from the start, and on that basis, any means of getting there is worthwhile and "virtuous" in their twisted world. Consequently, their duplicity in this effort must be made fully known. Once leftist posturing for political leverage is properly and unequivocally identified, it is drastically weakened, and on the way to being neutralized.

Rule No.4: Never accept baseless leftist assertions of "cause and effect," which are vehemently proclaimed as inarguable truth, but are only enabling propaganda.

In their incessant political grandstanding, and in subsequent "news" accounts given by their media minions, leftists will spew bold but *baseless* assertions, thereafter treated as facts which are ostensibly substantiated beyond question. "If funding is cut, children will starve." "Old people will die as a result of this legislation." "This move is an assault on the rights of women." "*Millions* will lose their healthcare if..." And the list goes on in seeming perpetuity. As with the rest of their lies and duplicity, the baseless nature of these fabrications needs to be spotlighted, and their "credence" immediately refuted. And on every ensuing occasion in which leftists reassert such disinformation, it must be tirelessly and consistently identified as the fraud and lies that it is. Granting them any degree of "credibility" (think: finding common ground) only serves to elevate the leftists to their vaunted perch on that all important "moral high ground." Once they worm their way into that position, every subsequent attempt to return to a sane and honest discussion will be deemed as a callous disregard for those they assert as victims of conservative initiatives.

Instead, the focus needs to be diligently brought back to the hideous realities of life in any region where leftist policies actually dominate. Without exception, the plight of common people in such locales is a sufficient testament to why the leftist agenda must be strenuously opposed. It is absolutely imperative to link prominent leftist political figures with the disasters that result from their policies. So much of the leftist strategy amounts to issuing proclamations of imminent utopia once they achieve uncontested dominance, while dodging any consideration of the grim consequences of leftist policies that are actually in place and bearing their evil "fruit."

CHAPTER EIGHT ~ THE RULES, PART I

It is no mystery that leftists abhor being labeled as leftists, but invariably attempt to adopt some other title for their ideology, at least until the latest "banner" under which they travel is thoroughly discredited by the effects of their policies. In truth they have not changed from what they were, back when the term "Marxists" was the norm. Over the years, they've demanded to be called liberals and, once that moniker was too readily associated with the usual disasters associated with the left, they opted for the less threatening term of "progressives." Here again, their neurotic dislike for the term "leftists" is proof of their fear of being associated with all of the inevitable repercussions of leftist policy, and is precisely why they need to be indelibly labeled as leftists, the moment they reveal that their ideology is such. And their track record of failed policies must be just as diligently attached to their ideology and their agenda, rather than allowing them to frame the issue of the day on their terms.

In "healthcare" for example, leftist caterwauling of the supposed millions who would suddenly keel over in the streets, the moment a dime is rescinded from the money pit of Obamacare, is a total deflection from the millions who *actually lost* worthwhile health coverage, or whose coverage suddenly became far more expensive, once the nightmare of Obamacare descended on America. For Republicans in the Congress and Senate to ever be on the "defensive" over the empty promises of Obamacare, and the bureaucratic monstrosity that it entailed, was a huge ideological victory for the left, and thus a disaster for the American people, whose hopes of being extricated from the Obamacare morass were essentially ignored and abandoned by the political class, which includes both parties.

The same principles hold true in regard to the "Global Warming" scam, border security, and a host of other issues on which leftists grandstand and incite panic with apocalyptic warnings that have no basis in reality. In every case, their alarmist assertions must be tied to the policies they actually intend to implement in response. As always, those policies involve seizing private property and exerting dictatorial control over the common citizen. Sadly, our side typically responds by retreating to a defensive posture, and attempting to prove our benevolence and heartfelt desire not to be guilty of baseless accusations made against us, instead of highlighting the contempt for reason, the unbridled duplicity, and the shameless manipulations which those accusations represent.

Rule No. 5: Never reflexively accept leftist definitions of good and evil.

Per the discussion of "moral certitude" in Chapter 6, leftists are always ready to jump to the front of the line, as if they have an unassailable power to define the boundaries of right and wrong, ethical and unethical, civil and uncivil, that which is beneficial or detrimental to society, and every other standard of morality. This is of course a neat trick for people who, when expedient, will contend that morality itself does not exist. And even as they issue their edicts, it must be understood that such "standards" are completely flexible, and can be counted upon to suddenly morph in a totally contradictory manner as ensuing situations warrant. Last week's lies were only intended to "win" last week's debate. All previous proclamations of what ostensibly constitutes "virtue" in the minds of leftists are instantly ignored and discarded, the moment it becomes expedient to violate them in the midst of the latest leftist onslaught.

Therefore, whenever leftists try to claim moral supremacy, they need to immediately be called out on the behavior which reflects their innate hypocrisy. At that point, *all* of their sanctimony must be dismissed. Their only purpose in such phony moralizing is to hamstring our side from standing against their agenda and the real harm to society which it represents. And despite how seemingly eloquent they are as they extol and glorify themselves for their supposed "virtue," it should never be acknowledged as anything more than empty political posturing by the minions of an ideology that is totally devoid of actual virtue.

Never accept any leftist premise of where the "threshold" of moral outrage should be set. The only purpose of this stunt is to advance their agenda, and if possible, to cause some on our side to turn on our own people, by accepting any precept of their case, and proclaiming that they "have a point." Their real intention and end game in these situations must be recognized, which is invariably to concoct their phony "moral high ground" on such a basis that they and their ideology are its undisputed occupants, and that any deviation from their agenda must therefore constitute the gravest of sins against nature and humanity. On such bogus premises, they grant themselves "license" to engage in any behavior, no matter how deceitful, vicious or depraved, in order to prevail. From lies to personal attacks and degradation, and even to the point of advocating violence, their venom is totally "justified" since it enables them to pursue the "greater good" as they define it.

Historically, this predictable strategy required them to overcome an enormous hurdle. For leftists to be able to proclaim the countercultural rot of their agenda as "good," they first needed to eradicate the time-honored norms of a healthy society that had previously defined such ideals. Their onslaught against the American culture over the past several decades was perpetrated with just such intentions. Much of it has been based on the tenuous notion that since an exact boundary cannot always be determined between what was asserted to be "right," and what had been deemed "wrong," no such boundary existed. Leftists have successfully invoked such ambiguity (often totally hypothetical) as an effective negation of clear cut principle

Wherever leftists were allowed to establish this "toehold" of contrived ambiguity on any issue, it was only a matter of time before they were invoking it as a "precedent" to attack every related moral precept on which a healthy and functioning society had been based, supplanting well established principles of a decent and functioning society with new and perverse "norms" of their own, which they thereafter profess with blunt certainty. Consequently, something as innocuous as a Nativity Scene in the public square will inevitably be attacked by the leftist "American Civil Liberties Union" (ACLU) on the premise that it is a violation of the First Amendment, and therefore a threat to our Constitution and America. Meanwhile, under the guise of artistic expression, the leftist counterculture creates the most vile and sacrilegious *anti-Christian* exhibits. Not only are these insults to common decency prominently displayed on public property and extolled as an expression of "free speech," they are frequently financed with taxpayer dollars. Meanwhile, let anyone even suggest a similar affront to the Koran or the tenets of any religion *other than Christianity*, and the entire cadre of leftists instantly run for the nearest microphone, competing with each other to vehemently and "righteously" denounce the effort as "un-American."

Predictably, leftists issue their moral edicts with an unrestrained air of authority. And this is most apparent in the manner that they instantly and exuberantly latch on to every major cataclysm which they believe they can spin into winning propaganda. Any mass shooting, alleged "hate crime," or other emotionally charged tragedy, in which even the flimsiest or most oblique element of bias or bigotry against a chosen leftist special interest group can be insinuated, is guaranteed to make the evening news from coast to coast. The story will be incessantly repeated until leftists believe they have extracted every last drop of sympathy, anti-conservative anger, or any other political capital from it. To the degree that leftists seek to put uninvolved conservatives on the defensive at such times (which is inevitable), they maliciously and heartlessly exploit real calamity and tragedy suffered by others for purely political gain. To the degree that our side goes on the defensive and becomes apologetic, conciliatory, or otherwise tries to posture its way out of the leftist firestorm rather than boldly and directly confronting it, we tacitly accept their twisted premises and thus further empower their shameless propaganda.

Passivity in any form is a losing proposition. A response that is defensive in any respect suggests an acceptance of "guilt." Failing to boldly call out the left for its insincerity will give it an unwarranted appearance of being on that phony but fervently sought "moral high ground." Leftists are in a far better position to attach false motivations to our side on any given issue, the moment we fail to properly identify their real motivations for concocting their phony "morality." At this point, many casual observers in the disengaged "middle" are more likely to presume that leftist talking points are statements of fact.

Leftists carry this ploy to an extreme, persuading the public of an overall mindset among conservatives based on nothing but their own prejudices. Eventually, they impute underlying "motivations" on the thinking of conservatives with seemingly absolute certainty. And of course, such thinking is presumed to take place on the most blindly irrational and *immoral* basis. Recall Barack Obama's denigration of mainstream Americans at a Democrat Party fundraiser in April of 2008:

"You go into these small towns in Pennsylvania and, like a lot of small towns in the Midwest, the jobs have been gone now for 25 years and nothing's replaced them. And they fell through the Clinton administration, and the Bush administration, and each successive administration has said that somehow these communities are gonna regenerate and they have not.

And it's not surprising that they get bitter, they cling to guns or religion or antipathy toward people who aren't like them or anti-immigrant sentiment or anti-trade sentiment as a way to explain their frustrations."

Outrage over Obama's statement was immediate and justified. It quickly became known as his "Bitter clingers" comment, and has been recalled ever since to highlight Obama's aversion to Americans from the Heartland who own guns, read the Bible, and don't want to see their communities and their nation fall into ruin. But another major component of his detestable statement was not so immediately recognized, yet needs to be addressed, just like all similar efforts to advance an indefensible political premise. Callously brushing aside all of the problems Americans have actually suffered as a result of open borders, Obama flatly asserts that Americans only oppose the situation because of a disdain for "immigrants" who "aren't like them." Given Obama's fixation on race, and his incessant efforts to stir up racial discord at every opportunity, it isn't hard to know exactly what he was implying. In Obama's world, opposition to open borders has nothing to do with lost jobs, the spread of gang violence, overcrowded schools, overburdened welfare rolls, or anything else. It's *all* a matter of American bigotry. Ignore the real issues or the need to actually address them. Replace them with an inflammatory accusation, issued in a thoroughly "matter of fact" manner. It will be tacitly accepted by a major portion of those who hear it. And while Obama is among the most brazen of such manipulators, he certainly is not alone.

With Pavlovian predictability, any conservative efforts to cut bloated government and reduce its cost to those who pay for it are instantly attacked by Democrats as "mean spirited." It is common sense to allow hard working citizens to keep more of the money they've honorably earned, and to limit the threat of encroachment posed by an unfettered state. Doing so should be universally recognized as the justice that citizens deserve in a free society. Instead, attempts to cut the size and burden of government are deliberately mischaracterized as being "mean spirited" on the grounds that the loss of revenue to government may restrict its "benevolence." In truth, the concern is that doing so would limit its ability to maintain the blind loyalty of the dependent class which it cultivates *and controls* with targeted handouts.

It is essential to immediately identify and confront all such baseless leftist presumptions. The proper response is to diligently reset the discourse by unabashedly refuting the leftist lies, and reasserting the real boundaries of good and evil in every situation. It is imperative that conservatives recognize when the phony leftist "moral high ground" is *phony*, and steadfastly refuse to give it *even the slightest* presumption of credibility after that. As often as leftists assert any contrived moral "edict" as inarguable truth, it needs to be flatly rebutted and properly presented as the perverse and politically motivated sanctimony which it is. At that point, the real nature and intent of leftist attacks becomes glaringly evident, which is to deflect from the actual issues by refocusing on bogus premises in order to demean and destroy their opposition by putting them on the defensive. Undiluted truth in the face of this underhanded scheming makes leftist posturing much more difficult to defend.

Finally, it should be recalled again how the mockery and blanket condemnation of ideological enemies is such an indispensable component of the Alinsky strategy. But leftists can only define what "deserves" to be mocked and condemned if they are first given the latitude to decide what needs to be applauded and extolled. Refusing to accept unsubstantiated leftist tenets of either can quickly and thoroughly dissipate the momentum of a leftist onslaught. And this is true, no matter how vehemently such things are declared, or how viciously leftists attack those who dare to reject their orthodoxy.

CHAPTER NINE
THE RULES, PART II

The realities of proactive conservatism may seem anti-climactic, especially in consideration of the intensity and ugliness of the leftist onslaught. But this aspect of America's current situation should hardly be deemed as discouraging. Rather, it suggests precisely the opposite. It is an indicator of just how winnable the battle against the leftists really is. Once the pitfalls of the Alinsky strategy are successfully navigated, as outlined in the previous chapter, the advancement of conservatism need not be an overwhelming task. Rather, a succinct presentation of the truth in its undiluted reality represents the most devastatingly effective weapon against the elaborate but inherently fragile facade of leftist lies.

When conservatives are able to recognize the particular pitfalls the left has created and exploited, they can easily be avoided, leaving the leftists to squall to their own, with the limited effect of any "preaching to the choir." Those on the right can then proceed to promote truth and restore reality to the political discourse among the mainstream of society in spite of leftist hysterics which, when properly framed, can then be dismissed as totally lacking in legitimacy. Eventually, they are relegated to the status of background noise.

Currently however, conservatives are suffering from something akin to "battered wife syndrome," where over time they have been conditioned to tacitly accept absurd and morally abhorrent leftist accusations, under the misbegotten premise that voicing any opposition will be instantly branded as heretical, and those deemed "guilty" of such will be the targets of fearsome and merciless attacks. Again, this does not represent any inherent "strength" of the leftists, but instead reflects their overriding vulnerability. The seeming "ferocity" with which they voice their opposition is more akin to fear and hysteria, as they face the prospect that their ideological strongholds are fatally flawed and indefensible in the face of concerted opposition.

It is thus imperative that conservatives recognize the ultimate strength of their ideology, which is its foundation in truth. The intent is neither to hide the goals of conservatism, nor to deflect attention from any of its real ramifications, as leftists are forced to do with theirs. And the best manner by which to keep the conservative message on course is to declare it, boldly and unabashedly, accepting none of the phony leftist accusations against it. This approach gives conservatives the greatest opportunity to deliver their message to the public despite the opposition of leftist politicians and their media lackeys. It also puts conservatives in the best position to properly rebuff leftist efforts to "muddy the waters" by personally attacking them and skewing the message.

Rule No. 6: *Power that is not asserted when necessary and appropriate is forfeited. Eventually it is lost forever.*

Any honest assessment of the current political discourse reveals an absurdly slanted playing field. For far too long, leftists have enjoyed a wholly unwarranted advantage in the social and political discourse, and consequently in the eventual outcome of political battles being fought in front of the public, merely on account of the vehemence of their baseless assertions that certain things cannot be said or done in opposition to them. Compliance with their edicts under any premise (usually as part of some misbegotten effort to "end the rancor" or "move forward together") only serves to solidify their hold on their phony "moral high ground" and allows them to further define the boundaries of the contest in purely self serving terms. As a result, they win.

By continuing to operate within such dangerously skewed boundaries, leftists and their policies are allowed to enjoy far too much of a "good reputation" overall, specifically because they often go unchallenged. Our side is far too easily silenced by vehement leftist assertions that we are not permitted to stand in opposition to their latest onslaught, or even to voice any doubt or criticism of it. Often, conservatives are put on defensive by an unexpectedly shrill and venomous attack over the ostensibly evil nature of our opposing stance, which frequently makes too many on "our side" feel compelled to move on to the next issue, naively presuming that it might be fielded on ground that is more politically "safe." Then, predictably, those who have allowed themselves to be manipulated in this manner find to their surprise that they are once again being accused of "callousness" against the downtrodden group at the center of the next issue, and every issue thereafter. Over time, the constant barrage of baseless and vile accusations, when not rebutted as such, begins to stick.

> Our side is far too easily silenced by vehement leftist assertions that we are not permitted to stand in opposition to their latest onslaught, or even to voice any doubt or criticism of it.

Meanwhile, leftists are rarely held to account for the manner in which they actually spew hate and venom, violate the law, trample the Constitution, or any of the other resulting disasters they've actually inflicted on innocent people in that manner. Instead, by virtue of their truly cold-blooded and shameless opportunism, coupled with the hesitance of conservatives to bluntly call them out for the actual pain and suffering they cause, it is increasingly easy for leftists to present themselves as worthy benefactors of humanity.

During the years of the Clinton presidency, the constant barrage of new revelations of rampant and flagrantly criminal corruption in the Clinton White House, with little or nothing being done in response to them, gave rise to the term "scandal fatigue." This descriptor was used mostly by conservatives to suggest emotional overload as the reason the

Clintons never seemed to suffer any political fallout from their abhorrent behavior. It was widely presumed, and often repeated by several prominent figures on the right that the individual instances of Clinton malfeasance were so numerous and incessant that it was simply impossible for the average person to absorb all of it or stay sufficiently focused on any single episode, and therefore most people simply tuned it all out. Yet this was hardly the case.

The scope of Clinton corruption, before and since, has been truly appalling, from the numerous actual assaults and abuses of innocent and vulnerable women by Bill, to the manner in which Hillary scammed and manipulated the system for personal gain and to ensure that she and Bill escaped justice. Recounting this vast litany, it becomes clear that the Clintons strategically leveraged their sheer audacity to the point of "weaponizing" it, portraying themselves and their crimes as "too big to be held accountable," and daring those whose responsibility it was to bring them to justice to actually follow through. The Clintons gambled on the overriding cowardice of those individuals as the reason justice would never be served. Sadly, on so many occasions throughout their corruption riddled public lives, this has proven to be a safe bet. The consequence of this pattern was that the criminal activity in which they engaged has permeated every organization with any responsibility of legal oversight. From that point forward, those organizations have been paralyzed from fulfilling their actual intended purpose, thereafter rendering them as equally corrupt enablers, not only of Clinton crimes, but those of other unscrupulous Democrats as well. That pattern continues to this day.

Certainly, the frequency and brazenness of the Clinton scandals was fully intentional, and part of a strategy to overwhelm their political opposition. But it was not merely the sheer number and depth of Clinton corruption that achieved this tactical advantage. More significantly, it was the lack of any real effort to deal with the Clinton scandals. And that includes the sham "impeachment" effort, which the House diligently conducted, but the Senate deliberately undermined and eventually abandoned without ever actually examining the evidence, despite Republicans being in a majority there.

It is not that conservatives on "Main Street" simply grow weary of ever more accusations of corrupt and scandalous behavior, eventually becoming disinterested. Rather it is that conservatives become frustrated over the fact that for one reason or another, *nothing* of substance ever happens in response. The moment real justice seems imminent for the guilty parties, conservatives become energized and engaged. Unfortunately, in virtually every instance to date, the predictable faces among the GOP "establishment" suddenly start backing away from taking any real action, and instead offer yet more of their empty platitudes, along with a good deal of shameless back-slapping for having "stood on principle," blah blah. Unrequited anger cannot be maintained in the face of such indefensible inaction. In the end, the rage that would have been directed at those on the left, whose behavior warranted it, is instead redirected at the usual cadre of RINOs, who invariably are more concerned with finding ways to run and hide from their responsibilities than they are with actually upholding justice and the rule of law.

The corrupt and malignant means by which leftists in public office have kept themselves in power and continued to implement their agenda could never fly with the American people, were those individuals diligently and thoroughly characterized as who they truly are, and their standard operating procedure exposed in all of its sheer ugliness. More recently, Obama FBI director James Comey could *never* have covered for the flagrant crimes of Hillary Clinton with the transparent excuse that he couldn't find any "intent" to commit them, had our side not allowed so many ostensibly "benevolent" liberal institutions including the "Clinton Foundation" to remain free of oversight. Had the "Clinton Foundation" been diligently spotlighted as the nefarious scheme that it was, with

Hillary's criminal *intentions* properly characterized and regularly proclaimed to the public with absolute assurance, her facade of innocence would have much more quickly been rendered laughable, and thereafter impossible to project in any manner. Likewise, Comey would not have dared to appear in front of the cameras oozing bias from every pore of his body, while holding such an obvious smoking gun.

In like manner, Democrats can only get away with their incessant calls to impeach President Trump because they have been granted the authority to make such proclamations by the hapless *Republicans* who ran both the House and Senate since 2014. The moment former House Speaker John Boehner (R.-OH) and Senate Majority Leader Mitch McConnell (R.-KY) went into full retreat, at the mere suggestion that "racism" might be their motivation for any opposition to Obama's unconstitutional abuses of power, they essentially proclaimed that during Obama's tenure, he would be immune from any threat of impeachment. In so doing, they abdicated the constitutional authority of the Congress to hold corrupt office-holders accountable. In that sense, they were *as guilty* of trashing and abandoning our nation's founding charter as was Obama in his regular abuses and over-reaches of power. And once that ground had been surrendered by the Republicans, the Democrats were quick to move in and seize it for themselves, and to incessantly wield it as a purely political bludgeon ever since.

Had Boehner and McConnell instead done the *right thing*, which is simply to uphold the Constitution and the rule of law, they would have reaffirmed impeachment as a matter of justice and a guarantor of governmental integrity, not of politics. However, their response to the situation was itself purely *political*, with the Constitution and the good of the nation relegated to a back burner. And in the process, the door was opened for the Democrats to seize the upper hand, thus ensuring a continuation of their corrupt "business as usual."

Rule No.7: When leftists rally around one of their own who has been exposed for engaging in reprehensible or corrupt behavior, all who support the individual need to be identified as being equally corrupt, and thereafter diligently tagged as such.

Leftists have become extremely adept with their selective "moralizing," by taking often obscure events among conservatives, blowing the significance of those events vastly out of proportion, and thereafter claiming them to be indicative of conservatism in general. This "broad brush" approach to characterizing conservatism in the most vile of terms has become thoroughly predictable in this age of unfettered leftist media bias. Every mass shooting is followed by immediate suggestions that the perpetrator must have been a conservative, who was surely motivated by every hateful and nefarious precept of the conservative philosophy, or by embracing some statement from a prominent conservative that may bear no real relation to the incident in question, but which can be construed (with media "guidance") to reflect a similar mindset. Of course, the actual perpetrators of such atrocities have most often either been avowed leftists, or mentally unstable and totally devoid of any discernible political alignment. Real conservatives simply don't engage in such behavior. Nevertheless, the malicious effort to link insane or murderous individuals with those on the right is pervasive among shameless leftist politicians and their media minions.

Consequently, every alleged crime ostensibly committed by a conservative, or even something so inconsequential as a careless misstatement by any prominent conservative, is immediately plastered across every leftist media venue as if it constitutes an unpardonable sin that will forever stain conservatism in its totality. From that point forward, leftists demand that every member of the conservative movement either publicly recant, or ever after be grouped in with the accused. But it is a grave mistake to accept the premise that the latest episode of leftist outrage is legitimate and sincere in any respect, or that conservatives should make any effort to agree with such premises, which amounts to genuflecting at their altar. In so doing, leftists are further solidified as being in a place to define which sins are "real," and which ones are trivial. Regardless of any specifics of the situation, such determinations are of course always made in favor of the leftist orthodoxy.

Since leftists recognize the absolute importance of maintaining their phony perch on that "moral high ground," when real and provable episodes of lies, bigotry, corruption, and other abuses committed by leftist icons become widely known, the response is always to rally around the perpetrator, and contrive any means, no matter how ridiculous or obtuse, to completely exonerate them. Even in the cases of the insane leftist terrorist Ted Kaczynski, (the so-called "Unabomber") or the hard-left and pathologically bigoted "Reverend" Jeremiah Wright, leftists never rendered any blanket condemnation, but offered only tepid and conditional "criticism" of each, always accompanied by some explanation of why their hateful sentiments and behavior contained a element of supposed legitimacy.

As with all leftist hypocrisy, this ploy has enjoyed success because historically, our side tacitly allows it by dutifully accepting leftist assertions of the supposed need to "move on." Not only should the reprehensible behavior be made "front and center" in every future discourse of related matters, but the actual character of every leftist who sought to trivialize or dismiss the action should ever after be recognized as defining them as well, based on their support for the perpetrator. All those who stood with Bill Clinton, in the face of his many abuses of power and the appalling denigration of his office, both in his role as president and in his "private life," proved themselves to be his willing enablers, and therefore just as morally reprehensible.

The same can be said of officials and spokesmen who maintain loyalty to any corrupt politician, of which there are many. The goal here is not to get them to admit their errors, which they will never do with actual genuineness. Rather, it is to focus public attention on their unwillingness to *substantively* address the wrongs that have actually been committed. Consequently, any leftist grandstanding on related matters is provably lacking in sincerity. From that point forward, none of them should have any claim of "credibility" as paragons of justice or decency.

Over the past several decades, the left has indeed established a track record of every dubious character trait from underhanded and disingenuous issue advocacy (Think: Alinsky), to intimidation and violence, to the absolute fraud by which previous leftist policy disasters are excused or denied. It should be apparent that the rampant corruption in their ranks is ultimately a reflection of the thoroughly corrupt nature of their ideology. And this is why one of the most important strategic moves is to quantify why leftists involved in scandal and corruption enjoy the support of the entire leftist apparatus. Whenever the American people can be reminded of this, it puts the left totally on the defensive.

Rule No.8: Identify friend and foe. Once a determination is legitimately made that a political player is doing the bidding of the enemy, do not allow it to be altered on the basis of emotion or polished subsequent politicking and pandering.

Anyone with even a cursory knowledge of military strategy understands the significance of the "element of surprise" on the battlefield. From the time of Sun Tzu, it has been well established that the enemy which is not properly recognized *as an enemy* enjoys an enormous advantage as long as its cover can be preserved.

Yet although this same principle directly applies in the political realm, it too often goes completely ignored which is a particularly outrageous oversight, since maintaining a "friendly" facade is specifically the method of those who seek to advance their political aspirations under fraudulent premises. And it need not be explained here which political camp operates in that manner.

> From the time of Sun Tzu, it has been well established that the enemy which is not properly recognized as an enemy enjoys an enormous advantage as long its cover can be preserved.

However, this is not meant to suggest that such fraud and deceit exist on a partisan basis, confined solely to the Democrat Party. Indeed, it is too often among liberal *Republicans* that this particular form of treachery and duplicity wields its greatest destructive power against the conservative movement (See Chapter 6 *"RINOs: The Essential Alinsky Fifth Column"*). It must be understood that those in the political realm who don't fight to win, *don't want to win*. In the same sense, those who claim a desire to find "common ground" with leftists in face of irreconcilable differences *are leftists*. Focusing more specifically here on the inner workings of the Republican Party, it is necessary to take this principle even a step further. Those who seek party unity by asserting the importance of "common ground" with RINOs *are RINOs*.

Recognizing the predictable nature of their duplicity, and thus correctly anticipating their betrayals is essential to dealing effectively with them. This requires both the attainment of wisdom that supersedes standard "establishment" mantras, as well as the courage and resolve to confront their deceit in the face of even more lies and criticism, which they will instantly wield towards anyone who dares question their sincerity. The old axiom, predictably invoked at this juncture is that criticizing avowed "Republicans" foments disunity, and expecting them to abide by any reasonable conservative standard constitutes a "litmus test," or is too "divisive," and will only succeed in "making the perfect the enemy of the good." And of course there is that monotonously predictable reference to "Reagan's Eleventh Commandment," which ostensibly prohibits the criticism of Republicans by Republicans. Not surprisingly, this is the reflexive "fall back" position of RINOs, the moment conservatives finally tire of being back stabbed by them, and respond to their treachery by returning fire.

Admittedly, too strident or "purist" of a perspective could conceivably occasionally overreach, thereby cutting out potential allies. Certain supposedly "conservative" players have at times established overly stringent standards, not for any worthy purpose but simply to grandstand as to their elevated degree of professed "virtue." And this is invariably counterproductive.

However, in the current political climate, the admonition against holding up too high of a conservative standard is most often uttered by those seeking to totally abolish any standards whatsoever, in order to undermine any safeguards against their duplicity. In this manner they give themselves cover by which they proceed to deliberately subvert conservatism under some phony premise. The risk of being undercut as a result of being stridently conservative "to excess," has proven to be far smaller than the risk posed by leftist "Trojan Horses" and their RINO accomplices who continually confuse and dilute conservative efforts. Over time, their real agenda and allegiances become apparent. They are in collusion with overt leftists, and only maintain a facade of "conservatism," or alignment with the GOP, in order to more effectively inflict harm by undermining the conservative movement from within. From the moment this becomes evident, their real nature and intentions must be diligently tagged onto them every time they seek to intervene and sabotage conservatism, regardless of how eloquently they tout the "virtue" of their efforts to play the political game.

Diligence and discernment are absolutely essential if conservatives are ever to regain their footing and advance their interests without being continually betrayed at critical junctures by professed "allies" against whom they've naively remained unguarded. On too many fronts, conservatives are still blind-sided by seemingly "inexplicable" sudden defections, which render defining political agenda items dead on arrival at the hands of politicians who had loudly proclaimed (especially when back home on the campaign trail) that they were staunch supporters. In the overwhelming majority of cases, the political track records of such politicians, if honestly examined, should have given sufficient warning that their treachery was inevitable. Allowing them to escape culpability on any grounds only sets the stage for further betrayals.

Their patterns of duplicity are usually not hard to identify, if genuine conservatives are willing to risk the wrath of those among the political "inner circle" for daring to stand against them. But as the political "establishment" seeks to perpetuate itself, many phony veneers are pasted over such treachery, some of which are even embraced by hapless conservatives. Yet regardless of excuses and denials, such actions should be noted and cited as identifying traits. For example, a professed "conservative" is only as truly conservative as the sources he cites to make his case. Those supposed "conservatives" who regularly find it convenient to regurgitate the leftist worldview as espoused by CNN, the *New York Times,* and *Washington Post* are clearly not interested in gathering worthwhile evidence to make their case, but are instead attempting to transform the agenda of the political right by insidiously conforming it to the premises of the left.

Frequently, such players are given a "pass" by the conservative base because their treacherous dealings appear at first glance to be a departure from the conservatism they eloquently espouse. However, it is specifically such individuals whose behavior is the most pernicious, and reveals the most defining evidence of their duplicity. The fact that they are so adept at espousing the conservatism they betray is itself proof that their behavior is deliberate and premeditated. It is not an accident that, on a consistent basis, their seemingly brief lapses invariably redound to the benefit of the left. Properly identifying RINO traitors, and ensuring that their reputations are well known, is the best way to minimize their ability to participate in any leftist/Alinsky attack, particularly when it comes to the effort to "freeze and isolate" a targeted conservative. If the source of "Republican" criticism has a well-known track record of collaborating with the left, the effort to give credence to the leftists doesn't carry near the weight it otherwise would. In the same manner, RINO efforts to extol the veracity of leftist players aren't nearly as successful when the endorsement comes from someone who has been diligently identified as a leftist pawn.

The present, lopsided nature of the political playing field is a grim consequence of the failure of the Republicans to sufficiently deal with this tactic. For example, leftists have long enjoyed unwarranted success in undermining the credibility of Republican cabinet and court nominees with their partisan opposition, making sure that confirmation vote margins are razor thin. This is particularly effective because in contrast, Republicans have historically been too willing to rubber stamp Democrat nominees, when many should have been rejected as unfit for office on account of their hard left political agendas. *Every* honorable Senator should adamantly refuse to support any nominee to the nation's high courts, who lacks a track record of upholding constitutional principle, since the Senate oath of office includes a specific vow to "support and defend the Constitution against all enemies, foreign and domestic." Thus a potential judge with a typical leftist background is *inherently unqualified* to gain access to such power, regardless of pedigree or credentials. If leftists want to condemn such a response, they would have to make the case that upholding the Constitution is an example of "partisanship." Bring it on! Let them thereafter attempt to defend their tacit admission that their agenda is inherently unconstitutional.

Unfortunately, leftist judicial and cabinet nominees who's track records are questionable at best, nevertheless enjoy Senate confirmations of overwhelming "bipartisan" support, while truly worthwhile conservatives, who actually uphold constitutional principle, are deemed "controversial" and treated as inherently unfit for office. In the current climate, the Republican "establishment" is so lacking in spine and principle that it absolutely refuses to take a firm stance on such grounds. Instead, it reverts to standard game playing as the essence of "bipartisanship." Thus the principles which ostensibly define the Republican Party are sidestepped by its key players, in hopes of avoiding controversy and backlash from the Democrats. Both parties are guilty of the verbal gymnastics needed to pacify an increasingly engaged public while the efforts of the ruling class to perpetuate its "business as usual" inside the Beltway continue, and always with itself as chief beneficiary. But it is among the Republicans that this constitutes a direct betrayal of the platform and supposed guiding principles of the party. And this is not only abhorrently dishonest, it isn't smart politics.

The enormous groundswell of conservatism that resulted in the 1994-95 "Republican Revolution" had largely dissipated by 1996, when Bill Clinton was handily reelected to his second term. Yet contrary to many popular assessments, the momentum didn't die because the American people had arbitrarily turned their backs on conservatism. Rather, it collapsed when Senate Majority Leader Bob Dole and House Speaker Newt Gingrich jumped ship, and rather than pushing for the drastic reforms on which they had campaigned in the mid-term elections of '94, they backed away from such measures once the Democrats and their media minions had made the case that they were too "Draconian," generating a contrived and drastically overblown public outcry. Rather than keeping their promises and making that the primary issue of the 1996 presidential campaign, the Republican Senate and House leaders abandoned the interests of their conservative base, and instead attempted to mollify critics by offering an ostensibly more efficient version of socialism in the way of "block grants" to states to continue the government handouts on a supposedly more cost effective basis. At that point, the GOP leaders essentially validated the Democrat agenda, concurring with the premise that government should be in the business of providing subsistence to common people, and only disagreeing on the best method of delivering it.

The pattern has only gotten worse ever since. At the inner circles of the GOP is a cadre of self-serving power brokers, who have become extremely adept at offering empty excuses for maintaining the status quo, invariably accompanied by pleas for patience and phony "assurances" that the onslaught of liberalism will finally be addressed and decisively opposed, but always at some future date. Recall John Boehner's lament, in the wake of his ascendancy to Speakership of the House of Representatives in 2010, that he was only in charge of "one half of one third of the government." In contrast, the real proof of a politician's true allegiance is not to be gleaned from the seeming intensity of that individual's "remorse" after having yet again betrayed the Republican base, but instead by his actual behavior at critical junctures when the leftist onslaught might have been, and *should have been* stopped.

The same principles apply to ongoing efforts to repeal Obamacare. While some sincere conservatives have been willing to face the inevitable "heat" of outraged leftist socialists and their dutiful media minions by demanding total repeal for the good of the country, many Republican Senators and Representatives are terrified at the prospect. However, reverting to the standard Republican "establishment" response, they once again attempt to find that mythical "happy medium" which will never work, and *always* signals ideological surrender. Whether the issue is government spending, securing the border, or rescuing the nation from the nightmare of medical socialism, the defining question is not how well those posturing politicians can defend their duplicity on difficult issues, but whether or not they ever stuck to their principles and simply did the right thing when necessary.

Standing resolutely and boldly against the liberal agenda at such junctures, even when capitulation is promoted by certain prominent

"Republicans," not only puts the entire leftist ideology "front and center," where focused scrutiny will invariably do it the most damage; it spotlights key RINO players as the turncoats they truly are, regardless of party affiliation. If done with sufficient resolve, any facade of being "mainstream" can be dispelled and the leftist agenda they advocate can be consigned to the political "fringe" where it belongs. Conversely, conservative attempts to achieve "unity" with RINOs only sets the stage for those RINOs to be elevated as "spokesmen" for the GOP, presenting themselves to be the party's "mainstream." And this is an empowering role which they will readily seize. Typically, the moment they believe they have such standing, their very next effort is to push for "unity" with the Democrats. And at that point conservative momentum has been thoroughly neutralized, and its advocates consigned once again to the margins. The only option is to instead marginalize liberal Republicans, and to do so loudly and diligently enough that they are forced to face their voters after having been identified as such, whereupon they can then attempt reelection on that basis.

Recalling once again the original and simple defining standard of what constitutes a sincere conservative; that being which way they *actually* "move the ball down the field" (whether to the left or to the right), the track records of the vast majority of key political players can be confidently established, and should thereafter be recognized as defining their real character with indelible certainty. A single minor "misstep" may not be grounds for permanent rejection of any particular individual, though it should raise cautionary "red flags." However, once a pattern of betrayal becomes evident, it must thereafter be recognized as thoroughly characterizing such individuals, no matter how vehemently or eloquently they dispute the claim when Election Day approaches.

Throughout the entirety of modern social and political warfare, this is perhaps the most difficult concept for ardent conservatives to properly grasp. As a result, over time the conservative agenda has suffered needless setbacks. Political adversaries are most effective when they are not recognized as such. The transparent facade of collegiality exhibited by two-faced politicians, while universally disparaged in jokes and cynical portrayals of politics in general, is rarely directly applied to specific individuals. Yet it is there where it must be done when warranted, and where failing to do so results in the greatest lurking obstacle to conservatives in their quest to turn back the evil tide of the leftist agenda.

Rule No.9: Stay on Target. Whenever engaged in an effort to advance the conservative agenda, or seeking to confront leftist fraud and duplicity, it is crucial to stay on point, and not allow leftists to complicate the issue or distract from it.

Given how thoroughly the leftist ideology is steeped in fraud, from its foundational premises to the lies and duplicity by which it is implemented, it is a virtual impossibility for the leftist agenda to advance where facts and truth prevail. And this, more than anything else, is why leftists will not allow themselves to be engaged in an objective and intellectually honest debate on any topic, but will instead attempt to distract and confuse the issue at hand. Whether they are seeking to lend credence to their philosophy as a whole, or merely attempting to gain dominance of a particular issue in the political arena, leftists will "bob and weave" to an amazing (and truly shameless) degree when given any opportunity to do so. Unfortunately, such behavior has proven effective against a hapless and blindsided conservative opposition on far too many occasions.

Thus the most devastatingly effective means to counter this ploy is also exceedingly simple. Sadly, it isn't employed sufficiently to prevent leftists from frequently gaining ground or thwarting conservative opposition on a thoroughly fraudulent basis. Simply stay on message, and do not allow leftists to complicate things with emotionally charged, but invariably *irrelevant* deviations from the reality and truth of the situation or issue at hand. Leftists are most obsessed with distracting from a conservative message when they feel most vulnerable to it. Thus, the seeming shrillness of leftist "outrage" over a conservative position or rebuttal, rather than highlighting its flaws as they claim, is instead most likely an indicator of its validity.

When a factual news report deals a blow to leftist ideology, the reflexive response from the left is to denigrate the source, avoiding the facts of the situation at all cost. On this basis, Fox News (which the left deems to be a "conservative" mouthpiece) is incessantly attacked and disparaged as if it is universally recognized to be a coven of right-wing disinformation. Yet no analysis of the information presented there is ever made by leftists in a direct "side by side" comparison with the distorted presentation of events from their favored sources. Instead, Fox is simply mocked and dismissed. Invariably however, the grounds for such mockery and dismissal are baseless, by which leftists instead reveal a dishonesty on their part that exceeds any boundaries of mere "bias" and proves them to be entirely agenda-driven propagandists.

> The shrillness of leftist "outrage" over a conservative position or rebuttal, rather than highlighting its flaws as they claim, is instead most likely an indicator of its validity.

So when facts are presented, and leftists respond with derision, the facts merely need to be forcefully reasserted, and the derisive (and typically puerile) behavior of leftists thereafter spotlighted as proof of their abhorrence for the truth and their vulnerability to it. When conservatives respond by remaining steadfast in the face of obviously contrived outrage and ridicule, leftists typically turn up the volume and shrillness of their tirades, and thereby actually end up "tipping their hand." It becomes obvious that they desperately seek to avoid a direct and factual debate of the issues. Their ploy is thus unmasked and from that point forward, the continuation and escalation of leftist antics actually *enhances* the credibility of those on the right.

Throughout the decades since Roe versus Wade, the leftist counterculture has pursued every disingenuous means of justifying abortion by shifting the focus from its grim reality to the supposed liberation and societal elevation of women, feigned "compassion," concerning the "quality of life" of the child, and the seemingly virtuous and utopian promises of embryonic stem-cell research. Abortion itself is extolled as "choice," (ostensibly connoting "freedom") and even cloaked with a contrived mantle of civic virtue as reproductive "rights."

Yet despite the absurdity of such meticulously constructed talking points, even the slightest concession to them thoroughly weakens the most diligent efforts to stop the wanton slaughter of unborn children. Among the pro-life organizations that have arisen to oppose the practice, one in particular has avoided this pitfall and thus enjoyed a success that vastly outweighs its size. The "Center for Bio-Ethical Reform," founded in 1990, delivers a simple message that totally permeates every official work it undertakes. This blunt but inarguable truth is that "Every abortion is an act of violence that kills a child."

While too many among the pro-life movement are inadvertently drawn into the morass of pro-abort "justifications," attempting to match genuine concern for the plight of the unborn and their mothers against the supposed "compassion" of simply eliminating those inconvenient lives, the CBR message instead leaves no "wiggle room" for excuses and deflections, no subjectivity for phony comparisons of which side ostensibly has a "bigger heart," and no allowances for pro-abort accusations of being "anti-woman." It is just cold hard fact, not as any expression of "religion" (as pro-aborts contend), but based in irrefutable biology and science.

By doggedly sticking to this message, CBR has enjoyed enormous success in actually stopping abortions. And of course, it is for this reason that the leftist counterculture abhors the organization. Unable to refute its brutally simple claim, the effort is instead invariably focused on somehow silencing CBR altogether. Ultimately, the ferocity and virulence of the opposition to CBR stand as a testament to the potency of its message.

Conversely, consider how an incident of horrendous treachery against the United States was trivialized, and eventually disappeared almost entirely from the recollection of the American people. During Bill Clinton's tenure as president in the 1990s, highly sensitive technical information was given to the Chinese, which enabled them to successfully develop reliable intercontinental ballistic missiles. Their advancement of this capability represents a huge danger to the security of the United States which looms over us to this day. The information transfer took place with the full knowledge and participation of the Clinton White House. Yet when questioned on the matter, Bill Clinton dismissed the enormous security breach and betrayal as inconsequential, on the basis that the missile technology would only be used for "peaceful purposes," such as satellite launch vehicles. So instead of being pursued for a flagrant betrayal of America's security and military interests that rivaled the crimes of Julius and Ethel Rosenberg, Bill Clinton could proceed under the mantle of "helping" China to improve the lives of its citizens for the good of all humanity. At that point, both the complicit "news" media, *and* Bill Clinton's political opposition on the right dropped the matter. Nothing was ever done to follow up on his treasonous betrayal of America.

In truth, anyone with even a cursory knowledge of rocketry knows that the ICBM technology is completely identical to that of satellite launch vehicles. The structure and function of the launch vehicle for a nuke is *no different* than it is for a satellite. The only distinction between the two is the targeting data in the vehicle's internal guidance system. One is targeted to inject a payload into earth orbit, while the other is targeted to send its payload to a foreign location on the ground. As a matter of fact, up until the later stages of America's moon program in the 1960s, every major satellite and space-capsule launch vehicle in NASA's fleet was in fact an ICBM, with the only modification being its programmed trajectory and the payload it carried. Yet on the basis of his flimsy excuse, Bill Clinton was able to give highly classified information directly to the Chinese, who then used it to improve their ability to wage nuclear war against the United States!

During his impeachment, Bill Clinton was incessant with such deflections and obfuscations, deliberately complicating and thus diluting the issues at every turn, with his infamous contortions over the meaning of the word "is," and the thoroughly clouded definition of "sex." The brazenness of his antics is most significant, given that when all of the deliberate evasions and deflections had finally been cleared up, Clinton had indeed actually engaged in the sordid behavior of which he was accused.

In like manner, so many of Hillary Clinton's own criminal actions have been put nearly out of reach of the law, simply because she always responds to inquiry in a manner that forces further inquiry from those willing to take the bait, who should instead simply maintain their focus on the original issue of interest. As Secretary of State, Hillary Clinton deliberately sequestered and trafficked in classified information for her personal use. At the same time, she was receiving enormous "donations" from foreign governments to the Clinton Foundation. These "dots" are not hard to connect. Yet she effectively neutralized those seeking to learn of her behavior by incessantly engaging in one stonewalling tactic after another, including her most reliable ruse of former years, feigning sheer ignorance of that which she was clearly knowledgeable, *and guilty.*

The grim lesson to be learned here is that those on the left will throw out any flimsy excuse in their efforts to send our side down some time-consuming but inconsequential rabbit trail. In the process, energy, resources, and *public interest* are the "casualties." The last one is perhaps the most significant. If those responsible for upholding the law are actually more concerned for their own political fortunes than with the primacy of truth or justice, they are likely to drop the ball the moment they perceive that the public is no longer engaged. And that is why this ruse is frequently successful.

It is abundantly evident that Saul Alinsky viewed open and honest debate as a liability. One of his rules reveals inarguable proof of this: "Whenever possible, go outside the expertise of the enemy." In the leftist universe, the inherent worthiness of their agenda and the need to implement it supersedes all else, including *the facts*. And this is why it is imperative for conservatives to stick tenaciously to the facts, not allowing leftists to cloud them, suppress them, or deflect attention from them for any reason. Truths regarding abhorrent actions that aren't too ugly for leftists to commit, cannot be too ugly for conservatives to bluntly and factually discuss and portray in all of their inhuman gruesomeness. The same goes for any other criminal activity, but especially in regards to the real consequences of the leftist agenda in any region of the world where it has prevailed. The horror and squalor that ensues must be made known to the American people in order for them to see past the imaginary bliss that leftists promise. Otherwise, when conservatives attempt to step lightly in order to avoid "controversy," and such topics are only obliquely referenced in the euphemistic manner that leftists demand, the leftist position, no matter how corrupt or abhorrent, is eventually presumed to be "validated" in the absence of diligent opposition.

Rule No. 10: Focus on winnable regions and issues to build momentum.

In the same sense that it is a total waste of time to attempt to persuade leftist ideologues of the truth (See Rule No. 2), conservative political momentum can best be generated and maintained in those regions of the country where enough of a connection with reality exists that leftist propaganda cannot thoroughly overwhelm it. While the goal of the conservative movement is to see the entire country set free from the societal cesspool that results from leftist policy, excess effort should not be wasted on converting those places where leftist attitude and arrogance have become so ingrained that truth and reality no longer have influence. Per the well known proverb, we need to choose our battles wisely. Nevertheless, it must be understood that victory is still the goal, and that the battle can still be won in such regions, but just not by means of a direct "frontal assault."

In the present day, a total facade of "public sentiment" is often created by the left out of thin air, triggered by either a real or contrived "crisis," followed by a rapid Blitzkrieg of shrill "news" reports and accusations, coordinated among liberal politicians and their media minions, often with no connection to reality. Next come the predictable public opinion polls ostensibly reflecting overwhelming public support for the leftist point of view. Of course the real issue at hand is never their actual concern. Rather, leftists only seek to exploit it for maximized political gain. In truth, the thoroughly disingenuous nature of leftist opportunism and sanctimony in such situations constitutes glaring proof of the actual indifference of the left to any actual victims of the crisis.

Making the case of this leftist duplicity should be a guaranteed winner for conservatives, except that it instead often hits them hardest at their "Achilles Heel," which is the Republican establishment. Unfortunately, the GOP has over time proven itself to be easily manipulated into jumping aboard the latest leftist bandwagon. This gives credence to even the most absurd and transparently politicized leftist characterization of any calamity, as well as its proposed solution. And on this basis, the declared "public sentiment" (which of course favors the leftist "solution" and thus empowers them) is thereafter proclaimed as immutable.

In contrast, the "flash in the pan" grandstanding and hysteria of leftists, which is their standard response to any real or imagined crisis, will not prevail against an unwavering and stridently stated conservative stance. In this manner, the posturing and pandering of the left can not only be defused; but those who perpetrate it will be discredited in the process, and if they are diligently identified, thereafter will find it much more difficult to gain any political traction on this or *any other* substantive issue. In this manner, conservatives can and must establish "beach heads" of truth, where the standard leftist/Alinsky efforts to mock and dismiss them significantly lose their effectiveness.

As this level of resolve and momentum is established and enhanced across the nation, beginning in conservative strongholds and eventually reaching out to those regions deemed to be "middle ground," it will reverberate among any reasonable individuals, even in such far leftist enclaves as California and New York. And it is in this manner that the message can best inspire and motivate them to stand their ground against the onslaught of leftist insanity, that will otherwise be deemed "normal" by default.

It must be emphasized here that the goal is *not* to ignore or abandon conservatives in areas where leftists are concentrated, but to build energy from the outside, where it can actually gain ground on a widespread basis. By presenting a stark contrast to the increasing crime, squalor and tragedy of leftist dominated regions, it can exert its greatest influence on them, where a direct effort would be otherwise silenced or suppressed.

For this approach to work, it is crucial that the truth be presented in an undiluted form, from a position of confidence and strength. Any effort to make it more "palatable" by softening it, in hopes of better appealing to the local demographics, will only weaken it. That's why "moderates" never fare well in liberal areas. While they alienate real conservatives, they remain insipid and totally uninspiring in the eyes of those who might believe themselves to be liberal, but are willing to honestly examine alternatives.

Instead, the glaringly obvious "cause and effect" relationships of the disasters of leftist policies need to be diligently connected to leftist ideology and its real impact on the situation. Here are just a few examples of how leftist insanity has manifested itself in human suffering and social dysfunction on a massive scale: Failed inner city schools that turn out "graduates" who can barely function in the workforce, social policy that leads to shattered families, delinquent youth, and burgeoning crime, environmental policies that prevent the clearing of undergrowth and dead wood, thus contributing directly to massive wildfires. In every one of these cases, leftist doctrine was the basis of such atrocious policies. It can and should be directly identified as the root cause of the catastrophes and tragedies that ensued. Only in this manner can individuals living within leftist dominated regions have any hope of awakening to the dangerously dogmatic belief system that instigated the disasters and was the ultimate cause of their suffering. This is the most powerful message that can be delivered to them as they contend with the horrible effects of leftist ideology and its resultant policies.

In the same sense that certain regions of the country are currently so steeped in leftist ideology that they can no longer be changed by direct confrontation in legislative bodies, those indoctrination centers known as government schools now represent a bastion of leftist thinking that must be confronted, but in a feasible manner. While a concerted effort to clean house in public "education" is a worthy idea, actually undertaking such a task would be extremely difficult, owing to the vastness of the effort, and the overwhelming resources of the entrenched leftists who control those institutions and the enormous pipeline of money to them. Rather, the goal must be to teach young people *genuine* critical thinking, particularly *before* they face leftist indoctrination.

The goal is *not* to ignore or abandon conservatives in areas where leftists are concentrated, but to build energy from the outside, where it can actually gain ground on a widespread basis.

Sadly, so much ground has been ceded to the left in modern "schooling" that any actual examination of issues from the perspective of genuine critical thinking is not only being sidestepped, it is actively discouraged. Pupils are coerced to embrace leftist ideology, and those who may be reluctant to do so because they have doubts (the seed of critical thinking) are marginalized and demeaned. This truly reprehensible behavior by "teaching" staffs is ominously reflective of totalitarian "re-education" camps. Still, the very manner in which such manipulations are being perpetrated can be its own invaluable "education," the moment students are made aware of what it really represents. If they can be successfully taught critical thinking outside of such poisoned environments, even in relation to sports and other seemingly unrelated topics, they can apply such principles to any other topic with which they are confronted.

It is no secret that over the past several decades, leftists have thoroughly infested "academic" institutions, from kindergarten through the post graduate level. And they now have in place a well established "educational" regimen that has little to do with actual academics, but is instead all about indoctrination through manipulation. Hence, those increasingly abysmal educational test scores of recent years. But once the victims can be made aware of how they are being manipulated, and once they are able to see the inescapable flaws of the leftist socialist ideology, and the duplicity with which that failed system is being promoted despite its disastrous track record, the task of indoctrinating them by leftist dominated academia becomes nearly impossible. But even more importantly, from that point forward, every ugly coercive tactic employed by the left has exactly the opposite effect, and can actually solidify the awareness of their fraud and inconsistencies. Instead of further convincing those truly liberated minds of the "validity" of leftist thinking, each ensuing effort stands thereafter as a testament to the vile nature of the ideology, and proves what an intellectual and moral abyss awaits those who adopt it. Absent critical analysis, leftist tenets remain intact only as "religious" articles of faith. But they cannot withstand objective scrutiny, at which point they collapse completely.

Admittedly, this is a major undertaking. And it is made still more difficult in that the "educational" establishment already teaches its own alternative version of "critical thinking," which actually involves broad-based attacks on traditional America, and its traditional values, while leaving leftist orthodoxy untouched and "enshrined." Breaking through that fortification requires enlightening students on the sheer absurdity of this supposed critical thinking in which the leftist overseers tyrannically dictate which ideas can be questioned, and which questions are not allowed, lest the questioner be deemed guilty of heretical deviation from leftist orthodoxy. Nevertheless, it is to our decisive advantage that light can break through the darkness, but darkness *cannot* overpower the light. Fraud and the brutish suppression of contravening facts are essential to all leftist machinations and to maintaining a consistently leftist mindset. A student who is made aware of just how necessary they are can never be made ignorant of them thereafter.

This is not as overwhelming of an undertaking as it might initially seem. Once the agenda of the propagandist is recognized, his efforts to mislead become transparent and are far more difficult to accomplish.

CHAPTER TEN
CONCLUSION

It is inarguable that leftists have gained enormous ground redefining virtually every facet of American life during recent years, due in large part to their diligent implementation of the Alinsky strategy. And their ability to dominate the discourse has been exponentiating throughout that time. Yet despite the growing influence they wield on the American cultural and political scene, it is an absolute certainty that at some point leftist efforts will completely fail. No cancer ever outlives its host. For leftist policies to work, even in the short term, they must have access to the lifeblood of a healthy society from which to sap the resources and energy they need to survive. As their ideology gains dominance, it will invariably undermine and cripple those very aspects of the society on which they feed, to the point of dragging it into ruin, and themselves along with it.

> It is an absolute certainty that at some
> point leftist efforts will completely fail.
> No cancer ever outlives its host.

The only uncertainty in this scenario is whether or not the culture upon which leftists prey is able to recognize the potentially fatal threat they pose in time to throw it off, or if that culture will succumb to the leftists, paralyzed by a fear of derision, at which point its fate is all but guaranteed. So our nation has only two options. It will either proceed on its current downward course and suffer the grim consequences, or it will awaken to the societal sickness embodied in the left. Only then can America rebuff and reject every perverse leftist dogma, to restore the principles of a healthy, just, and morally functioning society. Clearly the goal of leftists is to keep the blinders on as many people as possible, until the outcome they intend becomes irreversible.

So it is that the greatest battle to be faced, even at this late date, does not constitute physical warfare. Rather, it is a committed effort to expose the vileness and enormity of the leftist threat by getting the word out to an often disengaged public that is largely unaware of the real threat facing it. Once sufficient numbers are awakened to the looming danger, the essential task is then to thoroughly instruct them on how to prevent being overcome by the leftists and their insidious agenda. Indeed time is short, and action must be decisive. Otherwise, the erosion and eradication of American culture at the hands of leftists will accelerate, the moment the relationship advances from parasitic to malignant; from confusing and polluting to fatally poisoning. Nevertheless, the mere fact that open opposition to the left still exists on a wide-scale basis is proof that a successful counter-effort is still completely feasible. The rules for effectively accomplishing this, as expounded upon in the previous two chapters, are as follows:

The Rules

Rule No.1: Never apologize unless an actual wrong has been committed. And then, if an apology is truly warranted, remain very specific as to the issue that is actually being addressed.

Rule No.2: Never engage leftist leaders and activists for the purpose of persuading them with the truth.

Rule No.3: Never allow leftists to move past their hypocrisy and lies.

Rule No.4: Never accept baseless leftist assertions of "cause and effect," which are vehemently proclaimed as inarguable truth, but are only enabling propaganda.

Rule No.5: Never reflexively accept leftist definitions of good and evil.

Rule No.6: Power that is not asserted when necessary and appropriate is forfeited. Eventually it is lost forever.

Rule No.7: When leftists rally around one of their own who has been exposed for engaging in reprehensible or corrupt behavior, all who support the individual need to be identified as being equally corrupt, and thereafter diligently tagged as such.

Rule No.8: Identify friend and foe. Once a determination is legitimately made that a political player is doing the bidding of the enemy, do not allow it to be altered on the basis of emotion or polished subsequent politicking and pandering.

Rule No.9: Stay on Target. Whenever engaged in an effort to advance the conservative agenda, or seeking to confront leftist fraud and duplicity, it is crucial to stay on point, and not allow leftists to complicate the issue or distract from it.

Rule No.10: Focus on winnable regions and issues to build momentum.

These rules are neither complicated, nor do they require profound intellectual insight or enormous individual sacrifice to be effective. They certainly don't represent any "magic bullet" by which the liberal disease might be miraculously expunged from our nation forever. Such is the human condition that a significant number of people will always gravitate towards evil and lies, as a seeming shortcut to get what they want. It is inevitable that at some point in the future, the deceit and lawlessness to which leftists ascribe can be expected to eventually coalesce and re-emerge as a "new" and alluring political ideology, just as it has periodically done throughout all of human history. Yet like many a vile strain of bacteria, leftists and their lies can only proliferate under cover of darkness, when they are enabled by the passivity of a host culture that has lapsed into moral ambiguity. Thus the task of counteracting them consists almost entirely of breaking through the extensive but fragile veneer of deceit hiding their real character, and exposing the ugly realities of who they are and what they portend for any society where they take hold.

It is thoroughly illustrative of who and what leftists are, that while conservatives always focus their energies on exposing and refuting leftist lies, leftists overwhelmingly seek instead to *silence* the truth presented by conservatives. The good news is that while the effort required to seal off every possible venue by which the truth might be told is massive, it only takes the counter efforts of a committed and morally upright opposition to diligently disseminate that truth among the American people. The rules presented here are merely a somewhat concise means of achieving this. The first step is to avoid the pitfalls leftists have concocted to stifle and ensnare conservatives in order to prevent the truth from coming out. Then, by being properly alerted to the deceitful ploys and scams of the left, conservatives are best equipped to stay on course, neutralize the onslaught, and share the realities of conservatism in its true and positive light with the mainstream of America.

However, while at first glance this characterization of proactive conservatism might seem a bit simplistic and uninspiring, it should be regarded as extremely encouraging, since it constitutes evidence that the leftist/Alinsky onslaught is hardly an unstoppable superhuman force requiring any monumental counterattack. Rather, it is a cowardly, devious, and insidious encroachment on normality that could only have achieved as much as it has owing to the lack of an appropriate and timely response. Like any would-be terrorist action, the leftist onslaught amounts to a relentless succession of cheap-shots and sucker punches, which could accomplish very little against a properly forewarned and forearmed opponent. It is inherently fragile and vulnerable to an opposition that recognizes its rhetorical sleights of hand and can muster the courage and resolve to confront them and bring the discourse back to reality.

The closest thing to any "magic bullet" in all of this is the ability to hamstring the left by diligently continuing to take the boundaries of the battle away from it and restoring those boundaries to reality, and the actual premises of right and wrong where they belong. This is why the repeated admonition that "the Alinsky strategy only works on those who allow it" is such an important concept to grasp, and that rejecting the leftist assertion of its phony "moral high ground" is so crucial to ensuring that truth and right prevail.

A single, well articulated presentation of truth can thoroughly devastate even the most elaborate construct of leftist lies.

Despite the magnitude and ferocity of leftist sanctimony, its power to persuade is finite. A single, well articulated presentation of truth can thoroughly devastate even the most elaborate construct of leftist lies, rendering them little more than a comical parody in the eyes of all but the most willfully blind adherents to the leftist ideology.

Genuine conservatives, who seriously contend for the future of our nation, should gird up and take heart. The battle for the future of America is ours to win, if we seriously have a mind to do so. Moreover, the *only* alternative is total capitulation to the insanity and tyranny of the left. Recall, once again, that in the opening of *"Rules for Radicals,"* Saul Alinsky sought to further outrage his opponents by offering a provocative but satirical "dedication" to Lucifer. Given the disastrous impact his work has had on society and the proliferation of sheer evil that resulted, it has become apparent that what Alinsky intended as a mocking affront to human decency ultimately embodied much more reality than even he might ever have imagined.

Nevertheless, neither the unparalleled perversity of the leftist/Alinsky ideology nor the sinister intentions and unfettered nastiness of its modern disciples constitute a final statement on the future of our nation. A power much greater than either is still available to those who will embrace it, ready to be wielded in a defining manner against the onslaught of the leftist counterculture. And it is a time-honored weapon that has endured even while corrupt kingdoms have arisen to seeming greatness and invincibility, only to fade into the dust. It is the power of truth to overcome lies, and to prevail over the toxicity by which those lies propagate and spread throughout an unsuspecting society, as the left now seeks in America. They need not succeed, if we are wise, courageous, and diligent in our opposition to them.

"Greater is He that is in you, than he that is in the world."- *I John 4:4b*